SHADOW MINISTER

Reflections of an Associate Minister

PASTOR PAUL LEACOCK

Largo, MD USA

Copyright © 2021 Paul Leacock

All rights reserved under the international copyright law. No part of this book may be reproduced or transmitted in any form or by any means, electronic or mechanical, including photocopying, recording, or by any information storage and retrieval system, without the express, written permission of the author or the publisher. The exception is reviewers, who may quote brief passages in a review.

Christian Living Books, Inc.
P. O. Box 7584
Largo, MD 20792
christianlivingbooks.com
We bring your dreams to fruition.

ISBN 9781562295097

Unless otherwise marked, all Scripture quotations are taken from the King James Version of the Bible. Scripture quotations marked NKJV are taken from The New King James Version / Thomas Nelson Publishers, Nashville: Thomas Nelson Publishers, Copyright © 1982. Used by permission. All rights reserved.

Contents

Foreword V

Preface IX

Introduction: Journey into The Shadow XIII

1: A Look Back: Marketing Vs. Ministry 1

2: Looking Forward: From Baptist to AME 11

3: Career Shift 31

4: An AME Licentiate at Allen 39

5: Called into the Shadow of the Bootstrapper 47

6: Designing and Establishing the Discipleship Ministry 65

7: Implementing the Ministry: From Conception to Inception ... 91

8: Pastoral Care: Discipling the Least, the Lost and the Last 115

9: Serving in Other Ministries 139

10: The GACNY MAP 167

11: Out of the Shadow – Into the Light 179

12: Looking Beyond Allen 187

13: Going Full Circle 247

Other Books by Pastor Leacock 281

Acknowledgments 283

Bibliography 285

Foreword

The advent of the mega-church phenomenon has led to layers of ministers serving under Senior Pastors, Bishops, Apostles, Chief Clerics, and Prelates, depending on the denominational tradition or the lack thereof. In the wake of these new developments, spiritual leaders have become or are expected to be Pastor/CEOs over large ministries. For many, these are new and unfamiliar corporate roles in unchartered territory. Nevertheless, theirs is the unenviable task of fulfilling the Biblical mandates, ministering to the congregants' needs, responding to society's ills, and addressing national issues in a global environment without losing sight of the compelling visions that bravely drive them forward. Many are bestselling authors. Some like myself had national offices that create public personas to manage while maintaining model homes with happy spouses and extraordinary children who aren't allowed to fail. As impossible as this may sound, it is the real-life experience of some who oversee such large ministries.

Naturally, in order to be successful, mega-churches require multiple ministers and ministries to address the needs of their extensive flocks, both in their physical and virtual congregations on the cable and social media networks. Such *Associate Ministers* and the heads of strategic ministries represent the second tier of persons who serve under the leadership of renowned pastors and spiritual leaders. How well they are accomplishing these roles is a question hardly asked as they become immersed in the business of ministry and growth.

The remarkable growth of ministries from, in some cases, basements to Cathedrals or from small beginnings to sports arenas is often so fast and dynamic that little time is taken to examine what is happening in the lives of the ministers themselves to ensure that they are able to fulfill the call of God upon their lives in personal and specific ways. If this is true of Pastors, who constantly struggle to find the delicate balance between sacred and secular, it is even more tragically true of their protégées in ministry. Therefore, there is a disturbingly noticeable failure among those who serve in the shadows of the great. It is a challenge to support the Pastor's vision, handle the exposure on national networks with its notoriety, manage the daily demands of overwhelming numbers of people, govern the financial aspects of church corporations, resist the temptation to imitate other successful ministries, all while searching for significance. Juggling all these moving parts can be a bit too much for some Associate Ministers.

There may be a desperate need among the "sons of the prophets" that can easily go unnoticed even by the most astute and caring Pastor. When one considers how a pastor may become caught up in capital works out of the sheer spiritual mandate on his life, it is not hard to see that such a minister could not always lend himself to the intensive one-on-one mentoring of junior ministerial staff. Allen became the largest employer in Queens through its 18 corporations, managed over $20-25 million budgets, gave Federal representation to a depressed community, ministered to some 20,000 registered congregants in three services each Sunday, and provided low-income and senior housing and centers of learning for poorly educated students in the community.

Nevertheless, the success and progress of those who serve under charismatic-visionary leaders need to be urgently promoted. Intentional empowerment is necessary for the present successful ministries to continue and leave a lasting legacy. The discussion of how to do so needs to begin now, especially when resources are challenged by prevailing global economic and spiritual factors confronting the church and its membership.

I believe this work, *Shadow Minister: Reflections of an Associate Minister,* has opened the conversation. Written from the perspective of the position he served, Rev. Paul Leacock expresses the tension he experienced serving as the Discipleship Minister of The Greater Allen (AME) Cathedral of New York while at the same time maintaining the personal sense of calling in his soul. He answers the question: Is it possible to be accomplished and successful at positions less than #1 with a resounding "yes!" It is possible to be (as a colleague, Bishop T.D Jakes expressed it) *a number 1 in a number 2 position.* Hence, *Shadow Minister* is recommended reading for every senior ecclesiastical leader and their subordinates. Both can synergize to accomplish their separate but interdependent roles. They ought to complement, not compete against one another.

Rev. Paul's *Reflections* here offer **excellent** insights expressing the often unseen struggles that junior ministers must face as they execute the tasks that help bring lofty visions into reality. These insights will have meaningful resonance with those who serve in such capacities. In some cases, they are unflattering and blunt, but such is the nature of personal reflections as conceived.

Rev. Paul's *Reflections* also offer good Biblical **exposition** so that the insights are not so unique and personal that they cannot be adopted and adapted by others. He does so by drawing on Biblical paradigms that can benefit his audience. He uses the Scriptures to shed light on complex situations and transcend individual contexts.

The Biblical principles he offers are means by which one can avoid ungodly choices. These reflections and discourses may prove invaluable in mentoring and group sessions.

At the same time, the insights are ***experiential.*** You will not find here mere platitudes that have no basis in reality. Rev. Paul served in several critical ministries as Discipleship Minister, Para-Chaplain Leader of the Allen Prison Ministry (Riker's Island, Danbury FCI/FCP; Woodbourne Correctional), Rites of Passage mentor, and Pastoral Care Counselor, among performing other ministerial tasks. His insights come out of this wealth of experience.

Above all, Rev Paul is an ***exemplary,*** sincere minister of the gospel, a good father to his three beautiful daughters: Joanna, Samantha, and Candace, a loving grandfather to Savion, Daniel, and Ava-Skye, and a devoted husband to Lorraine, his wife. He currently serves as Pastor of the First Baptist Church Barbados, where he may now cast his own shadow conscious, I am sure, of those who serve in it.

Rev. Floyd H. Flake, D. Min.
Retired Congressman

Preface

I didn't think of writing this book until Rev. Elaine Flake, my Co-Pastor of the Greater Allen Cathedral of New York, ignited the thought of doing so in me. I served as Discipleship Minister, and we were engaged in a discussion in which writing and publishing came up. In that discussion, she stated very candidly, "Oh yes, you have something to say." Her words were surprising and sobering given her stature and our ministry's scope under our senior Pastor, Floyd H. Flake. I hadn't actually given serious thought to becoming an author, far less considering what I would even write about. So what did I have to say?

As I pondered Rev. Elaine's words, I soon began to reflect on my own work under Pastor Flake, who had written "The Way of the Bootstrapper- Nine Action Steps for Achieving Your Dreams." In short order, his book had become a New York Times bestseller. Those who served as Associate Ministers under this nationally recognized leader felt honored and privileged to do so. He was not simply an outstanding Pastor of a mega-church but a Congressman who had revitalized an entire community into a viable economic zone. We, his ministerial underlings, saw firsthand how those action steps he wrote about were lived out in his ministry daily. The book merely gave a condensed and concise version of what we actually experienced. "The Bootstrapper..." gave others the principles to learn and put into practice, but we had their direct observation in practicality. Hence, I was learning in the long, imposing shadow of the Bootstrapper.

Awakened by these experiences, I began reflecting on my own life and ministry. This led to much introspection and reevaluation of Biblical paradigms to help explain my personal ministry experiences. I began to realize that I needed to act wisely, if nothing else. I could not squander the opportunities which lay before me as I labored in the shadow of an excellent Pastoral team recognized and respected by Presidents in the White House and other sacred and secular leaders around the country.

Before long, I began writing down my thoughts and the insights which were helpful to me personally. Then the writing took on a life of its own. As if driven by the Spirit, I found myself writing incessantly. I carried my journal everywhere and often spent entire plane trips writing or being awakened in the middle of the night to continue where I had left off or add more insights. First, of course, I studied whether my thoughts had credence, so I observed others in ministry and drew much from the monthly Pastoral meetings held at Allen to discuss matters that arose or to plan the way forward. I also gleaned from my sitting in with outstanding ministers from established ministries who often met with our Pastors to learn from their ministry model.

Most importantly, I was captured by the spiritual insights in Scripture that I must admit I had not adequately studied from the perspective of my tasks as an Associate Minister serving under a strong spiritual leader. Examples in Scripture abound, and the wise insights they yield are priceless. Without those scriptural reflections, I realized I was immersed in doing ministry, but how well? There are serious pitfalls to avoid, problems to resolve, and personal and private perils to navigate to serve both the leadership and the congregation well. But, then, that service needs to be pleasing to the

Chief Shepherd, who will reward each Pastor and Associate according to their work. I was struck by the need to balance all these factors as I thought and prayed and wrote.

Indeed, all I thought about or experienced is not written here, especially the scriptural insights. They require a separate volume in themselves under consideration as a devotional. However, my prayer is that my reflections will resonate with those who serve faithfully as Associate ministers, lay leaders, heads of ministries, and simply volunteers to churches and ministers. I hope to help those away from the spotlight beneath the pedestals of those revered.

Introduction: Journey into the Shadow

I came to the United States of America from my native Barbados, a paradise island at the furthest point east of the Caribbean Islands. I had no idea that I would meet and work under one of the most nationally respected pastors, the Honorable Rev. Floyd Harold Flake, and his wife and CO-Pastor, Margaret Elaine Flake. He later described himself as a 'Bootstrapper.' I first heard the term *bootstrap* used by Barbados' belated first Prime Minister, The Right Honorable Errol Walton Barrow. He had articulated what I perceived as a post-World War II American ideal of lifting oneself up by one's bootstraps. I always found it a curious term that didn't quite make sense. Perhaps some aspect of the concept was lost in the cultural transference; after all, given its geographical location, the absence of snow, hail, and sleet, wearing boots was not the standard model of Barbadian dress. I often wondered about the concept's genesis, giving rise to the term. At the time, it seemed to me to be an oxymoron since the one who attempted it was apt to fall. I came to understand it to refer to the phenomenon of lifting one's self by one's effort, by dint of hard work and determination. Hence the term was a dynatron, a hyperbolic expression used to emphasize the difficulty of near-impossible achievement.

Prime Minister Barrow had articulated the concept as part of the drive to encourage self-sufficiency in Barbados through industry and commerce. Having led the nation to independence from England in 1966, he established several Industrial Parks where he built light manufacturing plants to produce goods for the US and UK markets. Thus by self-generated efforts, the island would earn valuable foreign exchange, thereby amassing foreign reserves. The intent was to increase Barbados' GDP by its industry, therefore fulfilling its newly minted motto: *Pride and Industry*. It exemplified Prime Minister Barrow's stance that Barbados was not to be dependent on aid from the UK, the USA, or any other entity. His mantra *"friends of all, satellites of none"* underscored the national quest. Of course, I can only see this now, not as a youth then.

I guess, on reflection, that Barbados was to bootstrap to achieve collectively what Pastor Flake had achieved individually – success in the face of seemingly insurmountable life challenges as detailed in his book: *The Way of the Bootstrapper; Nine Action Steps to Achieve Your Dreams (Harper Collins, 1990)*. It may have been fortuitous to have had that book before I left Barbados in such a quest, but that was not the way God planned for my life path to intersect with that of Pastor Flake's.

Convergence of Paths

I can better explain *how* Rev. Flake's path crossed with mine than I can say *why* our ministries converged at the then Allen AME Church of Jamaica, Queens, where I ended up serving under his leadership. Looking through my natural human eyes without the aid of my spiritual lenses, I could see that our meeting was unlikely. My Barbados was a far cry from his native Houston, Texas. Both the USA and Barbados are former British colonies which presuppose that both Rev. Flake and I were more than likely descendants of slaves by a few generations. That may have been the only distant commonality; our lives were worlds apart. However, as I was to learn later, both of us lived lives facing similar socio-economic disparities that led us north to New York. He was perhaps following the historic, proverbial, Underground Railroad route to a more liberal area of the United States.

On the other hand, like most Barbadians, I was struggling to make ends meet even though I lived in a desegregated, independent country with no blatant Jim Crow laws and with blacks firmly in charge politically. Nevertheless, I needed to venture beyond my idyllic island's shores to achieve more for myself and my family, which I could not see myself accomplishing despite my hard work. Others around me seemed content to play out the unprinted mental scripts that circumvented their lives; I was not. I looked around and realized that I needed to escape the sociological box that limited upward social mobility, frustrated potential, and denied hope to predominantly black Barbadians.

From my vantage point for most Afro-Barbadians, life was a struggle to eke out a living in a post 'plantocratic' society still firmly governed by the vestiges of colonialism. For example, the white economic elite, composed of patently silent but influential Euro-Barbadian whites, commanded the nation's wealth. With increasingly notable exceptions, these power brokers were the privileged heirs of the 'plantocracy' that had ruled Britain's brightest jewel in Her Majesty's Crown throughout the Empire when sugar was king. Beneath them in society's class were Creole whites or near white whitey browns, as one early observer of Barbadian demographics called them, in varying gradations who lived at the margins of the white upper class. Below them was a small emerging middle class of fairer skin blacks and then the majority-black Barbadian, Caribbean nationals, and a minority of Indo-Barbadians. Nevertheless, they made up the bulk of the populace. By the time I was ready to go to the United States, tourism had succeeded sugar as the principal money earner, and Barbados had thrown off the shackles of British rule, as had the USA. However, the wealth remained with those who had diversified to other commercial enterprises as the economy moved further away from being a strictly agricultural economy to a service economy. That economic control was the primary reason I felt compelled to quit my job and leave for New York.

Frustration: Success Denied

Before leaving, I had worked for over eight years for the Goddards (one of the white Barbadian families) in their flagship store called Harrisons in the capital, proudly addressed as #1 Broad Street, Bridgetown. Reportedly, the Goddards were not enriched by the generational wealth which the planter class's heirs enjoyed. Theirs was a 'rags to riches' story among the poorer whites. The report says that old Joe Goddard walked barefooted with his cows to the market in Bridgetown, some 15miles away from his parish of St. John in the countryside. His yeoman efforts led to the acquisition of assets that enriched the Goddard family. However, that sympathetic reality was lost in the classism that dictated the economic divide, which separated them from their mostly black staff, even from those blacks to whom they were genetically related.

I had joined the company in 1979. I climbed to middle management positions in a few years by hard work, only to be frustrated by the glass ceilings strategically placed above black curly heads, however intelligent they may have been. In my personal experience, even though the company sent me to England to study General Management, I returned to utter frustration below the glass ceilings, which were now more painfully visible. I could not exercise my new expertise because my fairer Barbadian bosses told me quite candidly: "we don't know what to do with you." Why not? I was on their payroll while I was abroad; the company afforded my practical managerial training with the Littlewoods Organization because Harrison's submitted me to be a candidate for the study abroad opportunity, compliments of Peter Moore. He was the son of Sir John Moore of The Littlewoods Organization of England. I won the scholarship out of a field of hundreds of candidates from other companies island-wide. I suppose that management was proud and pleased that one of their 'boys' got the coveted prize. All my progress at Littlewoods was reported to my local superiors, who urged me on as I plunged into Management Theory, Chain Store Management, Mail Order Operations, Buying and Purchasing, Store Security, etc. I returned to the company with high commendations from my British supervisors and mentors, ready to demonstrate my knowledge to no avail. Instead, they sent me to dead-end jobs and positions guarded by incompetents (blacks, browns, and whites) who merely viewed me with narrow eyes jaundiced by their own insecurities and traditional white privileges as the case may be.

Despite presenting reports, surveys, and fact-finding studies to the Board of Directors (which they commissioned) that showed some departments were sinking the company's profits, I was ignored and left to feel like a mere pawn in a game of futility. Frustrated, I transferred out to the Food Service division of the company. Although not experienced in food purchasing, I put my acquired buying skills to work, purchasing all the supplies which the airlines flying in and out of Barbados needed through our Flight Kitchen. In less than two years, even though I had maintained a 60-70% profit margin, I was floundering not because of inabilities but because of the malevolent intrigues of junior and senior personnel. For example, the General Manager refused to let my assistant work in the office with me because she was white. She was reseated in his office upstairs instead, leaving me totally without help but charged with the task of maintaining his desired 30/70 cost to profit ratio. However, it did not stop him from allowing his wife to come to the storeroom weekly and give the supervisor her grocery list to supply his own home while the staff's bags were searched at the gate by security.

To make matters worse, the Assistant General Manager, who was afraid that I would ascend to his position, often sabotaged me. Therefore, he withheld critical information from me to prevent my planning ahead. My Store Room Manager, who had applied for the position I held and resented my being appointed, undermined me. Both of these were black, confirming that my experience was not merely because of color issues but more so because of character issues in a sociological environment that encouraged such counter-productive behavior.

My frustration only grew after I married the love of my life, Lorraine Maynard, I saw no future ahead for us because I worked in a company that held out a promise only to deny its fulfillment, and the wider, now independent economy was no better. Although blacks had ameliorated their condition to become Ministers of Government, the principals of schools, Senior Civil Servants, Commissioners of Police, Judges, Lawyers, and Doctors, occupying the commanding heights of society, the economic power elite looked to me as if it was unaffected. They remained in control of people's everyday lives. They controlled demand in the labor market (since they owned the stores). They monopolized the supply of goods and services, imports and exports, tangibles, and intangibles simply because they were the primary mercantile class. Consequently, along with the influence they inevitably exerted on government, it seemed as if they determined the affordability of necessities and luxuries in all of life, like Adam Smith's invisible hand in the marketplace.

Migration abroad seemed to be the one and only way out of the 14x21 'box' that was Barbados with a population at the time of 250,000 people, who were pawns to the upper 1%. The thought of migrating abroad was impressed upon me like a salmon needing to return to its breeding waters. Immigration has been a means of escape and advancement for Afro-Caribbeans for centuries. Thousands had migrated en mass to Panama for the building of the Canal. Thousands went to staff the hospitals and mass transit services of England. Other thousands went in seasonal cycles to the USA to pick fruit and harvest sugar cane, while others filled the job markets of Boston and New York as the British need for immigrant labor waned. Such mass exoduses and movements were long over a generation ago. Still, it was a journey I felt necessary to undertake, given my expanding family and limited prospects before me.

By the time I finally decided to leave Barbados, Lorraine and I had two young daughters, Joanna and Samantha; this only heightened my desire. We spent hours praying and thinking through scenarios and options. Several mentors were consulted, including my Pastor, and all indications pointed to me leaving. It was a painful parting, but it was now or never. Reluctant to travel to the USA with me, Lorraine agreed to move into my parents' home with the girls until I finished my studies abroad. The plan was to finish my studies in Global Marketing with the view of returning to Barbados to teach at the University of the West Indies (UWI). I was determined to raise a new cadre of indigenous, Afro-Barbadian entrepreneurs: men and women who would break the local elite's economic monopoly and shatter the glass ceilings in their fortress corporations by education, acquisition of competence, and business acumen.

This idea had germinated in my mind while I studied in England during the 1980s. Being there opened my eyes to the emerging, growing global economy and the commensurate need for an awareness of global marketing acumen. However, the Caribbean, Barbados included, was not prepared for the techno-driven tsunami initiated by the shift of the geopolitical tectonic plates. Fortress Europe, NAFTA, and other economic power blocks were established, and small island states like Barbados, dependent on tourism, were small fish in a new, huge, ever-widening ocean. I needed to get ahead of the wave before it made landfall.

Thus, with a fermenting passion in my heart and a sense of sadness and trepidation, I departed my beloved island for the enormous challenge of acquiring the necessary credentials in the marketing capital of the world - New York. My new residence at Uncle David and Auntie Hazel's home in Jamaica, Queens, brought me unwittingly into the congressional district of the Rev. Congressman Floyd Flake and his church community.

CHAPTER 1

A Look Back: Marketing Vs. Ministry

My Uncle David and Auntie Hazel allowed me to reside at their home while pursuing my education in Global Marketing. Auntie Hazel and my cousins: Amanda, Karen, Shawn, and Monique were members of Rev. Flake's congregation, but Allen Church was not my focus; it was perhaps the least of my concerns. I was determined to enter college, finish my studies, return to Barbados and embark on my career in the shortest time possible, which was ironic because I had always wanted to come to America to study ministry, not Global Marketing. Therefore, I could not help but cast a reflective eye over my shoulder as I pondered the new decision I had made. Here I was at a crucial turning point in my life, risking all to achieve success, and I could not help remembering a different path I was determined to pursue at another critical stage earlier in my life.

The Calling

As I recall it, I was 16 and had accepted a challenge from the late Rev. Ronald Trotman, the then interim Pastor of First Baptist Church (Barbados). He had preached that we should ask God what career He would have us pursue rather than simply choosing our own while in our youth. I began that quest earnestly praying each day for God to choose for me, to show me what He would have me do. I prayed that prayer until it became routine. I prayed that prayer until the initial passion was gone. The words would roll off my tongue like the Lord's Prayer or some other formalized, memorized scripted petition. Then one morning, sitting in the outhouse of all places, a distinct voice broke through my prayers and interrupted me to the degree that I was startled. *"Preach My Word,"* it said emphatically.

I can not to this day say whether it was an audible voice that I had heard with my external ears or whether it was an internal communication that had entered my conscious mind. What I do know, however, is that I was so aware of the voice that I responded as naturally as I would if I were speaking to someone in front of me in my physical presence. There was no thought as to whether I had heard things or not. The voice was as natural as my own: "You want me to be a preacher?" I responded incredulously. "I thought you would want me to be a businessman or something else like that, not a preacher!" There was no response to my insolent protest. "Well, if that's what You want, then I don't want to be a part-time preacher at church; I want to be a full-time Minister," I demanded. As the minutes ticked on and the reality of my vocation set in, I realized that was the answer I was seeking. Thus I had no choice. Reluctantly, I relented and asked God to give me a heart that loved and retained His word.

To this day, this encounter is sobering for several reasons, but principally for two. First, God spoke to me and told me what to do! There is no doubt in my mind about that. I cannot rationalize that voice away, no matter how plausible the explanations offered. I feel duty-bound to fulfill His demands. No other pursuit ever works favorably. No other path holds the sense of purpose and power as does preaching *His* Word. Second, my response was audacious given that I had asked Him, and yet I was unprepared to accept His choice. It showed the insidious wickedness of my carnal nature. All along, and unbeknownst to me, I had secretly desired to be a business entrepreneur. This desire seemed to have been lurking, lying below my immediate perceptibility. I was not showing any keen interest in any particular career, or was I? Apparently, I was because once He spoke to me, my subconscious preference attempted to supersede by presenting itself in protest. Then when I acquiesced to the divine command, it triggered my bargaining in an attempt to control how and under what conditions I would serve. My negotiations were puny, grasping for the wind in contrast to the voice that filled my entire mind space early that morning and stills echoes fresh in my soul daily. Once spoken, the call has taken up residence to ensure its execution and fulfillment.

It was not long before other messages came to do as commanded. Time after time, that unmistakable voice spoke into the internal channel of my perception and directed me when and where I was to preach God's Word. It came first to challenge my loyalty to God at high school. He commanded me to preach to the students at the lunch recess. "No, Lord," I begged, afraid more of the stares and the perceived loss of face before the other students than I was scared of disappointing Him, never mind it was through His mercy and grace that I was even admitted into that school. I was not willing to consider this fact at the time, but that is a story for another day. Preaching at schools was the frightening task that confronted me.

I can still recall the weeks of procrastination and trepidation leading up to the event, but the command stood firm as I came to meet the Lord in prayer each morning. I could not get past it. It stood firm like an unyielding sentinel in my way. Before long, I could not walk, sit, or stand without this burden to obey, weighing heavily on me. Thus to relieve myself, I gave in. I remembered my labored, wooden steps ascending a mound of dirt that elevated me above my peers. Hundreds of them were queued in a line that snaked in front of the outdoor canteen (cafeteria), waiting to purchase their lunch. As I had seen my father and mother do several times before, I instinctively began to sing a hymn. Then, as I relented to the Spirit, I preached to my fellow students, teachers, and janitorial staff members within earshot. Hardly a captive audience, students purchased their lunch and milled around; the younger students darted back and forth playing, casting the intermittent stare of disbelief at me. The weight seemed lifted off my shoulder once it was over, but not for long. It soon became a norm for me to preach all over the campus as the voice demanded. I soon became the Inter-School Christian Fellowship student leader at Ellerslie Secondary School.

After matriculating from Ellerslie, that voice came again at the Barbados Community College, where I had enrolled to pursue studies in Advance Economics and History. "Lord not here too," I protested. "I did it at high school. Wasn't that enough?" I felt embarrassed; wasn't college a place of higher learning and academia? I fruitlessly and illogically reasoned as if God, Godly living, and theology, in general, were somehow primitive and must now be left behind. Again, I moped and pouted for weeks. I was afraid that my peers would mischaracterize me as a religious fanatic, as crazy, or as some other label equated to being less than smart, bright, intelligent, and not belonging to that institution. Never mind that here, too, I had been admitted by His mercy and grace. Also, by His mercy and grace, I found another student on campus, Margaret Miller. She had attended Ellerslie Secondary School with me. I shared my undesirable burden with her and was shocked that she instantly agreed to go with me to share the gospel on campus. I was embarrassed that I had heard the Lord directing me to preach and was unwilling to do so, while Margaret, who didn't hear, was ready to go based on what I said, and so we did.

Soon an Inter-Varsity Christian Fellowship (IVCF) group of young people sprang up, and the witness by students for Christ intensified to the degree that some professors became concerned. The senior lecturer in the History Department met with me to discuss my spiritual extra-curricular activities; I believe he wanted to be sure that I was not breaking under the pressure of studies, though he never said so. He left me, seemingly pleased that I seemed sane but cautioned me to take it easy. After he left, I thought it strange that no one seemed to tell those who began smoking legal and illegal substances, drinking, wasting time, partying, and exploiting each other sexually to take it easy. Here we were taking a principled stand against all that, yet we were the ones who needed counsel? No wonder the voice sent me to preach.

After graduation, the voice also came unrelentingly, directing me to the streets of the city of Bridgetown, our capital, and the main concourse of business. I remember standing nervously on the sidewalk of busy commercial streets against the stares from faces that seemed to defy me before I even started to speak. I stood stoically against the vehicular traffic noise, competing against the chatter and clamor of human voices and the noisy shuffle of shoes as they hurried by on their business. Passers-by glared in shock at the youth who was shouting out Scripture at the top of his lungs to the traversing audience and demanding its attention. I remember one of the most challenging moments of my preaching on the street during my lunch hour. I was on the road pouring forth the gospel a block away from the store where I was recently hired when my boss walked by and stared at me curiously. I felt as if I had died inside and thought that I had lost his favor and respect, but perhaps that may have been precisely what the Spirit wanted.

I recalled the further prodding of the Spirit to speak to my neighbors about accepting Christ as Savior. Eventually, I had started a Sunday School class outside our house for the neighborhood children every Sunday afternoon. My mother graciously gave up her afternoon siesta to help her eager but novice son with them. Occasionally, I was asked to speak at our church, where I was subsequently appointed Youth President (equivalent to Youth Pastor). It was not long before I assisted at one of the branch churches in another parish outside the city. I was still somewhat unsettled by a question posed by the aged pastor, whom I was helping, when I announced my departure to New York to study. He asked whether I was going to study ministry. Pastor Clarke's question was fair, given the unofficial evangelical career that led me to his church.

That thought brought me back to the reality that I was not in New York to study ministry; I was here to explore my desire to right the inequity and unfair treatment I received in my management career. I was on my own bootstrapping mission to lift myself, my family, and my people.

Besides that, I had long given up the desire to study Ministry in the USA because of the enormous discouragement I received from all whom I expected to help me fulfill that noble desire. Having recognized God's desire in my life, I knew that I needed to prepare myself. I was well acquainted with Paul's words to Timothy:

> Study to shew thyself approved unto God, a workman that needeth not to be ashamed, rightly dividing the word of truth. (II Timothy 2:15)

This Scripture was indelibly printed in my memory. I interpreted it to mean that I should go to the USA to pursue theological studies. I looked towards the USA because that's where the missionaries came from. Plus, there was no Seminary in Barbados.

The now-defunct South Atlantic Baptist Mission had sponsored many an evangelist/missionary to minister seasonally in our churches. One such frequent visitor was Dr. Leon Maurer. He was a banjo-playing preacher who seemed sincere but was not as aloof as others. Dr. Maurer spouted Scripture fluently, quoting several texts from memory as he preached in his pronounced Southern accent. I recalled that he mentioned on one occasion that he was the President of a Bible college, so I took the opportunity to express my desire to study abroad to him, as the then Pastor David Hunte had done. Pastor Hunte was a local Euro-Barbadian that had married the daughter of the long-standing expatriate pastor, who had promptly handed over the reins of First Baptist to his son-in-law upon his return to the USA. Dr. Maurer was taken aback at my request, and I, being ignorant to the south's sociological complexion, didn't quite understand why at the time, but he recovered after stammering and halfheartedly promising to help. However, he placed a condition on it: "I can get you a full scholarship," he said confidently, "if you get a letter of endorsement from your Pastor." I was a little disappointed, but I calculated that I should quickly obtain a letter. Pastor Hunte knew my family well; after all, my parents had physically helped build the sanctuary we worshipped in. I am told that my father was the first deacon ordained in the new facility and had an unblemished, distinguished career as an evangelist and Choir Master throughout the churches. My mother was a deaconess, a women's leader, and a lead soloist in the choir. I thought a letter of endorsement should not have been hard to acquire with this legacy and service behind me. However, after chasing the Pastor for months (he was on an unofficial sabbatical), he interviewed me as if I were a stranger. I was dumbfounded. Although I was 17 or 18, I knew that he was unwilling to help me and was stonewalling with unnecessary, formal questions. For example, he asked me to relay my salvation experience as if he needed assurance that I was a believer. Perturbed but cautious, I responded, "You baptized me, Sir." I recalled the day he raised me proudly in the fount above the aperture wall since I was too short to be seen by the congregation. He held me up to testify to the assembly pleased that the youth were embracing the faith; then, he immersed me to the cheers of all. What was a life-altering moment for me was merely a distant memory for him. After a few more awkward questions, he ended the meeting, promising to get back to me but never did. Shortly after, he resigned under dubious circumstances and left First Baptist Church. I never heard from Dr. Mauer again either.

As if that disappointment was not perturbing enough, my parents also seemed to be against my American quest. My father was particularly unrelenting in his opposition to my going to American to study. I was stunned at his reaction, which I saw as contradictory to all he had taught me and trained me to believe and do. He gave me several reasons why I should not go that ran the gamut of the rational to the irrational, frustrating my desire to pursue my evident calling into the ministry. My mother was less vocal and sat on the fence, but her silence only made Papa's objections more daunting. Before long, I stopped corresponding to the colleges I had written.

Confused and disillusioned, I felt that God had unfairly put me in a duplicitous position. How could I honor and obey my parents and fulfill His will simultaneously? I was so discouraged that when the door of opportunity swung open before me, I didn't go in, which is precisely what may have happened one Sunday at First Baptist Church (Barbados). A visiting African American came to our church.

I and another young man, who began preaching with me on the street, went over to greet him after the service. He informed us that he had come to offer scholarships to black Barbadians who wanted to study ministry abroad. His organization was interested in raising indigenous leaders in the Caribbean. It was like an angel had visited the church to answer our prayers. We would have gone the next day! Without delay, I ran over to the then interim pastor, Bro. Crichlow and gave him the good news. His sharp retort was like the final blow to my mounting frustration. "So why didn't he come to us (leaders)" he snapped. "So why did he go to the young people and not to us?" His rebuke was so terse that it cast a total pall over the visitor's kind generosity. We came back to him unaccompanied with our proverbial tails between our legs; it was clear that the Pastor had no interest in seeing the man. He gave us his card to call him, were we interested, and left us. Now unsupported by my spiritual leaders, my spirit was broken by this. I held the card but never called. What was the point? Dejected and rejected, I turned inward to other interests rather than the purpose I was called to fulfill.

I went along, pursuing my academic education, contemplating my father's dream for me to become a doctor. Clearly, he was willing to sacrifice anything for me to become a doctor, but not a minister. Having been immersed in the faith from birth, I could not reconcile the inner conflict this presented within me. There were numerous unanswered questions. Why were my parents and Pastor so hostile to my desire to enter into ministry? In our home, we had family devotions daily, early in the morning and sometimes in the evening. My parents went all over the country preaching on the streets before dawn. They often woke me up to accompany them to these sobering events as they sang and preached to awakening but respectful people who treated them as if they were angels sent by God to prick their dull consciences. Why then was my father not proud that his seventh child wanted to follow in his footsteps, having been groomed in his shadow? Why were they discouraging me rather than encouraging me in my calling? The answer to these puzzling questions eluded me until I had made my transition to the United States as a young married man free from paternal authority.

Then, Eureka! It suddenly dawned on me that my father was afraid. He was fearful of losing another son! I had an older brother Barton, a handsome young man. He had Rheumatic Fever, I was told, but he never allowed it to stop him. He was a perfect gentleman with a well-defined physique, adored by several young women of the church. His dream was to live in America. After severe bouts of sickness, his opportunity came. He was selected to work in the US harvesting sugar cane at age 25. We said a tearful goodbye, never to see him again. Reportedly, he moved up to New York from Florida after his work assignment was done and settled there. One year or so later, we were informed that he collapsed in the streets, suffering a heart attack; his enlarged heart gave out. Tragically, we were too poor to ship his body home. We had to settle for a memorial service for him. I don't think my mother and father ever recovered from that. I began to realize that my request to go abroad at the tender age of 18 frightened them into saying no, not because they did not support my desire for ministry, but could not risk losing another son dying in his quest to be in the US. I now understood their fear and objections.

However, I was now in the USA, and I had to stop looking back. Instead, I needed to forge ahead to meet the challenges that lay before me. I had a carefully thought-out plan in my head, but of course, heaven had another that would soon begin to unfold. I was facing a contradiction. Despite my earlier desire, I was now in the USA to study Global Marketing, not Ministry.

CHAPTER 2

LOOKING FORWARD: FROM BAPTIST TO AME

At Uncle David and Auntie Hazel's house, I plunged into my studies. Once accepted at York College (CUNY), I began to refresh my Math and English skills in preparation for the placement exam. I was somewhat concerned, having been out of school for a while, and felt some fear of my inability to recall mathematical theorems and grammatical constructs. However, my preparation paid off because I passed both Math and English tests well. Furthermore, I was pleasantly surprised that I was over the first hurdle, not having to do any remedial, only some prerequisite classes in both subjects.

Although I maintained my Christian Faith, fellowshipping at a church was not the priority; my secular career was now my crusade. I was going to right a wrong that had victimized my people, and now me, for over three (3) centuries. However, I felt compelled to join a church in New York. After all, I had gone to church all my life. I didn't want to be another prodigal son that traded in his spiritual legacy for the sinful pleasures of the "far country," and I was indeed in a far country. I was far away from home, culturally and in every other respect.

Choosing a church, though, was quite a feat. My first impulse was to join a Baptist Church. After all, each year, when we renewed the Covenant at First Baptist Barbados, we vowed to join a church of *like faith* if we are ever removed from the local church fellowship. Thus, as a faithful Baptist, I began looking for such a church. I went from church to church wherever Baptist signs hung. I visited them within the limits of my knowledge and mass transit reach in Queens with great disappointment. The name said Baptist, but they were not so in practice; at least nothing I recognized.

I visited Calvary Baptist Church in New York City, which seemed closer to what I found familiar, but the distance was cost-prohibitive. Plus, it didn't fit my new overnight part-time security job schedule. Then I visited my eldest brother in New Jersey and found a Baptist church there. It was as close to First Baptist in format and style as I could want, but like Calvary, I could not possibly travel there for "like faith fellowship" because of the distance. Then something else began to dawn on me: the churches I recognized as familiar were predominantly Caucasian in population with a Euro-centric service liturgy, but the Baptist churches in Jamaica, Queens, were 99.9% Black with a strange service format. Their form of worship seemed more like the Pentecostal Churches to me (not that anything is wrong with the Charismatic style of worship). I was caught in a sociological dynamic that I neither understood at the time nor could reconcile at first. It took me a while to figure it out – Barbados, like many other colonized countries, were Christianized by white southern missionaries who transmitted their faith and superimposed their culture on that transmission. Thus, the music genre and style, the liturgy of worship, the cultural norms and mores, even the very lenses through which one was taught to view the Scripture were of those who were kith and kin to our former slave masters. Therefore, we were acculturated to respect a white culture as superior to our own indigenous, natural inclinations of worship. We were also incidentally or intentionally indoctrinated to revere their religious style. That explained why I subconsciously felt more at home in a *White Church* than in a *Black Church,* Baptist or not.

Disillusioned and disappointed at my futile attempts to honor my covenant, I was faced with the question of whether to join Allen African Methodist Episcopal Church or not. The entire appellation jutted out at me, challenging my theology and sense of self, so I began to process it mentally piece by piece:

Allen

What a strange name for a church, undoubtedly unbiblical, I thought, but thankfully not aloud. That was an absurd thought, especially after I learned the rich history that stood solidly behind the founder of the AME Church in the person of Bishop Richard Allen. That was the name and hence the honor accorded by those who were the heirs of his legacy, memorializing him in the church's name in Jamaica, Queens. To my shame, I was over-driven by my myopic search for a denominational equivalent that I couldn't appreciate that for which I have now come to have deep respect. The AME Church came into existence for the very historical, cultural, and religious tensions I was wrestling within myself.

African

The impact of British colonialism was so endemic that it disengaged me from what I inherently was. African, in relation to my faith, was foreign to me. As I tried to reconcile the two concepts, African and Christian, I felt something within me unraveled as if I was in a severe state of anomie- one that disempowers the essential self's full potential of being. On reflection, this had happened unconsciously through the inculturation and social conditioning of colonization resulting in an unsettled adaptation, a bravado that seeks to normalize the disquiet within the self.

I could not rationalize these insights at the time, but I did recognize that my cocky, Caribbean self could not entirely embrace that designation for a church. It was novel to me; Africa and Christianity didn't quite fit together in my ignorant mind, even though Africa's Christian heritage dates back to the Apostles. It was more comfortable in this foreign land to resort to the denominational nomenclatures with which I was more familiar. Some, of course, were wretched misnomers.

Thus, as I reflected on the term African, it forced me to think of descriptions, religious and non-religious, that I held to proudly without any analysis, including my description as a 'West Indian' instead of a West African or any other ethnic appellation which more aptly described me and my people.

In any event, 'West Indian' was a misidentification of the Arawaks and Caribs after whom the territory was named. Christopher Columbus who dubbed these indigenous people as West Indian was so obsessed with finding Marco Polo's India that perhaps he could not deal with the reality that the Caribbean islands, which he stumbled upon, were not what he sought. Unable to accept failure, he superimposed his pseudonym upon the lands and people, disregarding their own established civilization and the native reality in plain sight before his desperate crews. If this be not the India of the East, then these shall be called Indians of the West - *West Indians*.

Thus, I was taught to believe that I was a *West Indian,* even though I was more likely a *West African* by direct descent. We were not taught Caribbean history; rather, we were taught British History. The horrors the Europeans visited upon the indigenous people and their near extinction were never taught except to say that small pockets of Caribs and Arawaks were to be seen in the larger territories and islands of Guyana, Jamaica, Dominica, etc. Certainly, we were never taught African history that would have been counter to the English goal of mental slavery by indoctrination. Without knowing it then, coming to Allen and the USA exposed my displaced self-concept and awakened my full self: body, soul, and spirit.

Methodist

How was I to tell my mother I had joined a *Methodist* church, I wondered? Back home, we snotty Baptists sneered down our pious noses at other less evangelical denominations. "They were not serious Christians," some bigots would say. We peered through our Pharisaic eyes at some church folks' party going, smoking, drinking, and other worldly behaviors as hypocritical and unchristian. Now how could I join a different church? I felt I would be disloyal to my family, to my church, and to all I had believed, whether it was true or false. Again my religious prejudice blinded me to the fact that like the name Allen, The Methodist Church in America was so called because of the methodical discipling of new converts in classes to ensure their thorough instruction in the faith.

Founded by John and Charles Wesley this assembly was one of the few which allowed blacks to worship in their sanctuaries along with whites albeit in segregated areas. The methodical feature was retained when the African believers struck out on their own. Nevertheless, my family had only always belonged to the Baptist Church as a family, and it seemed destined to be so forever. As pragmatic and straightforward as it appeared, it was a significant decision for me at the time. I was out of my culture, experiencing different societal norms and mores, separated from family and friends, living a new experience in a vast city and country. I was a fish out of the warm, familiar Caribbean waters trying to navigate myself in the colder unpredictable currents of New York, USA.

Episcopal

This title was an indication of the church's government structure under the oversight of Bishops. Still, my immediate reaction was my memories of the Anglican Church with its beautiful but staunch liturgy and the pomp and pageantry with which the priests conducted services. To be sure, Allen was not so staid. It was a church full of life and its services vibrant, but even so, I was trained to focus on preaching; everything else was to be considered precursory, preliminary, and preparatory. The preaching at Allen at first seemed so political to me. I was accustomed to Biblical, expository preaching. Here was Biblical preaching, but directly interpreted and applied to the immediate, harsh realities of America's African Diaspora. Again, I was too blind at the time to see that my naiveté was fed by my religious experience in Barbados that did not address the wretched lives of a disempowered, disenfranchised black populace. I cannot recall any sermons addressing the inequities that my or my parents' generation had faced or were facing. The Scriptures were taught in pure original context with little attempt to bring the power of God to bear upon the society in which some struggled.

In contrast, others, equally lost, enjoyed exclusive social privileges. We were taught platitudes that tended to circumvent our thinking and behavior. It gave us a mindset to accept our lot and to respect the grander allotments of others. In the words of the Old Anglican Hymn:

> *The rich man at his castle, the poor man at his gate. God made them both together and ordered their estate. All things*

bright and beautiful, all creatures great and small; all things wise and wonderful, the Lord God made them all.

We were taught to be conservative dispensationalists in the Schofield tradition with Eurocentric music, unknowingly taught to suppress our own native cultural expression as unbecoming in worship. Not so this Allen A.M.E. Church. Their gospel choirs were robust in their cultural renditions. Their vernacular was theirs, and even their Senior Choir sang its proud Anthems with a distinctively African American dignity, albeit in high church pitch, but, again, my state of anomie laid bare my fractured self.

Here I was at the feet of the Honorable Congressman Floyd H. Flake, Pastor, and I didn't quite appreciate some sermons. At first, I thought they were Biblically thin, theological deficient, and seemingly more sociological treatise than the exegesis of Scripture, yet I felt compelled to join.

Interestingly, as I contemplated joining Allen, I recalled the words of a white evangelist I had hosted at Mt. Paran Baptist Church, Barbados. He advised me on learning of my coming to the US: "Don't join a black church; you know that already. Join a white congregation so you could learn something more, (something) different from what you already know." I thought of that advice as odd at the time, but I didn't quite understand its psychological impact until I was in America facing my cultural, religious dilemma. I didn't know 'that' already. I 'knew' a white-led black congregation in Barbados, but not a *black church* per se. Allen was an ethnically black church worshipping God in the full context of their African, black selves. I had only known a culturally white church, and I needed to find a real sense of self in my faith experience.

I could not quite reconcile his advice with the experience of my current Superintendent, Rev. Henderson Neblett, and his wife,

Diana. They had visited the home church of one of the missionaries we met before. He appeared so warm in Barbados, so willing to keep company with us, spiritual and sincere. However, much to Rev. Neblett's and his wife's dismay, when they excitedly went to visit the much-esteemed minister's church, they were treated like unwelcomed strangers. They were not visiting friends from the mission field; they were "niggras" who weren't supposed to follow the missionary home. At Allen, I felt at ease in a new and different way that I didn't fully understand.

Church

Well, that it was. At Allen, I felt new, fresh freedom I never entirely experienced before. For the first time for as long as I could remember, I was not being called to pray, sing, collect the offering, sit in a meeting, close the church, preach or organize something. I was free to come in, sit anonymously in the congregation, sing, pray, listen, and then depart at my leisure and pleasure, filled and refreshed. I needed this oasis, this black oasis. I was in a dry place in my life; I was as parched as a man who had walked through the burning desert sands. I needed this time to sit unencumbered and to be ministered to. My soul was empty. My marriage would undergo its most significant challenge. Lorraine was happy to be a wife and mother in the small two-bedroom house we were renting in Barbados. By contrast, I wanted to advance my career to better care for my family. I was spent and exhausted mentally. I needed to come apart and rest awhile (Mark 6:31). My storage was empty and needed replenishment or restoration.

I began to realize that subconsciously, I may have been angry with spiritual leaders who were too insecure to deal with my self-assuredness and confidence in ministry. I was disillusioned by the hypocrisy and sheer wickedness in the people I respected and others

I thought were respectable. They had split the church and allowed their egos and self-interests to throw God's good work and people in the mud. They allowed His name to be slandered and blasphemed by sinners. I saw a great church, First Baptist Barbados, become a *hiss and a by-word* (Jeremiah 19:8) from which it has not yet fully recovered. I was a victim of racial and class prejudice in the face of faithful service to a company that promoted family members who sunk profits through their incompetence, ignorance, and arrogance. All of what I believe was in a state of crisis. Yet, strangely, at the boiling point of a personal tragedy was a turning point of opportunity perhaps orchestrated by the Lord. I was moved to join Allen.

From another perspective, it seemed out of a sense of deontological obligation that I should join Allen. My Uncle David was not the earnest Christian he is now, but make no mistake; he respected God, the Bible, and the Church. After all, his mother, my grandmother, was a saint, salt of the Earth. He even went to a Seventh Day Adventist School as a child, but he was not a practicing believer. He was a good father, a faithful husband, and a hardworking man, but he had not surrendered his life to Christ.

On the other hand, Auntie Hazel was a faithful member of Allen and loved Rev. Flake. She took the children to church with her every Sunday, so it was only natural to visit Allen with them while I searched. Still, then I had a realization: If I joined another church while living in their house, I was going to be another adult male in the house that was breaking the ranks with Auntie Hazel, who was holding up the torch of faith in her family alone. I instinctively felt that as the children grew older – into their late teens that they would soon opt not to go to church and join Uncle David at home.

I reasoned that it would be easy for Shawn, his son, to say he would stay home to work with his father on the cars he fixed in the driveway. I could hear his arguments in my head: "Even Paul doesn't think we should go to Allen. That's why he found another church." I couldn't undermine Auntie Hazel's efforts to raise her children in the fear of God. I needed to close ranks with her. Two other factors confirmed my decision. First was a comment Auntie Hazel made confirming my suspicions. In her quiet way, she quipped, "You Baptists are all the same; you think nobody's church is better than yours." That convicted me. I was a Christian first before I was a Baptist. I needed to be committed to the cause of Christ before I was committed to the covenant of my church back home; it was more important to strengthen my cousins' faith and serve the cause of the Kingdom than to cater to my religious preferences. The second factor was that my cousins began to look up to me like the big brother they always wanted and never had. I couldn't shake that confidence. I had to be an example. I had to encourage them to remain in the church, in the faith, in Allen with Auntie Hazel. One Sunday morning, I made an awkward walk down the aisle and knelt at the altar when "the doors of the Church" were declared "opened" by the preacher at the end of the sermon. It spoke volumes to Auntie Hazel, it meant a lot to the kids, and it convicted Uncle David. I had joined the family, and I became an Allenite.

It was an exciting time to join Allen, though. Pastor Flake immersed himself in the quest to rebuild the South Jamaica Community. He was young, vibrant, handsome, charismatic, and abounding in energy. His deep-set eyes seemed to see far into the future needs of his people. His 6 ft. plus height hoisted him over the heads of other pastors and community leaders who seemed not to see the people's plight and the economic blight of their neighborhood. In his book, he wrote, "We perceive of our community not as a ghetto but as a paradise...instead of grumbling we decided to take our destiny in our own hands." (The Way of the Bootstrapper, pg. 98). When I joined in 1987, we were worshiping in the gymnasium of Allen Christian School, which started in 1983.

Rev. Flake and his wife, Rev. Elaine Flake, an educator at the time, had conceptualized the school from pre-K to 8th Grade to specifically offset South East Queens children's under-educating. The children's poor education was a sticking point and a political football. It dominated community discussion. It was a worrisome subject for parents, and it hung like a looming dark cloud over young people of our community. Unlike those who simply complained and griped, Rev. Flake did something significant. In the spirit of their ancestors, they built their own school for the community and their children. It was a private, parochial school. It wasn't free, but it would be staffed by people who shared the bootstrapper's vision to impart Christian values and quality education. It was built one block away from the older Allen sanctuary on Sayers Avenue. The congregation had outgrown it under Pastor Flake's outstanding leadership. Situated at the intersection of two busy thoroughfares—Merrick and Linden Blvds, that intersection became a beacon of hope to the members and the whole community. It is now called Floyd H. Flake Boulevard, in honor of the bootstrapper who made such immense change. Several members unenrolled their children from public schools and other parochial schools and enrolled them joyfully in Allen Christian School. Auntie Hazel enrolled Karen and Shawn, and her sister, Jackie, enrolled Richie, her son, who was living with Auntie Hazel.

Formerly, the school's site was a dilapidated lot where a liquor store and other defunct businesses stood. Now, there was a striking, attractive building where children were being educated Monday through Friday. On Sundays, the gym transformed into a church becoming increasingly too small for the growing congregation.

People had to stand on the stairs. Others had to look through the balcony's glass doors above into the gym.

Rev. Flake had already built a large Senior Citizen Housing Complex on 167th Street. That lot was another eyesore that had been vacant and empty for years. With savvy and steely courage, he had secured its release from the City to build the two Senior Citizens' buildings. Together they provided affordable one and two-bedroom apartments for the growing senior population who were often shut out of senior housing in the surrounding white neighborhoods. Hence, Pastor Flake tackled another critical problem in the community. There was a place where our children could be educated with Godly values, and there was a place where our elders could go when they were unable to maintain their properties or themselves with dignity.

Of course, these projects would not go unnoticed. Pastor Flake's vision to transform the community physically and spiritually was not ignored by his critics. He got plenty of attention from those embarrassed by his success and the lack of theirs. Thousands were joining his church yearly, and his political star was rising with meteoric speed against the darkened South Jamaica sky. The breaking point for many came when Rev. Flake challenged an entrenched politically secure Congressman for his seat in the 16th Congressional District. His success would be decisive. It would bring together the black church's spiritual power, the black community's historical engine, and the boundless ambition of a young black man with a proven track record of success, as evidenced by the significant capital works he had already completed. With his congregation solidly behind him, Rev. Flake cast his eyes on the congressional seat representing his congregation and community, but he attracted more enemies from some unexpected quarters.

After church at the dinner table, our talks soon began to include concerns over the growing criticism leveled against *our* Pastor. Several pastors were upset that they seemed eclipsed by Rev. Flake's burgeoning ministry. Allen was the talk of the town. Some community board members were furious that they were upstaged by the young man. He had quietly assumed the leadership of Allen. He enlarged its influence in key areas. Rev. Flake related many years later that one minister invited him to his house to discuss his acquisition of the vacant lot to build the Senior Citizens Complex. Rev. Flake went to the minister's home and instead was threatened to withdraw his project or face recriminations. Another came to the Pastor's Office ranting and raving and threatening to kill him. Other people simply were mudslingers and cast disparaging remarks against the Pastor. In his own words, Pastor Flake recalls that "this restructuring was no doubt the beginning of my trouble because, for some church leaders, it meant a loss of power and control. I was so certain of the vision that God had given me that I was willing to risk their short-term anger for the long-term strengthening of the church" (*The Way of The Bootstrapper: Nine Action Steps* Pg. 186).

As the modern-day drama unfolded, it took on Biblical proportions. Rev. Flake was cast in the role of Nehemiah; his detractors were the Sanballats, Tobiahs, Geshems, and Shamaiahs of our day. I recalled a fellow student at York whom I challenged for criticizing Rev. Flake. I was now duty-bound to defend him as *my* Pastor even though he often told us not to do so but to let people say what they would and only respond graciously. The student stated that he was the son of a minister in the area. He implied that he had it on good authority that Rev. Flake was not genuine. This was his way of deflecting my witnessing the gospel to him. He was a PK (Preacher's Kid) that had walked away from the church. I wondered if his father was also responsible for that departure. If he was maligning another minister's name before his son, what else was he doing that was unchristian? A business owner in the community also spoke negatively about Rev. Flake not knowing I was an Allen member. I was conducting a survey on Merrick Boulevard as part of a marketing assignment for college with a team of other students. He complained that: "Flake wanted to buy up all the property around" and that he would never sell his to Flake. He was two doors down from the Allen Christian School's property which the Church had already purchased and was now renting out a strip of stores across the street from his business. This man was indifferent to the number of jobs, new business opportunities, better safety and security, and the rise in property values that the Pastor's work was accomplishing and from which he was indirectly benefiting. As far as this man was concerned, he would not help Rev. Flake improve the neighborhood by selling him his property when he was ready to sell.

Like Nehemiah, the worst of Rev. Flake's detractors were those who proved to be enemies within the church gates. Nehemiah discovered, much to his chagrin, that the nobles of Judah were spies for Tobiah and kept him apprised of his words and activities. Some were in bed with the enemy and their sworn allies. One of them, Shechaniah, was Tobiah's father-in-law. His son was married to another of Nehemiah's enemies, Berekiah, who didn't want Nehemiah to succeed-building the wall to afford protection for God's people and ensure the rebuilding of the temple (Nehemiah 6: 17-19). Rev. Flake, too, had to contend with the backstabbers – his own people who were attacking him from within the same community he was trying to improve. He was doing it for their benefit more than his own. Unlike others, Rev. Flake was not feathering his own nest. His work in the community was unselfish. Herein lay the problem: Rev. Flake's ministry began to expose the fact that some people benefited from the decadence of society. Improvement meant displacement, and they would strike back.

Thankfully, however, they were godly people beyond Allen's congregation who lent their support. After entering the race for the vacant seat of the late Congressman Joseph P. Addabbo, Allen's congregation and the community of South East Queens rallied behind the Pastor. They catapulted him into the halls of Congress. Some ministers who made up the South East Queens Clergy for Economic Empowerment were solidly behind him as well. They became partners in community development. Now he was not just a dynamic Pastor lobbying for projects and programs for his underrepresented community; Rev. Flake was Congressman Floyd H. Flake of the 16th Congressional district. His community was not only South Jamaica; it now stretched from the gated communities of the Rockaways in the south to the prestigious Jamaica Estates in the north, bound by Ozone Park on the west and Rochdale in the east. In the place of power, Congressman Flake was out of his local critics' reach but not out of the reach of those in-house enemies.

He had often taught us that we will always be criticized by people; many of them will try to pull us down. Therefore he advised: "Keep climbing up higher on the rungs of success. Move up to the higher branches so that they have to keep reaching up to get to you. There will always be people criticizing you, whether you do something or not. I'd rather do something worthwhile and have them criticize me rather than nothing and be criticized", he would often say. As Congressman, he could negotiate with the Federal Government for programs to benefit his constituency. He was more than a local preacher agitating for a handout from manipulative politicians who needed favors in return. He was now able to wield power over many people who resisted, refused, or rebutted him. They would now have to come to him for help. He was the Joseph in the story. Hated by his brethren, he later became the 'go-to' person for survival. His rise to power was a turn of events that bore spiritual significance (Genesis 45:4, 5). It called to mind the messianic prophecy:

> The stone which the builders refused is become the head stone of the corner. This is the Lord's doing; it is marvelous in our eyes. (Psalms 118:22, 23)

Many who once were on the anti-Flake bandwagon jumped ship to be on the S.S. Flake. Whether for selfish reasons or out of sheer respect for what God had done, admirers were now willing to acknowledge his success and began to claim him as their own.

Generally, the Allen congregation took most things in stride. They took the criticisms of their esteemed Pastor as water on a duck's back. They handled his election to Congress as a blessing from God and a testimony to the one God raised to be their voice in Washington. At home, he was their beloved Pastor as touchable and down-to-earth as he had always been. He returned every week to preach two sermons each Sunday and was often present for significant services, clearing the week to the pleasant surprise of his grateful congregants.

Then the unthinkable happened. A scandal broke out that sent shock waves through Allen, shaking its foundations. A former secretary accused him in the press of sexual harassment. She was the Administrative Assistant who the Church Board insisted he hire to help him from spreading too thin. She may have been competent as an Administrative Assistant, but she was not a servant to the man of God who was a servant to the people of God. Instead, she was loyal to Sanballat, Tobiah, and their liaisons within the church's very leadership. She was soon terminated and resurfaced with a vicious and vengeful agenda from the devil himself. Rumors she fermented were flying everywhere. She circulated letters to the "officers of the church, Bishops, and other people in the denomination" (*The Way of The Bootstrapper*, pg. 196) alleging, among other things, sexual harassment.

Greater trouble began by the spring of the following year, 1988. The Justice Department initiated an investigation, a sexual harassment case was filed, and the State Commission on Investigation weighed in on the conspiracy to destroy the pastor. The newspaper and the media began a feeding frenzy. It was not uncommon to see reporters and photographers attending Church to catch a word or a photograph that could keep their stories alive. Enemies that were muted by the congressional success became active again. The Pastors began receiving death threats which they kept unknown to the congregation as they soldiered on. In an enormous show of intestinal strength and Christian character, he never raised the issue from the pulpit. He dissuaded Allen members from being embroiled in arguments with the public and cautious with the press, who tried to elicit responses as we exited the Sunday services. The court cases, the division, the church accountant, who turned state witness, and the scorn of the public, were painfully familiar to me. I did not need to be in a church with all that turmoil.

It catapulted me back to the most dreadful years of my Christian experience. I was a youth, but I can remember it vividly—a conflict that split First Baptist Church down the middle. The Senior Pastor and the new black Assistant Pastor began to have disputes that seemed so trivial to my youthful ears, but it blew out of proportion. Soon a group of people walked out in support of the young black minister to form a new church further up the street. Those of us who remained at First Baptist endured the slights, the insults, evil glances, and withdrawal of friendship from people who were our brethren and godparents. More painful was the betrayal of those who taught Sunday School at First Baptist or attended part of the morning service and then sneaked away to worship with the other group that now hated us without a cause. I reasoned that the conflict was between pastors. Why had it degenerated into bitterness among members rolling eyes or looking away from each other as enemies? As a youth, I was bewildered at the 'adult' behavior.

My bewilderment turned to shock and awe when the former members who had withdrawn their fellowship moved back into First Baptist one Saturday afternoon in a coup de tat that would make the CIA blush. They quietly descended upon the premises, broke locks, and promptly started to clean or rather *purge* the church from top to bottom. At the top, they confiscated files and crucial documents from the church office. At the bottom, they fanned out sweeping, mopping, and dusting everything, including the floors, pews, and sanctuary furniture. Then, they lit a bonfire (or was it a devilish fire) in the yard, indiscriminately burning papers, including several copies of songs from the cabinets where the choir stored them. Being a young member of the choir at the time, I could not help feeling appalled at their indifference and wondered if they realized that they may have been desecrating sacred materials. Many of the songs burned were not readily available, and some of the songbooks long out of print. The cleaners acted like automatons – wound up like toys sent to work mindlessly.

Imagine the utter shock when the First Baptist membership showed up for their regular service to discover that service was already in progress led by the departed who had suddenly returned. In the ensuing weeks, it got worse; the two groups were soon physically fighting in the sanctuary for control of the services and the congregation. Finally, the situation became so grave that police officers were assigned to sit in the assembly to ensure order in divine service. That was deeply embarrassing, but more shameful was seeing my father slapped in the face or hearing my mother threatened and ridiculed by people without and within the church. All this scandalous behavior made us odorous to our Christian brethren who treated us like untouchables; none sympathized or stood with us in our troubles; none sought to mediate the impasse between our estranged brethren and us. I can vividly recall an old saint riding by on his bicycle from his assembly. He was dressed in his suit as he peddled, wagging his head in disgust at us standing in front of the church. Another passerby blurted out in anguished tones, "Why don't ya'all close down de church, nuh?!" Those words and gestures struck a deep chord in me. I felt like the rejected Israelites; we had become a *hiss* and a *by-word* to our neighbors (I Kings 9:7, 8; Deuteronomy 28:37).

Needless to say, the matter ended up in court before a judge who had to decide which group was the rightful owner of the properties of the Fundamental Baptist Churches of which First Baptist was a part. We had the Corinthian virus; we had gone before an unjust judge to determine which group had the right to worship and legally operate as an incorporated church body. In the end, First Baptist was vindicated after a long stressful wait. Those who had previously moved out and attempted to move back in forcefully were deemed legitimate members. They could stay, their Pastor could stay, but they both opted to leave again. The sad thing is that they would most likely have been accepted before the takeover if they asked to rejoin the fellowship. Now that opportunity was lost by bitterness and acrimony. However, before that thought could be processed, we broke out in our battle cry song, which was sung constantly in hope but now in jubilation: *Satan You Can't Prevail*. The church, battered and bruised, marched on.

'What was to be Allen's experience?' I wondered. Here I was in the USA, in a church struggling against wretched behaviors of other believers who placed the fate of their Pastor and congregation in the hands of the courts again. I can still recall the then First Lady Elaine's incessant tears that flowed unbidden down her flushed face each Sunday as we tried to worship under the threat of incarceration of our esteemed leaders. Still, as in Barbados, the court trial allowed me to witness the resolve of the people of God under direct spiritual test and attack. I saw steely courage from the accused, disgraced Pastor, an intensification of prayer, a deepening of fellowship, more sincere worship, and the exercise of faith in God. The congregation went to court day after day with Pastor and his wife. They prayed on the bus, on the court precincts, in the court, and wherever and whenever they were permitted. In the end, the prosecutors' proverbial car ran out of gas, and in a miraculous turn of events, the press and people of goodwill recognized the injustice that was leveled against a good man. The case was dropped to the triumphant jubilation of a grateful church and community. Allen was the church where God's hand on God's man was evident. I guess I was in the right place after all.

CHAPTER 3

CAREER SHIFT

My attention to my studies continued unabated. I set high standards for myself and maintained my place on the Dean's List almost every semester. Then, after graduating from York College – CUNY, I was ready to embark on my master's degree in Marketing to complete my qualification and quest to return to Barbados. I had already secured assurances from the Dean of Business UWI Cave Hill, Barbados, that upon completion of my Masters, I would be welcomed to begin my teaching there. He directed me to Dexter University in Pennsylvania, which had a relationship with the UWI. I was about to enroll when suddenly I heard that familiar voice again. It said, "That's enough!" halting me in my tracks. "It's time," it continued, "Do what I called you to do!"

Turning away from my own dream, which was more fueled by anger and hurt than anything else, I relented to the will of God. I enrolled in the Bethel Seminary of the East to complete my theological education. I felt dislocated and diverted more so than directed. How ironic that I was in the United States of America, where I was yearning to be. I was not under my father's "jurisdiction," as he used to state it to his children, and the Lord led me to pursue my calling, which I was willing to do before. I did not need any endorsement from my former pastors (with the blessing of a scholarship to pay for the studies), yet I was not at the same place mentally and spiritually as back then. I was like King Saul, I guess, searching for the lost donkeys, oblivious to the interface of that search with divine destiny. Like Saul, I would come into contact with a premier leader who would identify me in obscurity, hiding "among the stuff" of my life and Allen's large congregation (1 Samuel 10:19-24).

My hiding among the stuff at Allen was becoming more difficult. More and more people began to tell me that I was evading my calling. I would shrug them off and continue my anonymity. However, I was soon drawn into the Voices of Victory, a newly formed Young Adult Choir. Eventually, my brother James (who had joined me in the USA) and I were singing leads and soon came to the congregation's attention and the Pastors' as a result. This was a far cry from being a minister, but this would quickly change by a series of seemingly minor events.

First, enrollment in the Bethel Seminary necessitated a letter from the Pastors of the applicant's church, so I was directed to the then Assistant Pastor, Brenda Hazel. To my surprise, she stated that she was not surprised at my wanting to take a step towards seminary as she had observed me from afar and expected my decision. However, she explained that the church had its own ministerial process and that it rarely gave blanket endorsement letters indiscriminately to individuals who simply wanted to go to seminary. Rev. Hazel then briefly described the AME ministerial track. I fell outside the parameters, though. I explained that I had not considered applying to be part of the ministerial process as I planned to return home to Barbados. I never envisioned myself as a minister in America. My face was always turned towards home.

The next event came when I joined the Allen Prison Ministry. Sis. Sumler (asleep in Christ), the Prison Ministry coordinator, went to a Voices of Victory rehearsal and appealed for us to come with her to Riker's Island. They needed younger blood in their waning ranks. I felt obligated to go, so I joined the ministry. We met at the church for prayer, then we boarded a bus and traveled to our destination, singing and praising God all the way. We were not allowed to talk casually or sleep on the way. Sis. Sumler was like a spiritual police officer, ensuring that we conformed. I recall my first trip to Riker's Island. It was quite a sobering experience. It was one thing to hear about it, but it was quite another to actually go there.

I watched with interest as the bus exited the main highway and meandered through East Elmhurst, then finally came to a guarded outpost at the foot of a bridge. For the first time, I realized that Riker's Island was really an island off the northern tip of Long Island. The narrow bridge stretched ominously away from the outpost, arching over the murky waters before connecting to the island on the other side in the distance. At the outpost, we disembarked and went to a trailer where an officer compared our identification with the names authorized to go through the first checkpoint. Once cleared, we could drive over on the bridge to go through another checkpoint before we were allowed to go to the specific building we were scheduled to visit. That was the other surprise we expected: a large jailhouse. I was shocked and saddened that there were actually 18 jails on the island, plus two barges anchored firmly in the frigid waters. It was a humbling experience to pass inmates in jumpsuits or to experience the searches, scanners, submission, or exchange of different ID tags as we went from point to point to minister to those confined behind the wall of the jails we visited each week.

My deep sadness at the plight of young men and women and the harsh treatment we experienced as we were repeatedly processed was only palatable because of the service we offered to the wretched souls there, including the officers who were as much confined as their charges. Along with a few other young men, we were made to observe what and how what was done for several weeks before we were allowed to do anything to ensure we understood and complied with the rules implicitly. Sis. Sumler made no allowances for error. However, one Sunday without warning, Sis. Sumler informed me that I would give the sermon to the men incarcerated at one of the sites where we ministered. Soon I was placed on the schedule to speak often. The frequency of my preaching was also escalated by Rev. Carson, who was the leading preacher but often stepped aside and allowed us to minister in his place. I was humbled by his graciousness and desire to promote the 'green' young men who had come into the ministry. The Prison Ministry stirred my gift, forcing me to prepare sermons and be attentive to preaching again. It was good training because we often had minimal time delivering the address. Sis. Sumler was a stickler for the rules, so despite our youthful zeal, she kept us in line with the rules and regulations; we could not exceed our time. Sis. Sara Hurst, a founding member, gave me her recipe to keep me in line. She put her hands in her 90-year-old hips and fired:

> *"Baby, let me tell you one thing. Aim high, strike fire, and si'down!"*

"Yes, Ma'am," I replied. I got the message: be brief and to the point. Before long, I was coming to the attention of the church leadership.

Another factor pressed me unwittingly to the front. When Rev. Mary Reed formed the first Praise Team, I was included. We were allowed to sing worship songs before the official AME liturgical procession began. Contemporary *Praise and Worship* was new to Allen as a music genre. Still, it was a phenomenon sweeping across the church's entire Christian landscape from Australia to North America. It cut across denominational, ethnic, and cultural lines with an uncanny universality of songs. The lyrics were very scriptural, and the music deeply spiritual. This new wave was viewed with suspicion by older Christians, who formed the vanguard of the faith, as some new fad, particularly among young people. They were more comfortable with the church's grand old Hymns and the choruses that were tried and tested testimonies of the saints. In addition to traditional hymns, the extensive collection of Negro spirituals and Gospel music rounded out the repertoire at Allen. However, more and more African American artists embraced the new praise and worship format and introduced them to the church. Ron Connolly and others were carving out a new path in this respect. More and more churches were singing Maranatha and Integrity music, and now there we were in Allen, asking people to stand and lift their hands and express their reverence to God. Some were responsive, but others felt choreographed and coached. They were more accustomed to the spontaneous demonstrative acts of worship evident in the African American experience.

Nevertheless, we pressed on with the support of our Pastors. This meant that we had to show passion and zeal in our singing and leading worship so that each of us had to be expressive. That in itself exposed more of our devotion to God, as taught by Rev. Reed in weekly workshops, to the watching congregation, which slowly began to embrace our ministry.

These three ministries unintentionally brought me front and center before the congregation and leaders. I was soon known by name, and my relation to the Farnums, my cousins, was quickly discovered. I was no longer an anonymous entity in the thousands that made up Allen. The thousands suddenly knew me. The Pastor greeted my brother James and me in the street, complimented our singing, and encouraged us to continue. More and more people kept hinting at my calling to the ministry I continued to evade. I was still content to serve in the shadows focusing on my secular education.

However, one year when the Stewardess Board selected persons to preach their trial sermons as introductions to the church membership for entry into the ministerial class, I was recommended. Trial Sermons Sunday was a formal event in which the candidates approved by the Pastors would preach a sermonette for 10-15 minutes before the congregation at a specially convened service. The purpose was to give the neophytes a chance to demonstrate their prophetic gift of proclaiming the Word of God. At the same time, it allowed the congregation to attest to their ability to do so. I was one of the five persons chosen: Beverly Smith, Christine Bridges, Richard McEachern, Horace Stewart, and myself. I spoke last. On that memorable Sunday evening, we were all approved to be Licentiates in the AME Church. My anonymity was over. I was now a *minister* at Allen. Rev. Flake had pulled me from the shadows to serve the congregation and community. I was unsure where this step was leading, but I felt compelled to take it. I did so conscious of the weighty responsibility it accompanied and uncertain of the future. All my career plans now laid in tatters with my family's needs predicated upon them. How could I meet them by becoming a preacher in America instead of a university professor or lecturer in Barbados?

Two further developments occurred that brought about more dramatic changes. The first happened towards the end of my second year. Lorraine unexpectedly decided to join me in the USA, which took me entirely by surprise. She had gone from a reluctant traveler to one resolved to leave Barbados for America. An economic downturn had rendered her unemployed, and she felt compelled to join me. I was flabbergasted. I shared a room with my cousins at Uncle David's, so I didn't know where we would stay or what would become of our children. Nevertheless, Lorraine was prepared to leave them behind until we were settled, where they could then join us.

What a turn of events! I did not feel that my parents would keep up with the rigors of taking care of my two young children. Therefore, I arranged for my sister Esther to take care of them until my studies were completed. She readily agreed to do so, and they moved in with her. She was married and had a young son, Seth, and we felt assured that the children would be well cared for with our support there. The fresh lance from the scalpel of that separation stung, though. The first wound was my painful leaving; now it was Lorraine's. This time the children would be left behind until we returned. We eventually rented a studio in a beautiful brownstone in Bedford-Stuyvesant, Brooklyn, where we cried ourselves to sleep many a night thinking about our two little ones adjusting to a new home for the second time. Although I knew I had to finish my studies, it felt so wrong. I accepted Lorraine's reason for leaving, but it didn't quite satisfy the gnawing uncertainty, doubt, and fears that had a habit of playing out dreadful scenarios in the all too anxious theatre of our minds. Finally, we resolved that we had to make our absence count; our being away had to make a significant difference. It had to account for something. Therefore, I pressed ahead with my studies, and Lorraine eventually found her passion in Cosmetology. We would be two professionals who together could escape the sociological trappings that hindered our children and us.

The second development occurred near the end of my studies at York. In the last month of my last semester, of my last year in college, my mother passed. This was a bitter pill to swallow. Instead of my mother and father coming to join me at the graduation ceremony of their first child from college, I had to join my other siblings in Barbados to lay my mother to rest. I returned with my father alone, but my beloved Aunt Dora, my Mom's closest sister, my cousins Brian and Andrea, Auntie Hazel and Uncle David, and Lorraine shared that moment with me. In the months that followed, I was consumed with a sadness that was difficult to shake. I had so many plans for her. I wanted her to cruise with my dad, travel to Israel, and learn to drive a car *in white gloves* as my father had promised her. Those were all deferred dreams. None of these were to be; she was gone. My pain only lifted when the Lord showed me that those plans were more for me than for her and that I could not give her more joy than she was experiencing in His paradise. What was a trip to war-torn Israel in comparison to the New Jerusalem? I traded in my sackcloth for a garment of praise and lifted my face from the floor to the skies of an all-wise God, whom my mother served faithfully.

Meanwhile, I needed to understand where my new destination as a Licentiate was taking me. The game plan was changed; the tide had turned. The currents were changing, and I was unsure where they would carry me now that I did not seem to be swimming against them. Instead, I was headed into a shadowy path. Unknown, but somehow not foreboding, it beckoned me to discover the mysterious destiny ahead where my quest for success and my calling to ministry would converge.

CHAPTER 4

An AME Licentiate at Allen

As Licentiates, we were pressed into service at Allen. With a Pastor of boundless energy and a growing congregation, there was no space for slouches; you worked or got out of the way. Licentiates, though neophytes, assisted in funerals, attended the needs of the ordained ministers serving in any gathering, and had to be ready to address any spontaneous request from the Pastors as they conducted service. One area where we were explicitly designated was the invitation to join the church, commonly referred to as the: *Altar Call*. This is where 'the doors of the church are opened' to receive new converts for membership. At the altar call, we would pray with or for those who responded to the sermon kneeling in contrition. Then, as the Pastor directed, we would conduct those who came forward to join the church or who wanted prayer to one of the classrooms upstairs of the Allen Christian School. Service was held in the school's auditorium. We would pray with the new believers in the designated classrooms and have them fill out contact information for follow-up. Given the nature and sensitivity of the respondents' decisions, this was a sober moment for us and one of great significance to the Church. Yet, I often felt that we didn't treat it with the diligence required. Perhaps it was because we were holding services in the school building that some of the sacredness of that moment was lost.

Worshipping in the school had its disadvantages. The auditorium lent itself well to be used as the sanctuary, but the adjacent classrooms were not accommodating for other purposes. For example, some of the classrooms were what the choir used to change or for the Church Officers to transact financial business. They were not equipped for such activities, which was understandable because classes would again be in session the next day. Too many changes would be disruptive and costly. Given these constraints, I found the altar respondents' reception in this setting to be most frustrating and upsetting. Usually, we prayed for a line of people who overcame the fear of walking from their seats under the gaze of thousands. Often, this was in response to a message dealing with sin(s) from which one needed to repent. Generally, people find it hard to make public confessions of faith depending on the context of the sermon. After prayers were made and some instructions are given from the preacher or Pastor, the respondents would follow the ministers upstairs for further ministry. Most people followed penitently, but some eased back in their seats for one reason or another. In our context, we led a line of people like ducklings in a row up a flight of steps, people unsure of where exactly they were going, leaving their friends, relatives, and at times their children or belongings behind in the congregation. Too often, because we know it is correct, we take those moments of decisions for granted without weighing their impact on people. Therefore, we are not looking for ways to reduce any negative impact on the birth of new souls into the kingdom. The thoughts of trepidation and uncertainty in those charged moments were only dispelled by the congratulatory applause of the congregation celebrating the new births in process.

Unfortunately, the rooms designated to process the new members were ill-advisedly shared by the serving choir(s) to change into their robes before and after the services. This was a bad arrangement. Perhaps someone thought that we would be finished before the choir recessed, and by the time service was dismissed. This often did not happen, given the numbers of new members joining and the current members coming for prayer. It would have been better if the choir and the altar respondents were designated separate rooms. Often and precisely, while we were praying with the new member prospects, the choir members would knock on the door or come into the room. They were not purposely insensitive, but they needed to change, collect personal items, or make way for the other choir serving in the successive service; it proved to be very disruptive. At times we were caught between services with one ensemble needing to exit, the other needing to enter to replace it, and both requiring to robe or disrobe, while we were there with weeping, broken, and fragile people in various states of despair. There was plenty of additional classroom space on the upper floors, but it was impractical for the choirs and new prospects to trek two floors on foot or cram into elevators to ascend to those rooms between each of the three morning services at 6:30, 8:30, and 11:15am.

Inevitably, a few members appeared insensitive to the critical process of receiving new members into the body of Christ. However unintentional, they tramped in while someone was sobbing, or were too noisy while we were praying, or they were simply rude and disruptive. In the worst scenario, a Licentiate team member went scurrying for the keys because the door was locked to secure the choir's belongings. In addition, the membership sign-up forms were not replenished before or after the service in anticipation of the respondents, or too few pens were there for the new member prospects' use. All these conflicts troubled me deeply, and I began to think of ways to combat them.

A more profound frustration was the follow-up process. It became apparent to me and other ministers, I am sure, that many respondents at the altar were in various states of distress. Allen's extensive ministry in the community and the visibility of the Pastor/Congressman attracted people in need of help to address a myriad of problems. Some were homeless, unemployed, drug-addicted, mentally disturbed, experiencing a marital breakdown, divorce, molestation, and a host of other sinful behaviors that drew them to God for deliverance from their misery. Praying the *prayer of salvation* and signing them up for membership was not enough. Many of them needed intervention from professionals. Others required a caring community of saints that would correspond with them and walk them through a process of discipleship until they were stable, settled, and secure within the body of Christ. This could then be built on to help them mature in the faith. Unfortunately, it seemed that we were growing so fast that our membership intake was outstripping our ability to handle or manage that growth well. We were flunking badly, at the school of all places.

I couldn't shake my frustration. My peers sometimes felt that I was perhaps too intense. I saw it in their eyes; I heard it in their voices. "Alright, Bro. Paul," I can remember Min. Bridges saying as I engaged a respondent in prayer and conversation. It was her diplomatic way of pulling on my reins as I apparently chafed at the bit. It was clear we didn't have time for "all that" someone else expressed, and in fairness to my peers, who were as equally devout, we may not have had enough time ministering in three services to give individual concern to each respondent. Therefore, I soon found myself giving my personal phone number, taking a phone number, or providing a phone number to assist respondents in finding resources. It became my burden. Was this of the Lord? I spent many moments pondering how to minister to our new members. I prayed about it and complained about it. I finally decided to submit a proposal to our Pastors suggesting how we may better address the matter. I drew up a 10 Point Plan of Discipling New Members who joined Allen Church. There was no direct response to me about it then, but little did I know what was to come.

Despite the difficulties, Allen pressed on raising funds to build a new church and community as our theme motivated us to do. Many members radically changed their lifestyles and spending patterns to contribute more. Others raised funds in creative ways and joyfully gave to the church. All the membership was motivated to give, and all chipped in. It was hard to get a seat with an ever-increasing congregation, even with three services. We needed a new church home, so with renewed zeal, the Pastors forged ahead with building a new facility on a site two blocks away from the school. I would often pass by the site to see the activity and pray for the work to progress.

While I prayed and waited for a better outcome to our new member intake process, I was preoccupied with managing Youth Service Coalition (YSC) in Brooklyn. YSC was a federally funded program that provided after-school assistance to at-risk youth underperforming in school and needing additional support to improve academically at their grade levels and above in English, Science, and Math. It was a challenging task with minimal resources, but my co-workers and I had the unlimited resolve to help the children. Against overwhelming odds, we found innovative ways to fulfill the program's mandate.

We were housed on the renowned Pratt Institute campus. That was an oddity in itself because Pratt's student body was primarily

Caucasian, but the Fort Green neighborhood where it is situated was predominately African American and Latino. The interface of these ethnic disparities provided some interesting cultural tensions, which often led to intriguing experiences. In my view, Pratt seemed to be using The Youth Service Coalition as its philanthropic tax write-off and its give-back to the community it occupied for enormous advantages. In turn, we were able to utilize some designated space. We reached out to the masses from this campus to help the neighborhood children. Many of them, as expected, came from economically poor homes and harsh conditions, which were the chief underlying causes of their underperformance. With a team of three tutors and two other support staff members, we were determined to tap and unleash that latent capability.

Within a year, we executed the programmatic goals and saw enormous gains in the students who attended. We visited their schools, met with their parents, and most importantly, we spent time with the students analyzing their difficulties, which were often more psycho-social than academic. In the summer, we held a day camp that ran from 9:30 am to 3:30 pm to the delight of parents who wanted their children in secure wholesome environments while they were on summer break and the parents themselves were at work. We did academic subjects in the morning, including English, Math, and Science, and fun activities in the evening. We traveled all over New York, showing the children sights near, yet seemingly so far, from their inner-city world. We were supposed to have only 50 students, but I had an assistant with a bleeding heart who could not say no to the parents pleading to admit their children, and so we ended up with 150 students! My boss, CEO of the Coalition, was livid, and the campus administration was mortified at our numbers. However, we kept pressing the envelope.

I was cheered on by Mr. Arno, a retired NYC Policeman and NYC Corrections Officer, our illegal drug counselor. He was a proud black man in the civil rights tradition. His booming voice and unorthodox style and approach either made him friends or distanced him from others, but the kids loved him. He always told them they were his replacements. His extensive book collection and attending every conference on African American youth made him an indispensable wealth of information. We became an instant team and spent every cent we received on the kids. I rearranged line items on the budget and applied for variances and modifications to have the resources necessary to pay for trips and snacks or any other thing needed to facilitate the program. This again angered my boss, whom I didn't realize used some line items for his personal benefit and perks. I was not going to mishandle Federal funds earmarked for the children of our disadvantaged neighborhoods. Despite our most gallant efforts, the program was defunded, and I was left with the possibility of transferring to another position. Then, the unexpected happened.

CHAPTER 5

CALLED INTO THE SHADOW OF THE BOOTSTRAPPER

In the fall of 1996, I received a call from Rev. Flake's secretary, Ms. London. She pointedly asked if I could come and see Rev. Flake that afternoon. It was a bit sudden, and I had no idea why I was being summoned to see my Pastor, but I agreed to go. I excused myself from work and drove to Queens. On arrival, Ms. London ushered me in to see Pastor Flake. The wait was not long, so I figured that he wanted to see me regarding my immigration status adjustment, for which I had sought his assistance through his Congressional Office. The Pastor greeted me and then asked about my current employment. After I told him, to my utter surprise, he stated rather forthrightly that he wanted me to resign my position and become Minister of Discipleship full-time on staff. I was floored! It was the opportunity of a lifetime. I managed to say yes without exploring salary, medical benefits, terms, and employment conditions, none of the usual bargaining points in the offer - acceptance employer-employee interchange. He assured me that my compensation would be better than my current salary, and the meeting quickly ended with a projected start date of January of the ensuing year. It seemed that my earlier proposal had made an impact after all. I returned to work in Brooklyn bewildered. Upon my arrival at home, I relayed the offer to my wife. In her usual phlegmatic way, she was not flushed with excitement, but cautious indicating that we needed to think it through as we contemplated the decision to work directly in the shadow of the Bootstrapper.

By the time I was invited to serve as an Associate Minister to Rev. Flake, I had received my first ordination. I was recommended to the Bishop for such orders by the AME Institute, where all Licentiates were referred for theological studies while attending seminary. It was hard juggling the two, but it was required. We often questioned the need for both and were told that the Institute provided the denominational protocols necessary to function as an AME Minister. At the same time, the Seminary afforded academic training at the Master's level beyond that of the Institute. Therefore, as the *Reverend* Leacock now, I accepted the Pastor's offer.

I never envisioned myself becoming a minister in America, but I was not doing the leading at this point. This was a radical change from the plan with which I set out. Instead of returning to Barbados to establish a career, I would transfer my family to America. Our daughters would now join Lorraine and me in the USA and be enrolled in the Allen Christian School. The way forward was unplanned, unexpected, unchartered, and unpredictable. 'Where will it lead?' I pondered as I stepped gingerly forward. I was now a full-time Minister not in the Baptist Church, not in Barbados but in America!

My father traveled up from Barbados to attend my ordination in New York to add to the unfolding mystery. As I knelt before the

Bishop to receive my Diaconate orders, the man adamantly against my coming to America as a youth to study to be a minister now stood proudly to see me accepting the charge to serve there. This turn of events gave me great pause as I assumed the new position.

My work on Pastor Flake's prestigious ministerial staff began on January 18th, 1997. As arranged, I met him at his old office in the former church building, now the Youth Church, Shekinah. Together with Ms. London, we walked over to the new offices in the nearly completed Cathedral building. Another thought flashed before me to add to the line of ideas I was already processing with deep contemplation as we entered the building. I realized that I was on holy ground, land bought by Allen's members who were now asleep in Jesus. This is where their new sanctuary would be built. They would never have the privilege that we, their spiritual heirs, would have, though it was paved with their prayer and struggle. Not only was I to worship in the Cathedral, but I was also to work in its hallowed halls. As the cadence of our feet sounded on the steps into the building, I recalled the praise team singing for the dedication service as the ground was consecrated. We sang: *This is Holy Ground... we're standing on holy ground.* Our imperfect harmonies were only forgivable because of the deep devotion with which we sang. The land was blessed, and the processional choirs and congregation ministered: *We've Come This Far By Faith*. Now upon this very hallowed ground stood the Cathedral, and within it, I stood to serve God's people, the first new minister appointed to do so. I was humbled by this honor.

Once inside the corporate wing, the Pastor escorted me to the office he had designated for the Discipleship Minister and took me to the large choir room, stacked with furniture donated by one of our bankers. He left me with the building manager to select the pieces I wanted for my office. Subsequently, we broadly discussed the mandate of the position. My primary tasks were to receive new members into the body and manage them through a discipling process to connect to the Allen congregation and grow spiritually. Secondly, I would prevent a revolving door scenario in which people came in and out of the church without commitment. The Pastor cautioned that I was not to dismantle existing structures but to liaison with existing Ministers that were already working with new members to ensure a smooth transition. Beyond that, he expected me to use all my gifts to achieve the mandate in keeping with his vision exemplified. With that, he dismissed me to get started.

The scope and depth of the mission were enormous. There were no predecessors to learn from, and there were no senior staff members to mentor me through the process. There were three Assistant Pastors: Rev. Elaine, who had entered the ministry, Rev. Dwayne Belin, and Rev. Anthony Lucas. However, all of them were immersed in their own duties. Rev. Elaine was Director of the Allen Christian School, which needed her direct daily involvement. Rev. Lucas was the new Youth Minister of the innovative Shekinah, a miniature church in itself. It was run as a full service with the youth performing all the liturgical functions like ushering, counting the offering, and distributing the elements on communion Sundays. The music was in their genre, and everything was conducted at their eye level. Then Rev. Belin managed the daily operations at the Cathedral and the logistics of the Sunday services in a new sanctuary with which all the participants were to become familiar. Their hands were full. The Pastor had always made it clear that he would not hold the hands and babysit persons through their job functions in his ministerial and staff meetings. He reasoned that he did not need that minister or staff person if he had to do so. I was thrown into the deep, and I was expected to swim. There was little transition time to design and try out fresh ideas because as soon as the Cathedral was opened, grateful members filled all the 1,500 plus seats at each service at

6:30am, 8:30a m, and 11:15 am. Additionally, prospects flocked in significant numbers to the new impressive building with state-of-the-art facilities.

Scope and Perspective

As I considered the enormity of the task before me, I also recognized that the Discipleship Minister position at Allen was a *national* position given the national standing of Allen Church and the wider AME denomination. Therefore if I failed *locally* at Allen, my failure would have *national* repercussions. It would be the equivalent of being responsible for new customers in a large corporation and flop in that position. Such failure would have an unavoidable, negative impact on the person responsible. For example, would the Bishop consider me competent to pastor a church, as my Itinerant status predisposed me if I could not manage a single ministry at Allen with all the corporate and ecclesiastical structure it offered? As a pastor, I would be responsible for all the ministries within that assembly, not one. What other church would readily hire me knowing my poor performance at Allen of all places? What recommendation would I receive from my Pastor? While these were not my ambitious preoccupations, somehow, they seemed essential considerations.

This was a peculiar way to look at my position. Still, perhaps it was the Lord's way of helping me comprehend the scope of my job function and task. I believe that the Holy Spirit began to impress some Biblical concepts on my mind. For example, the Great Commission was a global function, a worldwide undertaking, a universal mission even though it was given to a small group of disciples in Jerusalem. Hence, it would have been a mistake to look at my position only as a ministerial function *at Allen.* To do so would be to adopt a limited perspective focused on Allen as a local church assembly and take my position for granted. Rev. Flake usually referred to this as a storefront mentality (with no disrespect to storefront churches). Those who have such a mentality do not allow their vision to extend beyond their circumstances' limits and constraints. They form a benign resignation to such conditions and make no attempts to surmount them. My prior managerial experience would not allow me to think on such a limited scale. I, therefore, recast the post in my mind: the Discipleship Ministry was a division of a major corporation that had global reach. Thus, the Discipleship Minister was a middle to upper-level manager with the Pastor as President/CEO. It was clear that if I failed locally, I failed nationally, and if I succeeded locally, I did so nationally. My perspective was not merely formulated because of any secular business culture which the Pastor projected. Instead, this was my own strategic approach to accomplish the task at hand. I reasoned that this was why the Lord allowed me to acquire all the prior managerial training and experience in Barbados and the UK. With this mindset, I readied myself to begin.

Before I launched into the job, however, I felt prompted to assess Allen's corporate context and makeup to best determine where and how my role fitted within its framework. The staff structure was simple enough and relatively uncomplicated. Rev. Flake was the Pastor and CEO of the now 18 corporations nestled under the church's umbrella. His upper-level managers consisted of Rev. Elaine as Assistant Pastor and, simultaneously, Director of Allen Christian School, Rev. Dwayne Belin as Executive Minister, Rev. Anthony Lucas as Youth Pastor, Bro. Edwin Reed (now Reverend) as the CFO, and the late Howard Henderson as the COO. Then there was the regular division of staff personnel, administrative assistants, secretarial staff, accounting staff, maintenance staff, security staff, credit union staff persons, etc. Allen had become the largest employer in Queens after JFK Airport, which was no mean boast. I was the only other Minister on staff apart from the Assistant Pastors at the time (more were to be added later as Allen grew exponentially). All of our other ordained Ministers, Officers, and Stewards/Stewardesses were voluntarily doing yeoman service besides their regular secular professions. They were heads of ministries and provided expertise for all other operations; Allen could not function without them. Then, a myriad of ministries and specialized groups within the membership body developed and executed programs and projects that met the church and community's spiritual and temporal needs. I was honored to serve such wonderful people in such a dynamic ministry in such a crucial way. I needed a clear focus to be effective.

It was easy for me to become caught up in the glamour of ministry which mega-churches like Allen portrayed. It was easy to become heady about being on the Reverend Congressman Floyd H. Flake staff and all the prestige such a position brought. He was larger than life, brilliant in his work, long in vision, and many desired the opportunity to sit at his feet and learn from his astute business acumen as well as his powerful charisma in the pulpit. His ability to marry two huge sacred and secular offices into the mystique that was Allen became a sought-after methodology that few had understood and fewer yet had mastered as he had done. Consequently, Rev. Flake won the admiration of political leaders who clamored for his endorsement as they campaigned for local, state, and even federal offices. It became common for high officials to request permission to speak to the congregation in the hope of garnering the African American vote in Flake's South Jamaica community. Even after he had left office as a Congressman, his endorsement mattered. Mayoral candidates such as David Dinkins and Rudy Giuliani, activists such as Al Sharpton, Senatorial candidates like Chuck Schumer, and Presidential candidates like Bill and Hillary Clinton, among many others, all came calling, and ministerial staff had the opportunity to meet them.

Significant clergymen also came for individual sessions with the Flakes and as attendees at conferences hosted by the Pastors to share the Allen model of community development and ministry, which they wanted to duplicate. Many of these were nationally recognized and prosperous, but Allen's extraordinary success held the promise of improving their churches to the same national achievement.

A Dual Sensitivity

In all these contemplations, the Spirit was at work helping me to formulate a sound approach to my calling. It was made clear to me that I needed to design a ministry operation that was in keeping with the character and vision of the Pastor and yet one that fulfilled the mandate enshrined in the Great Commission, which is the paradigm for Christian Discipleship. This approach would characterize my entire ministry. It required a dual sensitivity that all who serve great leaders need to cultivate. First, I discovered that it was essential for me as an Associate Minister to be in the presence of God to know His burden and to honestly and adequately articulate His word (Jeremiah 23:18, 22). Secondly, it was also equally important to consciously serve the men and women of God whom He had entrusted with the vision and mission so that they may be successful. How to do so effectively was my challenge.

I thought of Baruch and the challenge he must have had as Jeremiah's aide. Jeremiah was called and ordained to be the prophet to the nations, the one sanctified from birth and the one whose mouth was touched to proclaim the word of the LORD (Jeremiah 1:7, 9, 10). Though none of these, Baruch was yet the one called to witness and preserve the words and deeds of the prophet (Jer. 32:12; 36:4). He was the one who wrote down in columns the utterings from the mouth of the prophet verbatim, and when Jeremiah was shut up in jail, he was the one who proclaimed the prophet's expressions in the temple and to the royal officials. He was the one who had to preach the Word of the LORD on Jeremiah's behalf as commanded. Jeremiah was the ordained prophet, and Baruch served in the shadow. He was the secretarial scribe who wrote and rewrote Jeremiah's prophecies, ensuring that the prophet's mission was accomplished. However, while he labored in relative obscurity, his work was outstanding before God, whose purpose he ultimately served. The LORD Himself recognized Baruch with a personal prophecy for his service in the shadow of His anointed but beleaguered prophet (Jer. 36; 45).

With such Biblical examples in mind, I positioned myself to serve under Rev. Flake and to do so wisely. I recognized that I needed to be a servant to the man of God by fulfilling the individual role which he assigned, but I was not to lose sight of myself as the service ultimately is rendered to God. Consequently, a guiding principle was established in my mind that followed this line of reasoning: the Associate Minister must faithfully serve the one under whom he is appointed to serve. This requires the giving of one's self totally to the task. It demands complete devotion to the leader. On the other hand, the Associate Minister needs to be fully aware of his own individual service to the LORD. While it directly caters to the earthly leader, that service must always reflect faithfulness to God.

At the risk of belaboring the point, I understood that I could not lose sight of the one in whose shadow I served because of my preoccupation with the details of the service, nor could I lose sight of the service to the LORD as I paid attention to the one I served on earth. This perspective guards against the unintended misunderstanding of the assignment, project, or ministry as an end in itself, where one could forget the primary function of serving the LORD and so miss one's own purpose.

As I contemplated this wise principle I believe the Lord revealed to me, I began to pay careful attention to Rev. Flake himself. Under the guidance of the Holy Spirit coupled with my corporate experience, I studied his management style and approach, his likes and dislikes, his standards and preferences, and his expectations and demands. I was not trying to be him any more than Baruch was trying to be Jeremiah by repeating his words exactly, but it was essential to work in tandem with the Pastor. As our motto stated, he was *Building a Better Church and Community*, and I needed to understand the builder to help build what was in sync with the overall plan. The Discipleship Ministry was to be complementary to and compatible with the main ministry thrust of the Church without compromising its theological integrity as mandated in the Scripture (Matthew 28:18, 19).

Balancing Act

This was quite a balancing act. It is okay to take the ball and run with it, but that run must stay within the game plan. How would I serve the Pastor well without losing my own straightforward personal service to God regarding what He called me to do and be and what He required of His ministers in general? This was the challenge I observed that many an Assistant Pastor, Assosiate Minister, Youth Pastor, Adjunct Minister, Deacon, Trustee, Armor Bearer, etc. often faced as they served under pastoral leadership. It is not hard for junior ministers or managers to become so immersed in the job that they lose focus on the senior minister or executive's corporate vision. Equally dangerous is forgetting one's personal calling within the scheme of things. This often ends in disaster. The process of balancing one's service to the chief minister and the Master pointed up some key essentials that I noted to help me serve well. They may prove helpful to those serving under luminaries, particularly in large assemblies or ministries. They are listed here but elaborated on in the *Shadow Minister Devotional*:

Key Essentials

- Know yourself and the certainty of your own particular calling.
- Study the leader and learn how God is or is not operating in his life (Ex. 24; 33:1-11; I Sam. 2; 3; 18; 19).
- Wisely navigate the via media between these two factors (I Sam. 18:5, 14, 15, 30).
- Don't second guess the leader with your own judgment, however justified (II Kings 5:19-27).
- Don't underestimate your own significance (study the importance of Aaron and Miriam to Moses).
- Don't go beyond the mandate you are given (Num. 10:1-3).
- Don't challenge God's choice, however legitimate your grouse seems (Num. 12; 16; 17).

These principles were not pulled from a book from seminary; they were gleaned from the experiences God orchestrated early in my career as the new Discipleship Minister. In the initial months, God gave me a period of quietness and calmness. Few knew that I was in office and on staff. I, therefore, had time to pray and to plan. I used this period well. I would spend hours early in the morning in my office on my knees praying long before the office staff arrived, but soon the public demands of ministry began to escalate, putting my learning to the test.

Deputized to Visit

One urgent issue facing the pastorate was members calling for visitation from the Pastor personally. Some were sick, some were in various mental and emotional distress states, some needed encouragement and spiritual support, all seemed to need Pastor Flake. By this time, the Pastor resigned his Congressional seat to focus on his flock's needs, but the needs exceeded the man. Thus, in true 'Flakian' style, staff were deputized and dispatched in his stead to address the congregants' needs. In short order, I was visiting the sick and meeting with various people, congregants, and community members who wanted to see the Pastor with requests ranging from prayer to partnership in businesses which they were convinced required his personal involvement. We could not always give them what they wanted but provided what they needed with skill and spiritual guidance.

This delegation of duties was particularly difficult to accept for some long-standing members and those who felt that given their loyal service or personal relationship with the Pastors, he would personally see them. For example, I visited one Stewardess who had been quite ill and quite upset that the Pastors had not seen her at home. I was going into a buzz-saw of anger and disappointment seeing her but well-received when I arrived at her house. Her husband was there. I was always concerned when spouses, children, and relatives were upset or disappointed, particularly when they were not church members or believers themselves. These would have observed their loved ones' sacrifice for and to the church often at their expense. Therefore, when the church does not reciprocate, it could send the wrong message that their loved one's work was in vain or unrecognized. That's when damage control had to be exercised swiftly, honestly, and prayerfully because these souls were at stake, and the name of the Lord could be sullied. I did not want that to happen on this visit to the stewardess's house.

On entry, we greeted each other and exchanged pleasantries. I enquired about her well-being, and she explained. I apologized for the Pastor's absence but was careful not to say that he was too busy or that the membership demands precluded him from being there. While all this may have been true, they were irrelevant to this member's needs. That's what I focused on and helped her refocus on- her needs. "I am here because the Pastor instructed me to come to see about you on his behalf," I stated sincerely. That offered her some temporary relief, but it did not satisfy her. She explained that the Pastor and Co-Pastor were often entertained in her home in their early years of ministry; therefore, she felt a personal connection to the degree that they would have rushed to her bedside in the time of her illness. Her husband quietly agreed. I empathized with her and promised to convey her deep sentiment to them. Then, we turned to the task at hand. We prayed, sang hymns, communed with the elements, and then prayed again. The fellowship was good, and we parted more at peace with ourselves, our God, and our Pastor.

Another member, a senior usher, was equally upset, but my presence and ministry on the Pastor's behalf engendered fellowship and assuaged anger and disappointment. It was clear that the older members were beginning to feel the loss of the direct attention they were accustomed to from the Pastor, who was now less accessible as the church grew. Still, their demand for his personal attention remained unchanged. They were pouting like an older child would when their parents become consumed with a new addition to the family. The recent members were the new babes in the church family and the care for these diminished the amount of time the senior members enjoyed. There was less time for social visits. There was a greater need to delegate ministry tasks to others, and Rev. Flake courageously did so.

The Funeral Detail

The impact of the church's phenomenal growth was also seen in the funeral services for members who fell asleep in Jesus. Again, each wanted Rev. Flake, Rev. Belin, Rev. Elaine, and Rev. Lucas to eulogize them, and I was often sent to represent them. That was the key: *represent* the Pastors. It was important not just to officiate in the service, preach the sermon, give a prayer, or share a moment of bereavement; it was essential to do so in the spirit of the Pastor. This level of representation required a conscious, concerted effort.

On the one hand, it was important to recognize that I was not the Pastor; hence, I must not imitate him. That would make me a mere cheap copy (he was a hard act to follow anyway). Instead, I had to use my own gifts and voice. For example, I sang, but Pastor didn't, and often that added difference was an asset. On the other hand, I needed to minister to the level of excellence he demonstrated. Pastor Flake was personable, spontaneous, and skillful at drawing names and personal data into his eulogies or speeches to make the sermon custom-made for the family. That pattern may be adopted and adapted to good use, but it required much practice and experience, which the Bootstrapper had gleaned since he began preaching at 15 years of age! Thus, I needed similar training and experience in these delicate areas, such as funerals. These are not events to mess up. Calling the deceased by wrong names or making bad blunders to grieving, hurting families is intolerable. Like Elisha, who understood the mission and used Elijah's very mantle to part the swollen waters of Jordan to gain passage saying: *where is the God of Elijah,* I prayed to navigate these complex early ministry challenges, and God sent help.

Seeing my inexperience, I was adopted by the unofficial 'Allen Funeral Detail' as Bro. Jenkins jokingly referred to it. This self-named group of individuals was the core of Allen's ministry to the bereaved. First, there was Bro. Lawrence Young, an accomplished organist, the then Minister of Music, and the Male Chorus Director. He had played for all kinds of funerals and therefore was a treasure trove of knowledge. He had a great sense of humor and delighted in teaching the neophytes, like myself, how to minister to the bereaved. He knew nearly all Allen members and could give meaningful perspective on the likely tone of the grieving family and the pitfalls to avoid. Also, he knew the Undertakers (Funeral Directors) and their peculiar idiosyncrasies and quirks. Since they were a significant part of the funeral, handling them was important; knowing how was paramount.

Then there was Bro. Charles Jenkins, soloist extraordinaire. His voice alone with Bro. Young's accompaniment was enough to soothe the many heaving bosoms and turned many a tearful moment into celebrations of praise. They were a team, and the stories they told were inestimable. Bro. Jenkins' love of laughter and his willingness to teach his experience with remarkable tact and skillful diplomacy was on the scale of a tribal griot or master teacher. He knew how to pull me aside and instruct without emasculating me with a deep, sincere respect for me as a young 'Reverend.' The third wheel was Sis. Dixon, the then Manager of the Allen Print Shop and long-standing member, Lay Organization Official, and so much more. She knew the members well and interviewed the bereaved as she compiled, typed, and printed the funeral programs. She would often call to tell me where, when, and how to approach each service effectively in ministry. Soon I was drafted into the Funeral Detail. I was taught how to stand with poise and dignity. I learned the pace at which to walk down the aisle, annunciate in a tone befitting the occasion, read signals, and greet the family. They showed me how to process in front of the stewards, stewardesses, and officers attending the funeral, how to recess, and how to manage the Undertakers who can often become 'over takers.' Because Allen graciously funeralized all who requested to have their final service there; we therefore hosted three to four funerals per week for members and non-members alike. I often officiated, read the Scripture, prayed, preached the eulogy, and committed the deceased with the Funeral Detail's able support. My marks of progress were Sis. Dixon's smile of approval, Bro. Jenkins' glowing accolades, and Bro. Young's teachable moments or the crowning joke of the day, even if it was at my expense.

Ministering to the bereaved was an enriching experience. It had a deepening effect on my ability to preach. Offering people hope amid their despair, clarity during the confusion, and faith in God in the face of death requires great skill. Bereaved people are often devastated by their loss. Their belief in God may be shaken with questions such as: why did God take my mother, father, sister, brother, son, daughter, husband, wife, friend? The list goes on. The process of finding the most appropriate Scripture to eulogize the deceased and minister to the bereaved family and friends at the same time in the same sermon is an invaluable process of learning. It produces diligent attention to details that differentiate between a stiff, formal funeral service and a soothing, compassionate one. It promotes devotion as one seeks God like Mary and Martha, the Widow of Nain, and Jairus. All these had desperate needs for God to speak to them what He would have them know in their time of loss (John 11:24, 25, 34; Lk.8:48, 50, 52). Hence I learned the indispensable ability to weep with them that weep and to bless those who mourn with comfort. In short, it gave my ministry depth and skill in the valleys of human despair. I soon came to see that if the Word of God can be preached well in the face of death, it may be better preached in life's more mundane issues. Thus, I was enriched and enlightened in the Scriptures and how they may be applied as we traverse the valley of Baca with those who had to pass through it.

On Behalf of the Pastor

Besides visitation of the sick and burial of the dead, there were other ministry demands in the broader community. On several occasions, Sis. London would send me to sit in for the Pastor in meetings, conferences, South East Queens Clergy forums, and community caucuses that he could not attend. Some of these were quite prestigious. I recall one occasion the Pastor came to my office with tickets in hand and said, "Why don't you take your wife to dinner and accept this award on my behalf?" Looking at the tickets, I saw that the award was coming from the New York Bar Association of Black Lawyers. It was a significant honor; the African American lawyers and Judiciary members had cited Rev. Flake as an honoree at their annual awards dinner. I was not only working in his shadow, but I was also standing in his shoes, far too big for my feet. Even these opportunities were instructive. Representing the Pastor in these forums showed me the vantage point from where he looked and how he was looked upon by those who invited him. In addition to that perspective, representing another person forces the representative to think, speak, and act in harmony with the represented one. It develops a deep sense of humility and the character of meekness in respect of one's self and role assignment as ambassador.

On reflection, I recognized that this was Jesus' experience. He repeatedly told his disciples and his detractors that the words that he spoke were not his own but that of the One who sent him and that the deeds he did were the ones he was sent to do by the Father (Jn. 5:19, 30, 31; 7:16-17). He often expressed that he did not seek His own glory but that of the Father (Jn. 7:18; 8:50-54). His discipleship program was the one that the Father dictated and directed Him to establish from beginning to end (Jn. 17). In like manner, I was called to serve this man of God not as I preferred but as he required.

In every respect, then, I was being molded with the people I was given to serve. I was becoming a disciple myself to administer the ministry of discipling others. I was to be sensitive to the leaders I served directly without losing sight of the spiritual mandate, and in a balanced way, serve the congregation according to the mandate given by both the Pastor and Christ. Specifically, my challenge was to design and oversee a Discipleship Ministry that fitted well within the existing structure of Allen; one that the Pastor was willing to endorse, to finance, and to promote to the membership for full participation. In addition, I needed to ensure that the ministry had the flexibility for growth and expansion beyond where Allen was at the time to where it needed to go as it fulfilled its Biblical mandate in South Jamaica, Queens, New York, across the nation and beyond, building a better church and community.

CHAPTER 6

DESIGNING AND ESTABLISHING THE DISCIPLESHIP MINISTRY

There was no prior Discipleship Ministry per se that I could improve upon; one had to be built and implemented. That is not to say that no New Member classes or Bible Studies prepared new converts to Allen to be received into membership. Certainly, there were. However, the Pastor wanted more than a prep class or a Catechism for initiates. He wanted me to initiate what I was later able to articulate as: *A theologically sound mentoring process that thoroughly transforms mere believers into ardent followers of Jesus Christ.* (*The Discipler, Teacher Guide* pg. 8-9). This definition was not such a clear-cut concept to me at the time; I discovered it in the process of building the ministry.

Discipleship Ministry Flow Chart

I started by resorting to the proposal I had submitted to the Pastor as a Licentiate. I studied it again; this time, it needed to become an operational plan from conception to inception, a list of actions to be activated, not only ideas. Thus it was necessary to begin to think through the logistics of each component stage of the plan. Every practical step needed to be walked through to ensure the achievement of the intended results. The Spirit led me to design a flow chart plotting each stage to study each one carefully and methodically.

The chart showed how the work was to be actually performed from A-Z. It mapped each logical step, what specific tasks were to be done at each step, and by whom to achieve the overall goals and objectives. It was a simple chart (see fig.1), but it proved to be a helpful guide which I slavishly followed throughout my tenure of office and which I hope I could expand upon wherever I may later be called to serve. It showed me the critical areas to address and the personnel to handle them. The chart also helped me think through the contextual nature of Discipleship to be implemented both theologically and sociologically. It answered some key questions. For example, does it conform to the Bible, and does it fit Allen's sociological milieu? Was it practical or simply theoretical? As the definition above shows, Christian Discipleship is a comprehensive method of teaching new believers to observe all that Christ taught and did (Matthew 28:18, 19). Therefore, the Ministry responsible for overseeing this process needed to be well-grounded in the Biblical mandate and pattern portrayed in Scripture. Each part of the proposed plan had to be vetted to ensure that it was true to the word. A written description of each stage of the method proved helpful as I thought through the outworking of each step briefly described here:

A vibrant worshipping community

First and foremost, I recognized that for Discipleship to occur, there needs to be a vibrant, worshipping community of saints to which disciples must belong and join. Jesus wasted no time after His anointing by the Holy Spirit to call disciples to Himself to follow Him (Mk.1:14-20). Hundreds responded until it seemed to the Sanhedrin that the world had gone after Him (Jn.7:47; 11:47-48). It was this separate and distinct group of disciples that people could join as true worshippers of God. On the Day of Pentecost, the **worshipping community** of Jesus' disciples in the upper room was recognized as the sect filled with the Holy Spirit poured out upon them. It was that assembly in one accord that all heard declaring the wonderful works of God. This group from the upper room attracted the diverse crowd by glorifying God in the native languages of the dumbfounded pilgrims. Therefore, it was that worshipping community of believers that the 3,000 new converts joined in fellowshipping, breaking bread, praying, teaching the apostles, and sharing possessions. Now they, too, were worshipping in the temple daily and from house to house, praising God and having favor from all the people (Acts 2: 42-47). It was also to that worshipping community that the Lord added new disciples daily (Acts 2:47; 5:14) so much that several priests *became obedient to the faith* and joined the followers of the Way (Acts 6:7; Acts 9:2).

Consequently, Allen's necessity to be a worship community and facilitate discipleship was brought to bear on my mind as I mapped the outgrowth of the Early Church as it carried out the Great Commission to make disciples beyond Jerusalem and Judea. Samaria was a good example as well. The Samaritans had experienced the ministry of Jesus earlier; they believed in Him to be the Savior as the woman who met Him at the well had done and turned from their ignorance and traditions (Jn.4:21-24, 39-42). However, they became a dedicated worshipping community under the ministry of Phillip, and the process of discipleship exploded, requiring the intervention and participation of the Apostles themselves (Acts 8:5-14). The same was true in Antioch (Acts 11:19-26), in Thessalonica (Acts 17:1-4), in Berea (Acts 17:10-15), in Corinth (Acts 18:7-11), in Ephesus (Acts 19:1-12), and on and on. Likewise, the Apostle Paul and his missionary team often started at the Greco-Roman world's worship communities and sought to add disciples to it (Acts 13; 14; 17:1, 17; 18:4, 19-26; 19:8). Allen was to be no exception.

Thus, Christian Discipleship is the primary activity of an established worshipping church community. Howard Snyder cites John Howard Yoder, who eloquently states that "Pragmatically... there can be no evangelistic call addressed to a person without inviting him to enter into a new kind of fellowship and learning if there is not such a body of persons, again, distinct from the totality of society to whom he can come and with whom he can learn" (The Community of The King, pg. 73-74). Snyder explains that "Spiritual growth occurs best in a caring community... Fellowship and community life are necessary within the church in order for their various kinds of witness and service" (Ibid, pg. 75-76). For sure, Allen was a congregation of saints whose vibrant worship was commended by all who experienced it.

Interception with the Gospel

Before a Discipleship Ministry could be established, it was essential to envision the entire church community actively creating the disciples we hoped to have. Each convert was to become a new kind of human being. According to Yoder, they would be the new humanity *distinct from the totality of society* to which the new believer comes having left the world (The Community of the King, Snyder, Howard, IVP, 1977). With this in mind, I was determined that the Discipleship

Ministry was not to be constructed as another auxiliary ministry of the church but the very central activity of it. This goal was very ambitious, making the task of building the Ministry even more formidable. How could such a main ministry be established in an already thriving church? In addition, Allen was more than a religious organization. As a hive of activity, it was the principal community-based organization in the Borough with 18 corporations making it the largest employer in Queens outside JFK. We certainly could not stop the church and restart the whole lot with discipleship as the primary goal. Still, we could position the Discipleship Ministry to project that message as it commenced its function within the existing framework. That seemed to be an insurmountable task at the time.

Undaunted, I reasoned that a worshipping Christian community under the Holy Spirit naturally takes the next logical step: *intercepting people with the Gospel to make them disciples.* In this way, the worshipping community becomes a witnessing community. Again I took courage from Snyder, who wrote: "Witness and community go together. A concept of evangelism that sees isolated individuals scattering the Word throughout the world without regard for the life and witness of the Christian community is truncated and self-defeating. Evangelism takes place through the life of the witnessing community" (Ibid, pg.103). I recall explaining the new ministry to Ministers, Officers, and other key leaders. The meeting's objective was to make the church leaders au fait with the Discipleship Ministry operations to support and help ensure its success when it was introduced to the entire church. I recall seeing a ministry colleague snicker to another. She mouthed the snide remark that the term, **Interception** seemed more like body-snatching than soul winning. For her, the word was inappropriate, but apart from the alliteration used to help me think through my concepts, the term was intended to convey how purpose-driven Allen needed to be.

Actually, the gospel is not spread in incidental and accidental interactions; it is shared intentionally and deliberately, *intercepting* people with the message, as the Spirit creates the opportunity to do so. Evangelists must stop people in their tracks with the gospel of Christ and persuade them to repent – to do an about-turn. Jesus expects us to interrupt the journey of people on the path to hell and destruction and share the truth with them so that they may choose Him instead who is the Way, the Truth, and the Life (Jn.14:6; Lk. 24:12-35; Mt. 4:17-25; Acts 8:26-40; Jn.4:1-7). Wherever the paths of believers and unbelievers meet on the plains of life, the believer should seize the moment to share the gospel to effect change in the unbeliever. Like a football player changing the opponent's game plan, we changed the enemy's game plan and turned losers into winners.

I observed that at Allen, *interception* occurred in a variety of ways: the Pastoral preaching at set services, the sale and distribution of CDs, DVDs, Radio and Cable TV broadcasts, the streaming via the internet, and the general witness of the members at large which is the most excellent witness of all. Of course, in the beginning, Allen was not broadcasting on cable, nor was it streaming online, but such was the scope of the plan; it anticipated these means of witnessing the gospel and the resultant converts to be discipled.

Conversion

The purpose of intercepting people with the gospel was to convert them to the faith. I reflected on this step considering the Apostle Peter's words, who wrote that it is God's will that none should perish but that all come to repentance (II Peter 3:9). Peter understood and realized this divine desire personally. The hope-filled words of Jesus rang in his ears on the fateful night of his betrayal, which said, "… but when thou art converted strengthen the brethren" (Lk.22:31, 32). Conversion (Greek: **strepho**) refers to the transformation of form, function, character; 'it is a spiritual change from sinfulness to righteousness' (Webster). That's what Jesus stated bluntly to the befuddled Nicodemus, who thought his piety through strict observance of the Law was enough to enter the Kingdom of God, only to realize that he needed a fundamental born-again conversion (Jn.3:3, 6). Since Discipleship involves affecting a fundamental change in people's lives so that they turn from their original carnal living to Christian living, then **Conversion** is a primary step to guide respondents through as we receive them (Rom.12:1-2). All who responded to the gospel then needed direction to make personal decisions to be converted. Our ministry needed to be ready like an Obstetric unit staffed with spiritual midwives prepared to receive the newborns in Christ.

Reception

One of the church's saddest lapses is failing to receive converts properly. In the more formal setting of services, our altar calls, that is, our call to audience members to come forward and show their desire to become disciples of Christ, are often unclear, confusing, or at times unsettling. Our communications to prospective converts are often too laced with religiosity and church jargon that does not engage the respondent as effectively as they should. I became aware that we needed to be more mindful of the process, considering that respondents are making the most crucial decision of their lives at the Holy Spirit's prompting and with great uncertainty of the road ahead and exactly what salvation involves. I recognized that there needed to be a deliberate readiness to accept new babies into the kingdom on the same preparation scale for our naturally born children.

In a realistic scenario, doctors are in place, nurses and midwives are ready, and parents deliver or support and coach each other through the birthing process. In addition, all the necessary and emergency equipment is sterilized and positioned for immediate use. If all this is necessary for a natural birth, how much more for spiritual delivery into the kingdom of God!

The Apostles demonstrated such a readiness throughout Scripture as the gospel went forth from Jerusalem to the uttermost parts of the earth. Samaria was one of the first significant stops of encounter and conversion. Once the Samaritans believed the gospel and broke free from the bewitching power of Simon, the sorcerer, it was necessary for the Apostles themselves to go there to receive the converts into the body of Christ. This was a significant step forward. Jesus instructed His disciples to precede from Jerusalem, then go to Judea, to Samaria, and to the uttermost parts of the earth. Now that Samaria had received the gospel, Jewish prejudices had to be laid aside. In the spirit of Jesus, who had demonstrated it before (Jn.4:1-42), the Apostles rightly went at Phillip's request to validate their faith and conversion.

The same **Reception** was necessary in the Gentile converts as the Gospel spread throughout the Greco-Roman world. Peter was dispatched by God to the house of Cornelius (Acts 10) and Barnabas to Antioch (Acts 11) and the primarily Jewish church of Jerusalem sent letters of confirmation to Gentile converts affirming their acceptance without the Mosaic encumbrances as led by the Holy Spirit (Acts 15:23-31). This letter dismissed the Judaizers who were unreceptive to the Gentile believers, but it brought much consolation to the Gentile believers at Antioch who rejoiced at their official acceptance.

Thus, Allen's converts were to be well received whether they responded to the pulpit's formal outreach via scheduled services or from the informal outreach via the witness of the membership. Those who responded at services were typically invited to the altar and then directed to the chapel, where a Discipleship Ministry team awaited them. Other respondents were met in specially arranged meetings designed to welcome converts. Evangelical groups such as the Street Ministry were even encouraged to return contact cards so that the persons they engaged on the street were to be called or written to communicate how welcomed they were to join the body of Christ at Allen.

This level of receptivity necessitated clergy and lay persons' training to be professional and proficient in their performance. Unfortunately, far too many souls are lost because new members are mishandled when deciding to follow Christ. It is incredible what a poor attitude, a judgmental posture, and an awkward or insensitive remark can convey and therefore affect a decision to convert or not. On the other hand, warm smiles, prayerful ministers, a gentle touch, or compassionate engagement can have an immeasurable effect on the outcome of the kingdom of God.

I was guided to consider how unreceptive some in the Church at Jerusalem were at first to Saul of Tarsus, the converted lead prosecutor and persecutor of the followers of Jesus Christ. He had been well received by Ananias and the disciples of Damascus, who initially were on his hit list. Still, his attempts to join the disciples were met with rejection from fear and disbelief on his return to Jerusalem. Thankfully, Barnabas, a compassionate, good man filled with the Spirit, was able to take him under his wing. He took Saul to the Apostles and testified to Saul's conversion and witness for Christ. As a result, Saul was accepted among the disciples, moving freely among them and speaking boldly in the Lord Jesus's name. What if Saul was rejected and refused entry into the church? What a loss! Notice that because of Barnabas' Spirit-led intervention and recognition of Saul's potential, the Gentiles were effectively evangelized. The Christian Church gained its most divinely inspired Apostle in his epistles alone.

The step of Reception was to be Allen's preparedness to win precious souls sent to it by the Lord Jesus Christ, Himself, as was

Paul. The Church must be in a state of readiness to accept them well. It is noteworthy that those receptive persons were first open to hearing from the Lord, making it possible for them to rise above their fears and personal concerns to do as the Lord commanded (Acts 9:10-19; 10). Many a lost soul travailing in the valley of decision may be lost because they perceive that they were unexpected and that the persons engaging them were unprepared to accept them. The rooms where they are directed may not be set up, the materials to be used may be insufficient, and personnel may be late or entirely untrained to handle new believers' peculiar needs. New member prospects unfamiliar with Church culture and protocols are ambivalent because of the sheer struggle of their commitment and must not be subjected to such bungling.

I needed to forestall such misfortunes by ensuring that clergy and laity were trained to achieve the intended outcome. This required that training sessions had to be scheduled. Then, any new materials had to be redesigned or developed to ensure the welcome mat was rolled out well.

Orientation

Once people were converted and graciously received, they would need to be oriented to the Church and the new Christian lifestyle they have decided to live. Orientation allowed new member prospects to be as comfortable as possible as they started their Discipleship journey. It was to be as immediate as possible. I have always visualized new believers as new babies in Christ. There is no time to lose once birth has occurred. The child is suctioned, severed from the umbilical cord, wrapped in a warm blanket, and checked to ensure its stability. Then it is immediately connected to its mother with whom the nourishing and nurturing can begin under the watchful eye of a beaming father.

Likewise, a new believer is weak and vulnerable, caught between two worlds: the familiar one, to which he or she may be tempted to resort, and the new one to which he or she must adapt. Allen's **Orientation** took into account this urgency so that it was held immediately the following evening or the Saturday of the week of conversion of the prospects' decision to join the church. The new prospective members would be introduced to each other and the church through an interactive presentation. They would need to understand the church they joined, the principles it stands by, and its mission in the community and beyond. Most importantly, the attendees were given a creative, interactive reiteration of the gospel message to ensure they understood what had taken place or what needed to occur in their lives as they decided to become members of the Church of the Lord Jesus Christ.

They were also given *Principles to Live By* – a unique method of maintaining their Christian faith beyond the group discipling process they were scheduled to undergo. Other materials that provided information on the Church, Christian living, and an opportunity to ask questions were also afforded. Before departing, they would be enrolled in the Discipleship Classes, which they were expected to attend as part of their education in Christian living, even if they were already believers joining Allen.

Christian Education

Of course, the conversion is not enough. Discipleship is about learning the teaching of Christ and applying those teachings to one's everyday life. I thought of the first converts on the Day of Pentecost. They were described by the writer as being devout. However, once they repented and were baptized, they needed to be educated in the Apostles' doctrine. The converts continued in it steadfastly and daily until they understood their error regarding Jesus Christ, whom they had previously rejected as Messiah. Jesus was clear that the imperative for His Church is the making of Disciples. Learners, students, and adherents were taught to observe everything He had commanded (Mt. 28:18, 19).

Thus new babes in Christ were to be educated in the *milk of the Word* until they became mature enough in Christ to masticate the *meat* of the Scriptures (I Pet. 2:2, 3; I Cor. 3:1-3; Heb. 5:12-14). **Christian Education** is the development and maturation of disciples by teaching Scripture and its practical application in the lives of those trained. This expressed purpose is the task of Apostles, Prophets, Pastors, Teachers, and Evangelists. These serve to edify, empower and equip the believers in the faith and knowledge of the Son of God to attain the complete maturity and stature of the fullness of Christ Himself (Eph. 4:11-13). *Christian Education* is discipling people with the Word of God so that they are no longer ignorant and vulnerable as children, susceptible to the whims and fancies of deceivers who, by cunning and craftiness, would lead them astray (Eph. 4:14).

As I pondered this necessity, I saw that this critical step required establishing an excellent curriculum taught by competent teachers in well-managed class modules to ensure that the mandate of Christ is carried out. It is this stage that tends to determine the sincerity of respondents. If people are curiosity seekers who join the church with ulterior motives, instruction in God's Word tends to separate the sheep from the goats. It distinguishes those who will worship in Spirit and in truth from those who merely want the church's loaves and fishes (Jn. 4:34; 6:26-27). I have seen people join the church simply to use the Pastors' names to acquire opportunities. Others joined to obtain a change in their Sunday work schedule; some joined to save their marriages because their spouses were threatening to leave them, so they *got some religion* to clean up their act. Still, others joined with malevolent intent- to prey on the brothers or sisters or to *case* the Church to steal the tithes and offerings in an armed robbery by gaining access to areas they would not be allowed in otherwise.

None of these, of course, are any good reasons to join the church. Those who responded to the Word of the Spirit of Life were seen as genuine members; all others who were not fully committed could regrettably go away (Jn. 6:66-69). In preparing the curriculum, the Pastor advised me to use some of the existing materials taught to new members and innovate as I went along. I realized that I would need to have ongoing Discipleship classes beyond the initial introductory courses, a Level II Discipleship.

Induction

Induction initiates and installs or introduces the new members into the general church body. Once new members had completed critical components of their New Members' classes, they were now ready to be inducted into the assembly by the Pastors. Most churches have a formal ceremonial process to mark this step. In Allen's AME tradition, eligible candidates are examined by the Pastors and extended the *Right Hand of Fellowship* before the congregation on a set Sunday during service (Gal. 2:9). This is a crucial step because people needed to experience an official, public welcome into the body by the leadership to know their standing. On this Sunday, new inductees were encouraged to bring family members and friends to witness them officially joining the church.

The congregation also witnessed the results of their own individual and collective evangelistic efforts and endorsements into the Lord's work. Most third Sundays were times of tears and great joy at the harvest, and many visitors joined. Often the wives, husbands, children, parents, and friends of the newly inducted members were moved to become Allen members also.

Ministration

The final step in the process was **Ministration.** It is not enough to induct new members, write their names on the church rolls, and hand them a Certificate of Membership. Part of the Discipleship process is to teach them to become ministrants themselves. In other words, having been discipled, it would be fitting for the discipled to disciple others as well. In this way, the process came full circle. Discipleship necessitates the disciple becoming as his or her teacher as Jesus expressed:

> It is enough for the disciple that he be as his master
> (Matt. 10:25)

This statement conveys sufficiency, completion, and competence when this is achieved. The Sanhedrin took council that the Apostles had been with Jesus, under His tutelage and influence. Thus, they could duplicate His works and speak with boldness and elocution of the Scriptures unusual for ignorant and unlearned men (Acts 4:5-13). Jesus had predicted this, having schooled them and imparted to them and in them all that they needed to be His witnesses. They would now do greater works than He, Himself, had done (Jn. 14:12). Thus at Allen, those who were served would serve others; those who were converted would seek to convert others; those who were intercepted with the gospel would intercept others with the gospel as well. They would assist in the discipling of others until they become mature in Christ.

As a result of the Flow Chart, I was able to think through each stage of the implementation plan piece by piece. Consequently, it was possible to follow a prospective membership through the system from a new member's point of entry, their info being collected and inputted, completion of their New Member Discipleship classes, receiving Right Hand of Fellowship to the ministries

Figure 1. Flow Chart

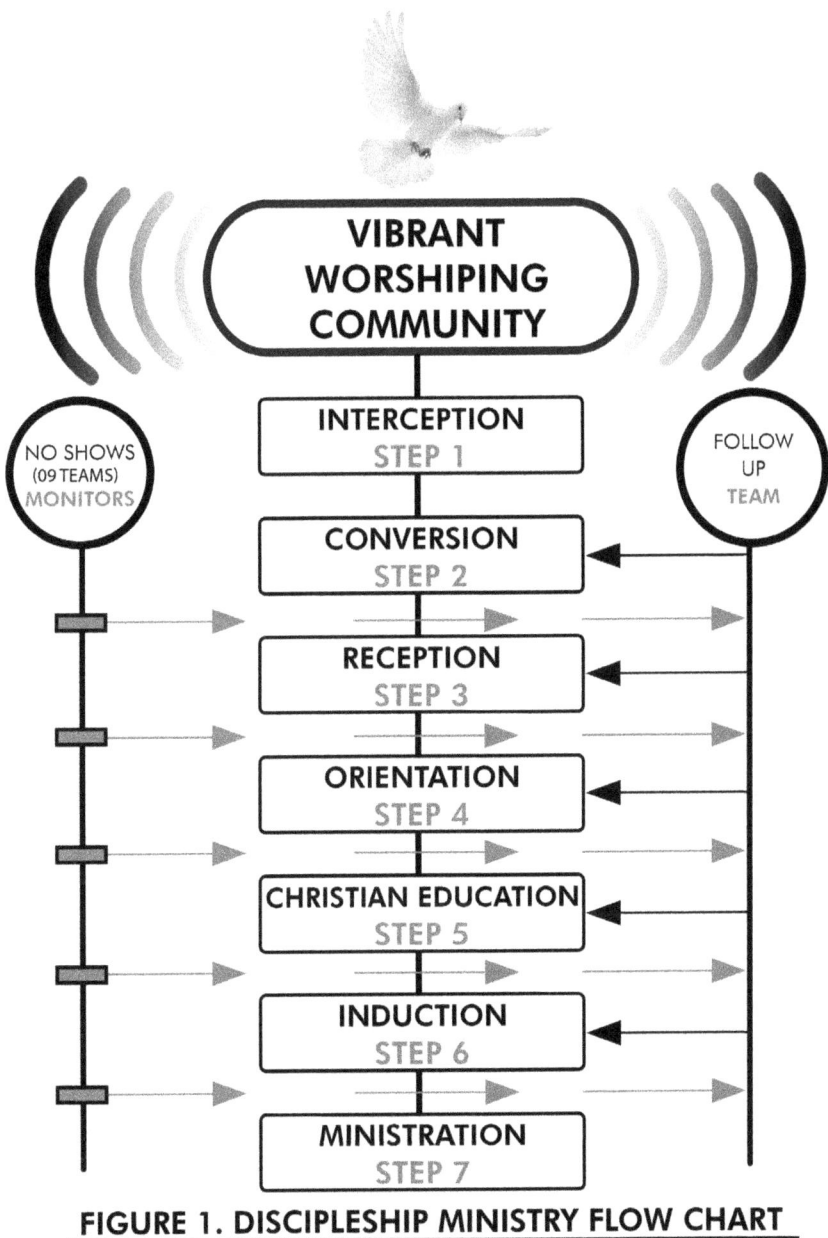

FIGURE 1. DISCIPLESHIP MINISTRY FLOW CHART
At every point of contact new member prospects are tended for maximum results

joined. Discipleship does not end with becoming a member of an assembly, though, so I was careful to design an ongoing series of classes that extended into three years of study.

After consultation with Bro. Andy Puleo of Navigators, I settled on *Design For Discipleship* (DFD) series of study booklets to be the basis of our Level II Discipleship Series. The DFD series (Book 1-7) were ideal because of their simplicity and fundamental truths. A skilled teacher could expand on the material for the benefit of his or her students. The DFD series was also used successfully by the Billy Graham Crusade follow-up teams and were tried-and-tested resources readily available. I also needed to study what my counterparts in other churches were doing, particularly mega-churches, to manage their Discipleship process. They may have lessons from which to glean.

Studying Other Models: Getting A Firm Grasp On Discipleship

As I set about establishing this system of discipleship for Allen, again, it became clear to me that it was important not to be myopic and insular in perspective and implementation. I felt a divine leading that it would be a mistake to develop a discipleship program that was so customized and fit for Allen that it did not lend itself to life application beyond Allen. I have seen church ministries that are so exclusive to their particular assembly that the language used, its doctrinal slants, the selected study materials, the illustrations, and the entire sociological ethos of the program made it almost irrelevant beyond the walls of that church context. Large churches tend to be susceptible to this phenomenon. They become entities in themselves, and if not careful, they tend to become insulated and isolated from the rest of the secular and religious world around them. I believe, in my heart, that God steered me away from such a religious bog.

Accordingly, I took the time to look at other models which churches of comparable size to Allen were practicing or contemplating. I traveled to Texas, for example, to see the ministry of T.D. Jakes at the Potter's House. I responded to the Altar Call at the appropriate time. I walked through their new member reception process, indicating to the lead minister what my purpose was, and he accommodated me. I next asked permission to observe the ministry of Dr. Tony Evans at Oak Cliff Bible Fellowship Church, Texas. I also followed the late Bishop Eddie Long's church, New Birth in Georgia. Back in New York, I attended Elim International in Brooklyn under the late Revered Bishop Wilbert S. McKinley. I was privileged to meet with Dr. A.R. Bernard at the 35,000 member Christian Cultural Center observing services at both their Linden and new pristine facilities in Flatlands, Brooklyn. I returned home to Queens and looked at Bethel Gospel Tabernacle led by Bishop Roderick Caesar. I often conferred with Andy Puleo, the New York Navigators representative and a discipleship specialist consultant to churches from Staten Island to Long Island across diverse cultural and ethnic lines in a way no one else could and did. Everywhere I went, I picked the brains of Pastors and Ministers on Discipleship, and at every church I attended, I looked at their program for and approach to Discipleship. I attended conferences on the subject and read on the matter until I became an au fait. I lived and breathed it, I reviewed it in Scripture and meditated on it, and I prayed daily for its success at Allen and everywhere else.

Of all the models I studied, I felt that Dr. Evan's was the most impressive. First and foremost, Discipleship is the stated priority of his assembly. It was made clear from the pulpit that Discipleship was required for all who joined. It was not an option. Secondly, Discipleship was mandatory for anyone who wanted to be an active participant in the assembly in any significant way. This prioritization of Discipleship in Oak Cliff's ministry was emphasized in two striking ways:

1. The Discipleship classes for respondents to the altar on a given Sunday began that very Sunday evening! This I had to see, so I went to lunch with my counterpart from Oak Cliff and returned a couple hours later to the church to see the response. I was pleasantly surprised to see several people gathered in a classroom dutifully awaiting their class to begin.

2. I watched in bewildered admiration as Dr. Evans himself came strolling down the hallway to teach the first class. He admitted to his appreciative staff that he was tired, but "I'm making it," he said determinedly. This acclaimed Pastor, successful author, TBN staple, etc., could have easily delegated this task to his staff as competent as they are. Yet, he wanted to ensure that each sheep added to his fold came under his direct care and understood the importance of following through the fully endorsed Discipleship process.

Another aspect of Oak Cliff's discipleship ministry I found admirable was its follow-up strategies. Discipleship permeated their weekly administrative activities. People who did not show up for classes were contacted with the compassion of a concerned shepherd looking for his precious lost sheep. Discipleship was not simply another ministry in the Church; it was *the ministry* of the church. As I studied Oak Cliff's model, I could only hope that discipleship at Allen could be as regarded and respected. I was impressed with the immediacy and urgency of Oak Cliff's model, but I knew that context was significant. New York and Texas had two very different populations, church traditions, and cultures that needed to be considered. Even northeastern practices had to be weighed for practical application as well. For example, I observed a church in New York whose immediacy was perhaps overwhelming. This church in question gave respondents to the altar call a ten-minute crash course in God's plan of redemption. Then they gave each a plastic suit and promptly baptized them. I was not sure that those who participated understood the depth and gravity of their decisions.

These models, concepts, ideas, paradigms, and traditions had merits. Where possible, the best practices were adopted and adapted to meet the need at Allen. To overcome the sense of being overwhelmed by our membership size, we engaged each person who responded to the invitation for salvation or membership in an adjacent Chapel. Teams of Discipleship facilitators and Ministers accompanied and attended them there. Once there, they were prayed for and divided into two groups: one for those who expressed interest in salvation or joining the church and the other for those who simply wanted more prayer for specific needs. Both were Discipleship groups- the first embarking on the journey and the second drawing on the community's collective strength to continue growing in Christ in the face of difficult circumstances.

The new member prospects were given welcome materials and invited to New Members Orientation the following day or the Saturday of that week. These alternative dates would be reinforced by follow-up calls that very evening to confirm their attendance and congratulate them on their decision to receive Christ as Savior or join the Church. Follow-up calls were made to no-shows weekly and then periodically by 30 days, 60 days, and 90 days to ascertain the commitment to discipleship. These no-shows were considered the *other nine* making up our O-9 list. This name was drawn from Jesus' question of where the other nine lepers were who had been cleansed but had not returned to Him. He expressed disappointment that only one had returned to offer thanks and praise to Him for His healing, and the others did not (Lk. 17:17). Having conceived the structure and researched other models, I decided it was time to move from conception to inception, in the words of Rev. Flake, to activate and accelerate.

Scope and Rope

However well-designed or intentioned, it was essential to ensure that the final Discipleship Program design was appropriate to meet Allen's needs within the operational framework which the leadership provided. This structure indicated the scope and rope each ministry was afforded to function within. It was necessary to keep the Pastor abreast of developments for his approval and support, and so meetings with him despite his busy schedule were crucial early on. The Pastor's monthly meetings with key staff personnel provided the opportunity to discuss strategies and procedures to shape the ministry to fit well within his Pastoral vision for our church and community. Additionally, his door was always open for quick decisions, which may have required his approval. He did not tolerate his time being wasted in aimless chatter, however. I learned early to treat him as a CEO as I had assessed the corporate structure. Therefore, when I met with him, I came prepared. I formulated the idea(s), studied the pros and cons, flushed out the critical issue, and arrived at a ready solution I believed was the best option for his consideration and approval.

More often than not, he trusted my judgment and gave me meaningful caution in areas where I needed to provide more thought. At other times he may have directed me to discuss the matter with other key personnel such as the CFO where finances were involved or Rev. Elaine (who soon became Co-Pastor) to ensure the plan's viability. Very rarely did he say 'no' even when he had reservations. Some yeses came with 'wait.' This was usually an indication that Pastor wanted me to rethink my idea or proceed prayerfully and slowly. He didn't like to kill anyone's motivation or creativity. Rev. Flake left room for his subordinates to grow and was willing to be wrong. He also disliked confrontation, and a cautionary *yes* took the tension out of most situations where strong feelings and passion existed. He was not an autocrat and never acted insecurely. He never exhibited the fear or concern that his staff may outshine him. Pastor Flake was a delegator and expected the one to whom the responsibility was delegated to deliver. He provided a large room (sometimes as large as a hanger) for development. While this gave great scope, it also meant that borders and barriers were often ill-defined and fuzzy.

Thus Allen was not for cowards. To succeed, one had to step up and step up boldly, always striving to do and say what was befitting the "Allen imprimatur," as the Pastor articulated it. The standards were high, and the demands were enormous. Success required courage and finesse. Courage provided the boldness to take the initiative and to be innovative. Finesse was necessary to artfully manage oneself as those steps were taken to not be a bull in a China shop or overstep one's boundaries, however ill-defined they may be.

It was just as essential to know when to step up and when to stand down. Two examples spring to mind. In one of our ministerial meetings, the Pastor announced that he would subdivide the Activities Room to allow the Nurses' Station to be housed there. I ventured to raise concerns with his plan. I stated that it ran the risk of overcrowding in one area and may be unsafe in an emergency. He indulged my concerns and said that he would not discuss the specific details at the moment. Others gave no scrutiny to the idea. I expanded on my anxiety which I strongly felt would lead to a bottleneck scenario impairing the medical personnel having to wade through congregants crowded in the activities room for tickets and information regarding a myriad of ministries and activities. Then, in a relatively terse voice, he looked directly at me and stated, "I said I will not discuss the matter any further, Reverend!" I got the message: *shut up!* I did. I was bold to challenge the idea, but I had not tactfully negotiated the political implications of my disapproval. This was an FYI, not an FYD (*for your discussion*). I tied a knot in the rope there to mark my boundary for the next time.

The other example concerned the Pastors' expectations of their Associate Ministers. For instance, they expected us to manage the services even when there was no printed program to follow. We had moved quickly from an AME Church with a fixed liturgical format to a very contemporary style with increasingly less traditional liturgy. Hence, when revival services or other special worship services outside of the regular Sunday Service were held, it was unclear exactly how they ought to be conducted. The Ministers who lead the service had to be sensitive to the Holy Spirit, intuitive to the Pastors, and cognizant of the congregation, choir, musicians, and other Ministers participating in the service. It was not unusual for the Pastors to come mid-way into the service with the guest speaker and ask, "Where are we in the service?" On a few occasions when we did not move the service sufficiently along through basics such as visitors' welcome and the collection of offerings, it was clear that Pastor was disappointed. He would never overtly express it, but I sensed it. I sensed when he seemed to feel that he could not depend on us to expedite the service, and we were waiting on him to do the obvious. Still, he would energetically run up onto the platform and move things along with ease and skill. At such times I felt conflicted and frustrated; I wished that we were briefed on and instructed about what exactly to do. Should the offering be collected before the preacher or after he spoke as some preferred? Should the congregants march to give their offering, or should the ushers collect from them while they remained seated in the pews? Who should be called to pray, greet the visitors, or read the Scripture? Was there a thematic Scripture? These matters were formerly handled by the Assistant Pastors, Reverends Belin and Lucas, who moved on to other ministries. Therefore, a vacuum of sorts was left.

However, the Pastors felt we each should be competent to do all these things, but at times we were unsure. I resolved not to be incompetent or incapable. When he made his entrance, whatever preliminaries were needed prior to the Pastor's remarks and introduction of the speaker would be done. I needed to understand his ministerial management style and function effectively under it, spoken or unspoken, defined or ill-defined, formal or informal. I checked out the length of my rope and the breadth of my scope. Needless to say, this path was fraught with danger. In high-profile churches such as Allen, ministers didn't have the luxury of repeatedly fumbling and bumbling without consequences, especially because some services were streamed live online. We were never bawled out or castigated, though; that was simply alien to our Pastors' nature. First-time baby steps were overlooked, occasional slip-ups were subjected to friendly banter, and incompetence was handled gracefully. The Pastors would simply suggest that the area of failure was not the offender's gift.

Grateful for the scope to grow, I stepped up and started the services, filled in and served, always careful to do so with good motives towards the Pastors and the people. Doing so meant keeping the Pastors and the people in my peripheral vision as I performed the activities, not overextending my rope. I learned how to read their faces, gestures, and body language. Rev. Elaine was easier to read; her lowered head and steady gaze were a sure sign of disapproval. It was like the incredulous look of the teacher peering over her glasses at a misbehaving student. At other times she crossed her hands and stood aside, or she shook her head. Rev. Flake, on the other hand, never showed his discomfort no matter how egregious the situation. He maintained a calm, composed posture. Pastor would publicly minimize the offense and use humor to diffuse any tension or embarrassment. He would often chide me for not masking my feelings but showing them visibly on my face when gaffs and clangers assaulted our theological ears or when proper Church protocols were violated.

I recalled one such occasion when we held a postpartum discussion with several ministerial staff present. We were somewhat unsettled by the remarks of a guest speaker. He had made rather crass comments during a Sunday Morning Men's Season service. He admonished the brothers to appreciate the black woman. Rather than drawing his reasons from Song of Solomon or Proverbs 31, where women's virtues were divinely valued, the preacher proceeded to charge the brother to appreciate the black woman for her luscious lips, curvaceous hips, and voluptuous derriere. "At least," he pointed out, gesturing, "you have something to hold onto when you're making love." A quick pan of the congregation showed the mortified faces of chiefly the older women who stared in disbelief. Others snickered incredulously. I had cradled my face in my hands as his message began to degenerate into a homiletic abyss. The Pastor had maintained his demeanor throughout, and after he took control of the pulpit, he piloted the service back to altar call and benediction. We laughed at our varied reactions, but Pastor Flake turned it into a teachable moment about not reacting because of the ripple effect on the congregation.

Finding my place and considering the mandate and the operational context to function, I felt ready to unfold the new Discipleship Ministry. Having planned the work, I knew it was time to work the plan. It was time to implement what was designed. Nevertheless, moving from conception to inception meant that one had to be strategic and astute in implementation. Since the Church's primary responsibility is the great Commission, one would think that making disciples would be given a welcomed place in the church's program. I soon realized that, alas, this is not always the case, even when it was the expressed desire of the Pastor. I further understood that each church has its own ethos, which must be carefully acknowledged. From the oldest denomination to the newest non-denominational assembly, each has a particular culture based on Scripture, traditions, societal influences, the specific circumstances from which the congregation has arisen, and the principal personalities that helped shape the assembly into a church group or religious organization. All these factors can help but can equally hinder the Great Commission's execution of making disciples. The early church found this true in their formative years and had to call their first conference to address it (Acts 15). I would run into Allen's.

I soon was awakened to the fact that not much has changed. Although the present Christian Church (now largely Gentile) knows of the priority of Discipleship, it allows certain men and women to resist the work of the Holy Spirit, especially in the area of discipleship. Today, the issue is not whether Mosaic laws should be observed or not. Instead, discipleship efforts, which are often innovative, necessary, and contextualized to reach new and different people, can often run counter to the staid, stiff, and stagnant waters of church traditions and politics. In this respect, Allen was no different.

CHAPTER 7

Implementing the Ministry: From Conception to Inception

Even though new members were pouring into the new Cathedral, it was necessary to convince some Officers, Ministry leaders, and the membership to orient the church to Discipleship to capture and manage the influx they undoubtedly were happy to see. Allen is a warm and loving church. However, more attention needed to be given to the efforts and activities which Discipleship demands, and those who control areas of power were not readily amenable. This is not to say that they were unchristian in their behavior or necessarily against Discipleship's priority. They were just resistant to the change in areas that ran counter to some of the traditional church habits they were accustomed to. African or not, we were in nature still Methodist and stuck fast to set ways of doing things in the meticulous Wesleyan tradition.

Avoiding the Big Brother Syndrome

I asked everyone to adjust the ministry priorities they felt passionately about. They had given yeoman service for the benefit of the church as they saw it and as they may have been appointed to do. Now I asked for their time, resources, energy, and space for this new ministry. For example, rooms had to be set aside for Discipleship classes; systems had to be established or modified to accommodate the demands discipling new believers required. New phones had to be installed to allow follow-up calls to new converts. Ministers were assigned to teach classes, laypersons had to be trained to minister to the new prospects, and Ministry leaders needed to be receptive and sensitive to new members joining their ministries. The General Office had to respond to questions and give the correct information. Pastors' schedules had to be adjusted to allow for their attendance at functions held for new members. The Business Office needed to factor new member statistics into their financial reports and allocate new expenditure accounts. Counselors had to schedule more therapeutic sessions for new presenting issues. Plus, the Maintenance staff had to set up rooms, reorganize furniture and space, and the list went on.

As can be seen, establishing the ministry affected the entire status quo and the established order, which is often naturally resistant to change. It is similar to the home scenario alluded to earlier when a new baby is born into a family. Everything and everyone's schedule and living patterns are disrupted to accommodate the new child's needs. As precious as the new baby is to the family, it is equally annoying, frustrating, demanding, expensive, and dislocating, requiring significant permanent adjustment. Similarly, church members (including the recently received) act like jealous siblings, upset that they are displaced by the new needy babes in Christ that are now receiving (as it would seem) all the attention. It is even possible for pastors to be conflicted because of the challenge discipleship presents. The tensions forged by the clash of the existing versus new members, the demand for new budgets, or even the allure of more finances from the more recent members all bring added pressures and new demands: more management, more ministering, more responsibility, more praying, more fasting, more sacrifice of time and on and on.

Care had to be taken to establish the Discipleship Ministry at Allen to avoid what I called *The Big Brother Syndrome* (Lk. 15:25-32). I was alarmed to discover that if the discipling of new members is not negotiated and navigated wisely under the Holy Spirit's direction, the church could become divided as the needs of the old and new believers conflicted. It became evident that one set of members could be shown concerted care and attention like a new baby that is kissed, petted, and pampered while the others feel kicked to the side as it were and ignored. Such an ill-advised approach would inevitably create two congregations within one assembly under one Pastor at odds with each other and unsure why. If not managed carefully, it could have created animosity against the newcomers. Many new members walk away from such situations feeling unwelcomed, hurt, and disappointed. Long-standing members can feel angry and mistreated in deference to more recent members who benefit from all the privileges they worked hard for and had made the monetary sacrifices to provide. It is easier for the latter to be felt since invariably, new members reap the ministry's benefits as it improves.

I recalled being pleasantly confronted by a long-standing member and ministry leader at a New Member's Reception we had hosted for recently received members. They were entertained, celebrated, and hosted in the Banquet Hall, where they could meet the Pastors without restraint and explore and join ministries that had staged information tables just for them. Sis. Dennis said to me, "We didn't get all this when we joined!" We looked at each other and laughed at the fact, but it was necessary to acknowledge her jealousy over the pleasantries that her efforts made possible. Others complained that their Membership Certificates were not as nice as the newer ones being issued with the church's new logos, which now read: The Greater Allen (AME) Cathedral of New York, not the old Allen AME Church. These encounters reinforced the importance of operating according to a Spirit-led plan sensitive to the entire congregation's needs. It needed to target and include leaders at all levels to ensure their partnership in the implementation, maintenance, and success of the new Discipleship Ministry. Therefore, in my Day Timers planner, I drew up a project sheet to set about winning the support of others critical to the Discipleship Ministry's work.

Winning the Support of Leaders and Finding the Faithful

Accordingly, I began introducing the ministry to critical leaders and increasingly held discussions with Rev. Elaine, whose portfolio had increased to oversee all the ministries and day-to-day affairs as Co-Pastor. Once this stage was established, selecting persons to do the work was next. For example, we needed a team to receive respondents at the altar during services and teachers for the New Members/ Discipleship classes. In addition, we required personnel to make follow-up calls, persons to take attendance, people to ensure accurate tracking through the class process, and persons to do analysis to measure outcomes.

We tapped into the existing pool of Ministers to be our teachers, and we began looking for faithful members who we could teach about the system of operation we had established. In my efforts to lay the groundwork, I discovered a critical truth: it was easier to plug people into a system but impossible to plug the system into people. Much effort was expended trying to do the latter, which only led to incredible frustration. People would eventually do what comes more comfortable and more natural to them, whether consistent with the stated plan or not.

Also, I learned that it is possible to teach faithful people new skills and competencies, but it is somewhat more difficult, if not impossible, to teach skilled and competent people to be faithful. Faithfulness is a virtue, not an acquired skill learned in a training session. Thus, it quickly became apparent that it was wiser to look for dedicated members than to run after skilled and competent staff. Such a person was Evangelist Doreen Prescott. She came enthusiastically and told me she came to help. Evangelist Prescott was a major encouragement. Her ready smile, graciousness, humility, love for the work of God and people was the perfect type I sought. Without prompting, she saw the need, served alongside me, and did so commendably before anyone else. We needed people who would show up on time and prepare to teach their classes or conduct the assigned session. 'No-shows' or ill-prepared personnel translated into a contradiction of the urgency we preached in our evangelical messages- the immediacy we impressed in the New Members' Orientation in respect of repentance and salvation. Such teaching is for naught in the face of poor performance or cancellations due to someone not showing up. A mediocre performance to a group of eager new members from a punctual facilitator was more forgivable than an outstanding facilitator who never showed up. It became evident that the training of the willingly faithful was essential to avoid the invalidation of efforts.

Training Disciples to Execute the Mission – the Pattern of Jesus

Training is often not given its proper value in church organization and administration. We usually provide minimum training to laypersons and Ministers in critical areas but expect exceptional results. This is absurd! We have a false belief that one sermon, one worship service, one meeting, one retreat, one prayer, one article, or one rebuke is enough to enable persons to miraculously do the work. It doesn't matter how difficult it may be. When this does not happen or mediocrity results from our minimum input, we resort to more rebukes, more sermons on the issue, and even more prayer and fasting for better outcomes. This is not the pattern set by Jesus, the ultimate Discipler. He trained all He called. He invited people to follow Him, but He promised them that He would *make them* fishers of men (Mt. 4:19). Often He called them aside to teach them, instruct and educate them not just in the mundane but in the mysteries of the kingdom of God (Mt. 5:1-13).

The famous Sermon on the Mount distinguishing the followers of Jesus from all others was taught primarily to the disciples that came and sat before Him (Mt. 5:1-2). The crowd often followed him out of curiosity, out of their own depravity, and the drive of their own material needs (Jn. 6:22-27). On the other hand, His disciples followed Him because He had the indispensable words of eternal life (Jn. 6:68, 69). He was more known to them as Rabbi (Teacher) than anything else. His teaching opened their eyes to who He truly is (Lk. 24:25-35, 45-49). He did not merely talk at them; He trained them in practical ways. He reached across cultural and religious traditions, gender, and generational lines to reach one woman at a well and taught the disciples how to see the resulting spiritual harvest (Jn. 4:35). Jesus came across socio-economic and moral barriers to speak to Publicans and sinners. He thereby taught His disciples that the sick needed the physician, not the well (Lk. 5:31). He reached across scorn, ridicule, and a disgrace to touch the halt, the lame, the blind, the leprous, and the dead, and He taught His disciples to restore them all (Lk. 5:12-14; 4:40-41; 9:1-2). Then when He saw fit, Jesus deployed His disciples to go without Him to do the very things that He had done in their presence. They returned, rejoicing they could heal the sick, exorcise demons, and preach the gospel of the kingdom just as he taught them to do (Lk. 9; 10).

Most importantly, He imparted *His* Spirit to clothe and empower them so that they may precisely function as He would and, in turn, to teach others to do the same. Thus, Jesus was a trainer of trainers, a discipler of disciples, and a teacher of teachers who poured Himself into those He expected to minister to the masses He wanted to reach. Hence, one of the hallmarks of Jesus' method of Discipleship is His impartation of Himself to His Disciples. (My reflection of this dynamic is summarized in the *Shadow Minister Devotional*).

In keeping with the Christological paradigm then, I began to train others to do the task of discipling. Being made the Discipleship Minister is one thing, but having trained volunteers to perform the ministry functions is quite another. Volunteers who graciously responded to the call were taught: how to receive persons at the altar, how to evangelize in the streets, how to pray with prospects, how to call them, what to say and what not to say, and how to deal with demoniacs or the mentally disturbed when encountered in our services.

Oneness of Spirit

At first, I was prepared to give a workshop or several to disseminate the information to the selected trainees, but I soon felt the Holy Spirit's rebuke not to. I was ready to release the trainees to their assigned tasks with some monitoring, of course, so that I may turn to another part of the ministry that needed building (and there were many), but the Holy Spirit disapproved of that decision. I sought the Lord on this matter because I could not shake the uneasiness I felt. He impressed upon my mind that if I wanted those selected to function as I desired and as He had directed me, then I needed to spend time with them frequently so that the way the Spirit was operative in me, He may also be operative in them. We needed to be of the same mind.

As I reflected on this principle, I realized that this was the essence of Discipleship. This is the reason Jesus spent time with the twelve. Of course, there was some spiritual transference to the disciples, especially Peter, James, and John, because of their apparent proximity and constant fellowship with Christ. Jesus' direct effect on His select Apostles and the testimonies of those Apostles themselves support the fact that Jesus imparted something of Himself to them that enabled them to function as He desired and determined in accordance to His Father's will. This was what the Spirit was intimating to me. Therefore, if others were to do the work of Discipleship, I had to train them to do so in the manner I was charged to do it. By so doing, there would be an impartation of the same vision, passion, and sense of mission in them as was given to me. This dynamic was a principle that proved to be essential in my experience, and I believe it is often underestimated in ministry elsewhere.

Furthermore, it became apparent to me that if Allen successfully carried out the Great Commission of making Disciples of all, those chosen for the task needed to be instilled with the same vision that the Pastor had given and entrusted to me. Therefore, it was now my responsibility to communicate it as Jesus had communicated His Father's will to those He had chosen to serve in the ministry. I felt the burning evangelistic zeal to reach souls each time an opportunity for soul-winning presented itself. I was consumed with the missionary zeal to minister to the lost, welcome the penitent, and help them reconcile themselves to God, their families, and themselves. My team needed to share that passion.

A Burning Passion

The glamour of ministry did not intrigue me. I passed up opportunities to meet dignitaries that visited Allen: President William (Bill) Clinton and the then First Lady Hilary Clinton, Vice President Al Gore, Mayors Dinkins, Giuliani, Bloomberg, Senators (Federal and Local), Councilmen, Government officials, Judges, renown Gospel Singers, secular artistes, and other notable personalities who were regular guests of our Pastors. As Associate Ministers, we had the privilege of meeting and interacting with them because of our Pastors' graciousness. More often than not, the Discipleship Team and I were caught up with some seeking soul, some lost lamb, some fallen saint seeking relief within the walls of Allen. More often than not, long after services were over, we would be in the Chapel ministering to those who responded to the call of salvation or to renew their faith in God.

I often exasperated the security staff waiting until we finally finished counseling a distraught parishioner or a walk-in late in the evening. While others were hurrying to go home, I was often detained or delayed with someone struggling for a breakthrough in their circumstances. My wife and children grew accustomed to the frustration of waiting for me to emerge from the chapel, from my office, from the sanctuary to take them home, or to join them late at the dinner table. The Spirit of God had seized hold of me and laid the burden of those seeking salvation heavily upon my heart. Yet, and still, it was a pleasure, a delight, a joy, my calling. Unmistakably, I was where I needed to be, doing what God intended for me to do at this time. It was impossible to convey that sense of mission to others in mere training sessions. These by nature tended to be pedantic, stiff, structured, formalized, tell-sell, linear communications of how to do what, where, when, why, and by whom. I needed to spend quality time with the team and build personal relationships.

As if the example of Jesus was not enough, the Spirit also reminded me of Moses, Joshua, and the Elders of Israel. God had called Moses and had empowered him by His divine Spirit to secure Israel's deliverance from Egyptian bondage and lead them into Canaan. However, the task was too much for Moses alone, so God did something extraordinary. He ordered Moses to appoint 70 elders from among the people and instructed:

> Bring them to the tabernacle of meeting, that they may stand there with you. Then I will come down and talk with you there. I will take of the Spirit that is upon you and will put the same upon them; and they shall bear the burden of the people with you, that you may not bear it yourself alone. (Numbers 11:16, 17 NKJV)

God did just that so that 70 elders prophesied, as did Moses. God's desire was that Moses would not bear the burden alone. Moses embraced God's plan, and rather than being concerned that the 70 would steal his thunder, he expressed that he wished all the people of Israel were prophets and that the Lord would put His Spirit on them all (Num. 11:24, 25). Thus, Israel's leadership was a shared spiritual responsibility, not a single person's purview. Most importantly, the same spirit operative in Moses was now operative in the 70 elders. They were able to administer the work of God, the will of God, the Law of God, the statutes, judgments and ordinances of God, the covenant of God, and the promises of God throughout the camp because they had the same Spirit of leadership with which Moses and Aaron were endowed (Ps. 77:20; Ex. 4:14-20). This same principle of imparting and load-sharing was applied to raise facilitators for the Discipleship Ministry. The same Holy Spirit that was operative in my life must also become operative in theirs.

However, while the Holy Spirit is common to all, the gifts, that is, the Spirit's manifestation in each, will differ as He chooses. In Moses' case, they all prophesied, proclaimed the LORD's Word to a nation newly delivered from Egyptian bondage and her various idols. In my case, the gifts operative in me to disciple those whom the Lord added to the Church were to be understood and complimented by those other gifted persons called to support the vision so that the process of discipleship would succeed.

Synergy

Closely associated with the need to impart the same vision, it seems as though the Lord was pointing me to another important principle in ministry that was practiced through Scripture. Though each circumstance and practice differed, the transcendent principle remained the same: *those who were led needed to function in the same Spirit as those who led them*. Elisha, for example, saw the essentiality of serving as a prophet *in the Spirit and power of Elijah;* the sons of the prophets all sought to emulate the patriarchal Seers who mentored them (II Kings 2:15; 4:38). Likewise, the disciples of Jesus were taught the necessity of being like Him (Mt. 10:25). The elders took council because there was an uncanny similarity as they confronted Peter and John regarding the miraculous work they had done. It was reminiscent of Jesus (Acts 4:13). Also, in the New Testament, Paul the Apostle charged Timothy:

> You therefore, my son, be strong in the grace that is in Christ Jesus. And the things that you have heard from

> me among many witnesses, commit these to faithful men who will be able to teach others also. (II Tim. 2:1-2 NJKV)

Notice that Paul expected Timothy to practice the principle of imparting what he received by the indwelling Spirit to other faithful men who were, in turn, to be taught to do likewise. This practice characterized Paul's ministry in the individuals he mentored and the Churches he founded. The Corinthians were also expected to function as Paul would and did as stated before (I Cor. 4:16, 17). They were to be Paul's followers as he followed Christ (I Cor. 11:1-2).

As I contemplated these ministry dynamics, I realized that their absence is perhaps why ministries often fail. The manner of the operation of the Holy Spirit in the Pastor, for example, may not be adequately communicated to the congregation by simply preaching one sermon, but more so in life-on-life Christian fellowship and discipleship as Jesus did, as the Apostles did, and successively as their converts did (Jn. 17:5-14, 20, 21; Lk. 1:1-4; Acts 1:1-3; 2:42-47). Even in their schism, the misguided Corinthians sought to align themselves with principal leaders, saying they were of Paul, Apollos, Cephas, and of course Christ (I Cor. 1:11,12). Paul reasserted his mission to restore proper order: *proclaiming the good news* (I Cor. 1:17). He stated his message: *Jesus Christ and Him crucified*. Then, his manner: *making known the mystery of the gospel in the demonstration and power of the Holy Spirit* (I Cor. 2:1-5). Again, the Corinthians could fall under his parental influence and ways in Christ as taught "everywhere in every Church" (I Cor. 4:14-21). This was to be done through Timothy, his son in the gospel to whom Paul's ministry was evidently transmitted and practiced (Acts 16:1-4; II Tim. 1:6-7).

Accordingly, by exploring these scriptural examples in ministry, I set out to train clergy and non-clergy alike in the ways Discipleship was best to be done within the sociological milieu of the Greater

Allen Cathedral of New York and following the Pastoral mandate and vision communicated to me.

As I began to train, I became conscious that the Holy Spirit's will was to be communicated, not only the materials being taught. I needed to be aware that the transmission of knowledge was spiritual and not merely intellectual. All too often, it is easy to fall into the rudiments of the lesson, the aims and objectives, the logistics, didactics, and dynamics of teaching and learning then fail to rise to the level of communicating transforming words that are Spirit and life to the hearers (Jn. 6:63). To my shame, I can recall times when I taught and preached, and homiletically and hermeneutically, the task may have been well done; the audience may have been well informed, but no one was transformed. None were moved to action; no one burned with the zeal to do or be what was proposed even though they agreed in principle to everything they heard.

This was not the case with the Discipleship Ministry; we would be Spirit-filled disciples. We were not simply moving people through a theological, religious experience satisfying catechism. We would mold lives in the demonstration and power of the Holy Spirit, so the faith of these sent to us was not in the wisdom of men, however noble, but in the power of God. That process needed to start with me.

Charting Church Politics: Introducing the Team

Training personnel is one thing; fitting them into an existing, functioning body is quite another. I kept in mind that introducing the new program and ministry vision was not an end; it was just an opening. Just as an introduction between two people does not constitute a relationship, a date, or a marriage, so too the installation of discipleship facilitators required more than an announcement but skillful, tactical deployment. We often falsely assume that because we agree on the church's primary evangelical mission, we are on one accord as to how that mission is to be accomplished once we turn up at the appointed place and time we agreed upon. These are fatal assumptions in churches filled with humanity, albeit redeemed.

In my UK management training, I had learned a fundamental maxim: the man who *introduces change has half a friend in the one whom the change will benefit and no friend in the one it will not.* This principle was taught to the would-be innovative managers in training to alert them not to be naïve to the human dynamics that come poignantly into play when they institute changes, however beneficial. This truth learned in my business career came sharply back to mind as I began to deploy Discipleship Team members and implement the ministry's primary features.

As the newly minted Discipleship Ministry personnel assumed their new visible roles, it became evident that they began to draw both positive and negative attention. It was essential to minimize any negative impact so that those assigned to tasks did not underperform or fail outright. For example, newly trained facilitators were deployed to minister to those responding to the altar call for prayer or as prospects for membership. When the invitation to Discipleship was extended after the preached word, these individuals were expected to rise from their seats and take up positions, usually at the head of the aisles, to help conduct persons to the altar. They would look invitingly to the congregation with extended hands and offer a warm reception to those conflicted, confused, and frightened to step out from their seats to sue for salvation. They may pray at the altar with respondents with a comforting hand on the shoulders of distraught persons broken over their life issues. Additionally, they were to help direct prospects and members alike to the designated Chapel for further ministry, which was usually prayer and applications for membership.

Apart from other people's expressions, the altar facilitators themselves were timorous, standing before Allen under the massive congregation's scrutiny and gaze at a charged moment in the worship service. For some, this was the first time they stood before such an amalgamation of people at such a serious time. Of course, making a public declaration of faith in God and Christ for many is intimidating, far more encouraging others to do so, but that was the task.

We soon began to hear some feedback from the congregation voicing, I suppose, their thoughts as they adjusted to those newly appointed facilitators set before them. They were comfortable with the Stewardesses who stood majestically in white before the altar and assisted the Pastors as desired. They were familiar with the Officers, Stewards, and Trustees who collected the offering and served the Communion on first Sundays; they were receptive to the Ministers who stood behind the altar rail and prayed with the penitent supplicants knelt there, but who were these? They needed to adapt to the presence and function of those who stood before them unrobed with only badges that read: Discipleship Ministry. "Who are they?" and "Why are they so ministering?" their inquisitive stares seemed to ask. It had not mattered that they were mentioned as members of the Discipleship Ministry by the Pastors; the congregation needed to adjust to them, and they had to adjust to the congregation in their new roles.

Despite all its changes, Allen was still an AME church by tradition. Our team was not part of that tradition, which allowed no one to walk about, especially during the altar call, unless designated by the specially appointed groups mentioned above. Accepting this new group in that capacity was a major mental shift that, to some, seemed as though it dislocated sacred traditions—that perceived change needed to be managed.

Change Must Be Managed

The introduction of a new ministry must be managed for a significant reason. Change may sometimes bring about a measure of displacement, albeit accidentally and incidentally. Such transformation must be carefully handled so that the ministry's intent is not misunderstood and misperceptions are clarified and resolved. For example, large churches and growing assemblies often quickly introduce new programs and changes to meet new demands and contingencies. Unfortunately, the pace of those changes sometimes moves faster than people's ability to adapt and adjust. Here, care needed to be taken to negotiate human foibles to ensure that required changes occurred without damaging the existing delicate fabric that made Allen as we knew it. Considering this dynamic, I had thought and prayed through several options. It would have been ideal for the new facilitators to come from the ranks of ordained Ministers, Stewards, and Stewardesses. In this way, they would be little or no adjustment within the service and perhaps less training since some protocols would already have been known, plus, a measure of spiritual maturity would already exist. However, several considerations were mitigated against such an ideal. For one, many of these serving in these capacities were already overly committed in several ministries and operating at all three services (6:30am, 8:30am, and 11:15pm). Additionally, in the case of several others, their other duties schedules, personal circumstances, personas, and personal preferences were incompatible with the demands of serving in the Discipleship Ministry.

Consequently, volunteers from the body politic of the congregation were called. Some were handpicked, while others were referred by Ministers and Officers. Some were directed to me by the Pastors, while others sensed what was being built and came and volunteered. However they arrived, a standard needed to be set so that those chosen to serve could do so as necessary, and the members of the congregation would feel comfortable in their care at the most vulnerable times in their lives. I was sensitive to the fact that people came to the altar in crisis. Marital problems, personal problems, family dysfunctions, health issues, employment/unemployment problems, mental, emotional, and spiritual matters drive them there. In the African American communities, the Church is still the sociological epicenter of the neighborhood.

In some other church communities, I observed that respondents were ushered immediately to different places for attention; they were often brought to the altar and allowed to pray in ours. How people are handled and ministered to undergo such tender circumstances is critical. If they are compassionately nurtured and supported through their crises with a sense of sincere concern for their personhood, that makes a crucial difference between attrition and Church growth. "People return where their needs are best met," our Pastor would always admonish us. They relate well to ministries that pour oil and wine into their wounds suffered on the Jericho roads of life. Then too, they refer others in their social circles for similar care. Many who watched this spectacle vicariously assess how they would be cared for if in the same or similar circumstances as their penitent fellow parishioners or neighbors. Therefore, it was essential for the Discipleship Ministry facilitators to be proficient, precise, and pristine in their execution of roles and, more importantly, to be spiritually effective as they did so.

A Discipleship Volunteer Application form was designed to ensure that this caliber of the facilitator was acquired. It established criteria regarding Allen Church membership, personal competencies, and spiritual gifts. It also required endorsements from respected congregants and members of the secular community. In this way, we could better assess the applicant's appropriateness for the tasks. In addition, it helped to ensure that we set persons before the congregation and the unsaved community, people who could command their respect. Without stringent criteria, hasty appointments often lead to embarrassing experiences for the Church. For example, the assembly may be unaware of an erstwhile member's ill repute until someone outside the immediate church community comes to join, only to be taken aback or refuses to join because they see such functioning hypocritically. Such scenarios cause potential members to pull back, and worst, they form a low image of the Church, its leadership, and the general Christian witness in the minds of the unsaved. Some of the applicants were somewhat disconcerted by the application's demands, but they served us well.

Setting High Standards

I was mindful of the high bar the Apostles set for the charitable distribution of food among the Early Church widows (Acts 6:1-7). In many cases, we fail to see the significance of spiritual qualities and the importance of the community's regard to do what we consider non-clergy functions. We foolishly relegate non-clergy functions to be less critical and set lower acceptance and achievement standards. Maybe that is why we have poor results in those areas. Not so in the Early Church; the Apostles required reputable, Spirit-filled, wise candidates *to serve food* equitably to the widows. Having set such a high bar for the first Deacons of the New Testament Church, the Scriptures note that the Apostles laid their hands on those who were so chosen, and the results were astronomical:

> Then the word of God spread, and the number of the disciples multiplied greatly in Jerusalem, and a great many of the priests were obedient to the faith.
>
> (Acts 6:7 NKJV)

The careful selection of the Deacons and the Apostles' concentration on the Word of God and prayer were so potent that even priests became disciples. What an achievement! Several of the seven Deacons grew into formidable ministers in their own right in other ministry areas. Stephen proved to be an irrefutable apologist performing signs and wonders among the people while Phillip carried the gospel to Samaria and dramatically delivered that city from the Satanic control of sorcery (Acts 6:8-15; 8:5-25).

As the Apostles had done, I was determined to put good Christian people in place to navigate any negative Church politics, and before long, results began to show. The Chapel became a place of intercession, deliverance, and miraculous experiences. Sicknesses were healed, demoniacs were delivered, illegal drug addicts and drug dealers found redemption, and many more found salvation. Some people regularly came as if it was a therapy session, and for some, it certainly was. The Church inevitably attracts the broken in all mental health/ill-health states. Their circumstances cause them to feel disempowered, hopeless, and defeated. Therefore, they are looking for influential people they perceive could deliver them or help them regain control of their lives. Therefore, these precious people are often drawn to Pastors and Ministers – the more notable, the more attractive they appear. They come in the press and in the throng of large dynamic congregations hoping to touch the hem of the garments of the man or woman of God desiring to experience a cessation of their conditions. Sunday mornings and formal services particularly do not lend themselves to private audiences with Pastors or Ministers. They are often too preoccupied with managing the services themselves or collecting their thoughts for their sermons. Hence, people with special needs are often referred to or directed to designated personnel who serve them with Christian compassion. Accordingly, the Discipleship Ministry facilitators were taught to treat these unfortunate seeking ones with respect and sensitivity. These were regarded as siblings with special needs and disabilities requiring additional attention and care. Of course, there are times when some who were disruptive or inappropriate had to be removed from a service or a meeting group so that the entire service/activity could continue.

In the process of time, the facilitators' confidence grew. They learned how to work alongside ministers in the Chapel and at the altar. The congregation became accustomed to their presence and ministry. Soon it was standard for the Pastors to say to respondents at the altar, "Please go with the Ministers *and the members of the Discipleship Ministry* to the Chapel for further ministry." We had become a standard part of the service format. That was a major accomplishment. Respect was earned, especially after the congregation began to see the harvest that the Ministry presented back to them each month to receive the Right Hand of Fellowship.

The successful deployment of the Discipleship facilitators was indicative of the ministry's success overall. New member prospects were being guided through the implemented process weekly and monthly. The Allen Church community impacted its world, and people came from miles around to join. As they did, they were received and directed through the process. Every third Sunday, with a few exceptions, 60-100 persons were presented to the Pastors before the congregation for their official acceptance as members.

Having undergone the entire discipleship process outlined before, they stood before their families, friends, and new Church family. The sheer sight of new members stretched across the front of the congregation excited, smiling, some crying and overwhelmed, warmed all our hearts. It earned respect for those who had welcomed them at the altar over three months and had managed them through a primary discipleship process that led them to stay and commit to being a full part of the body just as the Pastors desired.

New Members Reception: Reducing Allen to Size

Shortly after receiving the Right Hand of Fellowship, the new members would be invited to a New Member Reception, which the Discipleship Ministry hosted on behalf of the Pastors. These were the primary objectives: allow those who had joined the church to know that they were welcomed, meet the Pastors who ate with them and interacted with them in a social setting, testify about how and why they joined the Church, foster deeper fellowship, and join the various ministries which had mounted display tables expressly for them. Therefore, the New Member Reception achieved a diversity of goals:

1. It created a friendly interface between the existing and emerging members. The former were the hosts, and the latter the guests of honor. Thus both were unified in an up close and personal pleasant atmosphere.

2. It presented the Church's institution by the leaders of the congregation who were present to welcome the new entrants to Allen. Ministry heads were present to accept applications of new initiates. They did not have to stand aloof as new people merged into the mass of members, but they could direct them to places of service to further build the ministry based on their interests and gifts. They could also answer questions and explain operations, organizations within the Church, and the wider denomination. Hence they passed on the traditions and the institutional memory to those who would be their grateful heirs.

3. It provided insight into how the ministry was received and embraced by the broader community from which the new members had come. Allen was on Radio, TBN, and streaming live on the internet. Therefore, its message was being broadcasted in multi-media formats. How was it being perceived and received? The presence and testimony of the new members demonstrated the impact on the gospel's communication articulated by Allen. It showed the socio-demographic and the psycho-graphics of the population segments responding to the call to salvation and discipleship it issued. It was now possible to see trends, analyze outcomes, predict results, and point out patterns to make the message more compelling and determine what was working and what was not.

4. It facilitated an informal interaction between the Pastors and their newest members. In addition, the Reception introduced the Pastors to their new sheep and the new lambs to their shepherds.

The Flakes are very down-to-earth persons, mingling freely with their people. The New Members' Reception was no different. This informal interaction dispelled misperceptions about the Pastors and Allen members as a whole. We often laughed as new members confessed in testimonies the various misconceptions and mistaken beliefs about Allen and churches in general. For example, we learned of the rumor that applicants for membership of Allen needed to present their W-2 (tax statement of annual earnings) to be accepted as members and ensure full payment of tithes. We heard that Allen members were the bourgeoisie and needed to have a mink coat to belong; that one needed to drive an expensive automobile and on and on into the ridiculous. However, our Pastors' genuine humility and the reality that Allen's members came from all sections of society that the new members saw for themselves dispelled many false notions and led to better fellowship. These events, along with others, encouraged us that the Discipleship Ministry was functioning well as conceived. The training paid off, new members were integrating well into the congregation without adverse effects, new facilitators were commended, the vision of the Pastors was being realized, and we were all engaged in the achievement of the Great Commission.

CHAPTER 8

PASTORAL CARE: DISCIPLING THE LEAST, THE LOST AND THE LAST

As a natural outgrowth of the Discipleship Ministry, it became necessary to meet with and counsel members proceeding through their spiritual journey. I quickly observed as Discipleship Minister that each convert required Pastoral Care for one reason or another. Each person who joined the assembly faced fundamental decisions that often required help and in some cases, professional help. It is readily observed that people receive Christ at crucial points in their lives. Many are undergoing a divorce, marital distress, challenging dysfunction, unemployment or career meltdowns, identity crises, traumatized by molestation, abuse, or are suddenly becoming aware of it. Others are at the crossroads of life or in the valley of decision, halting between two opinions.

As a result, some new member converts often need the assurance and prayerful support of professionals to help them through the transformational process of moving from conformity to the world towards renewal of the mind centered on God's will. Many of these were seen and helped with Pastoral care or referred to Clinicians and Therapists as necessary. Although I was not a licensed practitioner, I did work in several social service settings and completed postgraduate courses in counseling, so I was sufficiently trained to offer Pastoral advice on the issues they presented. Still, another category of persons often gets overlooked if one is not careful. I refer to these as *the least, the lost, and the last*. These need special attention and care, and we were obligated to give it to them.

Ministering to the Least

As the ministry at Allen grew numerically and spiritually, we noticed a strange phenomenon. It seemed that there was a corresponding increase in people with bizarre behavioral patterns. It was not always obvious why they exhibited unusual behaviors. It was not always possible to interact with them as they sometimes stopped coming as soon as their exhibitions had played themselves out. Allen is a very tolerant church, and the Pastors were very accommodating to people who would probably be barred or significantly restricted in other places of worship. The leadership hated 'scenes' during services, so the security personnel was often not allowed to forcibly apprehend and remove those distracting in worship. They preferred to deal with disruptive people less publicly and compassionately.

On several occasions, Rev. Elaine would call me into her office to discuss one of our 'special members/attendees' to minimize their effect on the services. She would often jokingly refer to them as "one of your people." She had noted that her ministerial colleagues with large congregations were experiencing the same phenomenon. We hypothesized that these desperate folks were drawn to what they perceived as power centers and *people of influence*. It would seem that they felt that if they could connect themselves to those who exhibited 'power,' they would be released from their own powerlessness in their lives that were out of control. As a result, they often gravitated to the Pastors, whom they perceived as the most powerful persons. After all, they preached, prayed for the respondents at the altar, and laid hands on people seeking healing and salvation from various conditions. It stands to reason then that the distressed would want their attention. Unfortunately, their methods of getting that attention were often inappropriate, ranging from untimely, out of order, elaborate, aggressive, and even salacious. Such actions tended to single out such people from the congregation, which often characterized or mischaracterized them as demon-possessed, sick, and dangerous. Irene, a disturbed young woman, fell into this category.

In all groups, spiritual or otherwise, peculiar people are ostracized and marginalized to the periphery of society like the demoniac of Gadara was (Mk. 5:1-9). Irene was no different. I was often called upon to talk to her whenever she acted up or insisted on seeing the Pastor for the dubious reasons she seemed unable to articulate. It could've been that her reasons to see him never fit any of the acceptable categories we allowed. I spent many hours trying to make sense of her ramblings. I often stepped forward to help ease tensions when she encountered the Pastor in the hallways on weekdays and observed what seemed to be rational constipation with verbal diarrhea at the same time.

On one such occasion, Rev. Flake listened with a posture of rapt attention as Irene spewed forth what sounded like a barrage of words without coherent reason, rhythm, or rhyme for over five to ten minutes. It was as if she had been unloading her mental storage of Webster's dictionary. One could not help but be impressed with the litany of 'big' words that poured forth incessantly from her without a breath, eyes closed and all. After she emptied and walked off, the Pastor turned to his befuddled associates and asked: "Did you get all that?" We had no answers. We were still trying to process the interchange, and then he too walked off, saying, "I don't see why not," leaving us all the more stupefied. I processed this encounter as his pleasant way of defusing her constant desire to talk and have an appointment with him. He had given her time.

Irene's encounters with Rev. Elaine were, unfortunately, more harmful. For some reason, she was more violent and sought to maltreat the First Lady. Her unpredictable behavior relegated her to the restricted access list, the must watch list, and on one occasion, the banned list. Before she was expelled entirely from the sanctuary, I had two experiences with her I will never forget. First, I had come down to the lobby to speak to her because she was not allowed in the office section on the second floor. We went into the Chapel, and she proceeded to pour forth as usual. I was prepared for another long listening session, unsure of its usefulness. I felt that I was making some headway with her, though, because she began to warm up to me, although she seemed to be very guarded and did not want us to greet with the usual embrace or the kiss on the cheek which the Pastor had made a classic greeting at the Cathedral. Instead, she recoiled and stiffened, so I learned to keep my distance within the limits her body language indicated. She shared pictures of her family, her aunt who raised her, her family reunion photos, and, more importantly, a photo of her son, whom she explained was living with relatives down South. She also shared some of her writings on several subjects, some of which she wanted me to give to the Pastor, which I would do as the situation merited it. I was in a tenuous balancing act of providing her with standard care and courtesies given to all members yet being realistic given her abnormal behavior and imposed restrictions. Irene became lucid between incoherent verbal digressions as we sat in the Chapel. I strained to listen and make sense of the vocalic jigsaw puzzle she presented.

However, I was astounded as the picture of her life emerged that explained some of her bizarre behavior. I was almost reduced to tears. I understood that she was married and that her husband was abusive. It would appear that shortly after their first child, the abuse may have taken a toll on her, and she had a mental breakdown. As a result, she was placed on psychotropic drugs and advised by her doctor to not become pregnant while taking the medications as they would be harmful to the child. Unfortunately, her husband ignored the cautions, and she was impregnated again. No details were given regarding her prenatal care, but she was clear about one chilling fact. Irene related that she watched with horror as a doctor performed a partial-birth abortion on her emerging child. She questioned my ability to deal with seeing a doctor insert a scissor at the base of her child's skull and sever its spinal cord from the brain stem killing the child before it could take its first breath. I could hardly contain myself imagining what the reality of such a horrific act from a mother's perspective would look like. Having watched all three of my children emerge from the womb, I could not imagine seeing such inhumane cruelty done to one of them, no matter how impaired they may be. I instantly identified (or maybe over-identified with) her pain; I immediately understood her mental distress and distorted view of men, especially those in power. It seemed to explain her quest for control, especially over authoritative males or a search to be empowered by them. I needed to process the information within the full context of our interactions and put it all into perspective.

In the meanwhile, I found myself conflicted. I was smitten with grief and empathy; simultaneously, I felt a tinge of guilt as I reflected on my own judgments of her behaviors. Plus, I was bewildered about how this lost sheep may be restored (Ps. 23:3). I helped her in very tangible ways: called her Case Workers at the Protective Services program with which she was registered, dealt with issues related to her apartment, ensured that her funding was in place, conveyed to medical and other personnel that she was part of our community and we expected her to be treated well, gave her car fare when she mustered the courage to ask for it, etc., but those were minimal in comparison to this broken human spirit embodied before me (Prov. 18:14). I never treated her the same way after that and never allowed anyone to mistreat her if I could help it.

Before this revelation, on another ignoble occasion, I was somewhat frustrated with being called to contain or police her when she acted out in a service. It seemed that we were held hostage by her behaviors, and the worship service was enjoyed or not, depending on the actions of those who manifested strange behaviors. Then, of course, we questioned ourselves: 'if we did have demoniacs in our presence, why were we not utilizing our spiritual authority to address them?' It seemed to me that a congregation of thousands of believers should have been able to arrest the "ungodly" behaviors displayed in their midst! Thus, I went to war in my self-righteous "Godly" zeal. I asked brother Emanuel and a few other saints to join me in prayer and fasting to address them, particularly Irene. My prayer partners were not as enthusiastic as I because we had just come out of an extensive, corporate fast and were yearning to get back to the usual diet our souls were lusting for, but they obliged me, and we soldiered on.

As the days wore on in our seven-day spiritual wilderness journey, I had a sobering reality that I am convinced was from the Lord regarding his lost child Irene. As I prayed passionately before Him, asking for the power to heal and deliver and expel demons that were interrupting the services, I heard His voice curtly overriding my plaintive petitions or vain repetitions. He said, "You don't love her."

Without thinking, I retorted incredulously, "I don't love her? Don't you see the (major) sacrifice I am making on her behalf, and yet you say I don't love her?" "You don't love her," His voice scolded, unimpressed with my pseudo-piety, and as if to oblige me. He continued: "You want her to behave in the service, not for her sake, but for yours. You want her to behave so that it will be convenient for you and that you may not be interrupted". I was speechless. I felt naked and exposed, like a fraud. Then He graciously continued since I guess I was listening. "Have you ever wondered what it is like to struggle to put a clear thought together?" It was evident to me that He was referring to Irene's garbled and confused mental state. I did not need to answer as I pondered my own thoughts and contemplated my blind misapplication of spiritual weaponry (II Cor. 10:1-6).

Like the disciples who encountered Jesus on the Emmaus road were rebuked for their folly and slowness of heart to understand, I hurried to a meeting with my fellow sufferers. Before I could relay to them my divine encounter, they all admitted that they were unfaithful to the fast and apologetic. That was all inconsequential as I relayed to them my experience. We came away from our deliberation, having learned that there are some people who the Lord will send in our midst who are impaired, broken, sick, disabled, and in need of our loving care and affection. The Church is the family of God's people. Like in every family, there are children, siblings, parents, or relatives with special needs like the physically disabled, the mentally retarded, the autistic, the emotionally disturbed, the senile, the old, and the infirmed. Are they not to be loved, cared for, and accommodated? Should not their human dignity be respected and appreciated? We will all answer affirmatively and unequivocally 'yes!' to such questions. Many families do this devotedly daily. Must not then the same be applied in the Church, the family of God?

Some are lost and forlorn in the Church community, ruined and damaged by the world. There are broken people for whom Christ expects us to have compassion. We will need to dismount from our privileged, proverbial beast and go to them with neighborly love pouring into their wounds the oils of gladness and the disinfecting wine of fellowship and brotherhood. We are to lift them from the wayside where they were victimized and left for dead, and without regard for our own self-interest, we must set them upon our own proverbial beast and transport them to places and circumstances where they may be better cared for. These acts of kindness will interrupt our journey, slow our pace, incur unexpected costs, and deplete personal and corporate resources. Still, if we obey Jesus' greatest commandment, we are obligated to love the Lord our God with all our hearts, with all our minds with all our strengths, and our neighbors (especially those unlike us) as ourselves (Lk. 10:27). Jesus also cautions that we will be judged regarding how we treat the least of *His* brethren. We must be aware that what we do to the least, we do vicariously to Him (Mt. 25:31-46).

The Lost

As Discipleship Minister, those who are lost become the focus, and in some cases, winning them can be quite challenging, like Ms. Kelly Abdool. Before her conversion, she fell into that ignoble category of the *lost*. I first met her through a mutual friend, Alf, who called asking me to minister to her and her family at a disastrous time in their lives, and to be perfectly honest, I did not want to go. He informed me that her son was brutally murdered at her door and died at the foot of her stairs in the house's foyer where they were renting an apartment on the upper floor. He wanted me to speak to the bereaved mother and daughter and perhaps perform the funeral. I didn't know the family, and my experience told me that the death of a youth, especially an only son, is one of the deepest griefs to bear (Jer. 6:26; Amos 8:10; Zech. 12: 10). Added to this, the family was Muslim, and I did not know how to conduct a funeral that would respect their faith while maintaining my integrity. I did, however, offer to assist in any way I could. I sent word via him that the funeral could be held at Allen, and I would facilitate it if the family didn't mind. As per our policy, there was no charge for the service, including a musician, choir, ushers, security, and stewardesses to minister to the bereaved and guests. Space would even be given for a fellowship meal after the burial.

A few days later, he called back to say they chose to go to the funeral home. I was disappointed but relieved. He called again soon to say that he would like me to speak to the family because they were in deep distress. They were unaware of why their son and brother, Kiron, was murdered with no logical explanation. He was a very morally upright young man, an earnest college student, loved by all without any known enemies from all accounts. Why was he killed execution-style in his own house? There was no connection to drugs or other nefarious activities. His family and friends were bewildered. Alf convinced them to let me come to their apartment to minister to them. I guess in their desperate need for answers, they agreed. I recalled telling the congregation at a Pastor's Bible Study about the invitation and requesting that they pray for me as I went into this buzz-saw as I perceived it.

A week or so later, I traveled to the house and crossed the threshold; that very doorway had doubled as the tragic crime scene weeks prior. I gingerly climbed the stairs to the upper-floor apartment. I entered and was courteously greeted by a very somber Ms. Kelly and her daughter Keisha who mustered a warm, radiant smile. She ushered me into the dining and living room, where to my surprise, Kiron's friends were sitting poker-faced and angry. Alf's face was my only source of comfort as I sat feeling like a cat in a dog pound. Before long, it was my turn to address the gathering. I didn't know what to say, and there were no sure words from the Lord that I was confident He gave me for this family and friends. I cannot exactly recall what I said, but I told them of the need to forgive the evil perpetrator not for his sake but for their own so that they may heal. Unfortunately, my words hung in the air like unrealistic pious platitudes as they met with the cold, vengeful stares that made ears dull and unreceptive. They were unable to assuage the deep pain visible in the angry faces.

I can vividly recall that before I could finish, Keisha sat directly in front of me and peppered me with questions. "Rev. Leacock, where is my brother right now? Can he see us? Does he know what we are doing now and how we feel about him?" I admitted that I could not answer any of her questions as I didn't know her brother; I could only say what the Scriptures say in general about life, death, sin, and life beyond our temporal existence on earth. No generalities were welcomed here; no theological treatise mattered; all that she, her friends, and no doubt her mother, who kept her catatonic gaze, were concerned about was Kiron. Theirs was a desperate search for truth, justice, and meaning, having been impacted by the cruel hand of evil that executed a noble young man seemingly without cause and without a rational explanation. Yet, here I was advising the victims of this horrific murder to be rational, reasonable, and righteous even towards the twisted wretch that had done the dastardly deed.

To make matters worse, I also suggested that it was necessary not to make a shrine of his room and personal effects. This was necessary for their healing process to begin. I told them to put them away, give them away to worthy people and causes, and even discard some things. I hit a central nerve there because they had planned to keep his room exactly as he left it with all his personal effects in their exact places; everything had become sacred. None of what I said was spoken cruelly or indifferently, although it may have been premature. My inexperience in counseling and handling such a delicate situation was showing. I knew that I was walking on eggshells laid on top of thin ice. However, I was conscious that if I was faithful to my ministry, I needed to say the hard things no one in the family or in their circle of friends dared to say. It was necessary to lift their minds and hearts above the horror to a higher plain of living than the mere fragility of our human existence. They needed to hear the words of Jesus at the Mount:

> Blessed are they that mourn for they shall be comforted... Love your enemies, bless those who curse you, do good to those who hate you...For if you forgive men their trespasses, your heavenly Father will also forgive you.
> (Matthew 5:4, 44; 6:14)

His words, then as now, call us to life beyond the animalistic instincts of anger, revenge, hatred, malice, hopelessness, and despair. Of course, I suggested bereavement counseling that Allen offered to its members but was also open to the community, and they too were welcome to receive it. They were not excited about that either. Finally, I humbly requested to pray for the family. This they agreed to, and I prayed. Then I ask them to pray. Ms. Abdool decided to pray, but she stated that she could only pray in Arabic. I indicated that God recognized all languages, and she proceeded. I wished I knew Arabic to understand her request, but I did not. I understood Apostle Paul's words about how praying in an unknown tongue (language) excludes others and hinders fellowship. A common tongue allows all to enjoin and say in good conscience, *amen.* I was a barbarian to her. In that crucial moment, 'the twos and the threes' of us could have invited the Lord's presence into our midst. Where the Spirit of the Lord is, there is liberty (II Cor. 3:17). More importantly, she was not praying to me but to God.

I recall leaving the house feeling like a total failure. I thought that I was not an effective witness of the Lord. I rehashed the event in my mind and analyzed it to see whether I could have done things any differently. My mental toil was in vain; I walked away with a sense of defeat.

Weeks went by, and I heard nothing, which tended to confirm that I did not get through to this Muslim family and their embittered friends. I wished I knew then that Kiron had embraced Christianity and broke with his mother's faith to proudly wear a crucifix around his neck as a symbol of the One who he told her in his words, "Mommy, this is my God." This may not be a typical expression of Christian faith. He was raised as a Muslim, but had gone to Catholic schools as a child and may have been exposed to Church and Christian doctrines, so this was a considerable expression of his faith. However, I was ignorant of all this at the time. I was also ignorant that Ms. Abdool was crying out in her bewilderment and anguish of heart to God. She relayed to me much later that she asked Him, "How could you do this to a young man that said you are his God? What kind of God are you?" Her dialogue with God had begun. Unaware of all this, I reported back to the Bible study that I had heard nothing. Nevertheless, while there was silence on my side, God was being listened to on theirs.

About a month or more later, Alf called to say that the family wanted to see me again. Again, I was surprised, almost as equally bewildered as the first time. Nevertheless, this time with more eager steps, I pressed to go, inviting a fellow minister to go with me. On the appointed day, Min. Emanuel Haniah and I made our way with careful, prayerful steps to Ms. Abdool's house. I was determined to make up for my poor performance the first time. We arrived and were greeted a little more warmly. Once again, the living room was filled with Kiron's friends and well-wishers from Ms. Kelly's job; quite an assortment of people was present from diverse ethnic groups.

It was not long before the attention turned to us. We shared from the Scriptures and some anecdotal experiences of loss and the despair we, too, had undergone. There was no *Amen corner* here. No one was ready to agree to our suggestions; they wanted answers to the mystery surrounding Kiron's death. We were up against the fundamental questions of life, its purpose, its meaning, questions about evil, and its unrestrained preying upon the good. The question, 'was there a God who cared?' was playing loudly in the background of our conversations.

Again Keisha took the lead in asking questions, one of which was, "So what should we do now?" Because no one yet knew why her brother was killed and by whom, I suggested that she and her mother seek therapy to help them cope with their loss. Cold silence followed, and the incredulous look on some of the guest's faces indicated that they were not ready to move on yet. Kiron's peers had moved from shock and anguish to sheer anger; they were more inclined to avenge his death. We discussed the moral depravity of such thinking and its relation to the same mentality that led to Kiron's demise and gently questioned whether they wanted to be depraved. Once more, I had that sinking feeling that we were not having any effect. We were hitting a brick wall, or were it the gates of hell and needed to press the offensive. Sometimes it's hard to see what's happening spiritually. Haniah and I held our backs to each other, piercing our way through anger, hatred, strife, murder, pain, confusion, meaningless evil, hopelessness, despair, and different religious beliefs. Ms. Kelly was Muslim, as were her mother and brother visiting. Keisha and her fiancé were Hindi and had articulated some of their views in the discussion earlier. It seemed as though all these divergent forces, faiths, and psycho-social factors had taken up stronghold positions in that tiny apartment, and Emanuel and I were out of favor and out of sync with them. Relief came when we were invited to eat, and there was plenty of delicious food that broke the tension and allowed us to relate on a more basic, pleasant, human level. Haniah and I walked away, mulling over our foray into what seemed like enemy territory without any sense of victory.

Once again, days turned into weeks and weeks into months. Then suddenly it happened! One of the Discipleship Ministry's facilitators ran to me excitedly with the news. "Rev. Leacock, you know the woman you asked us to pray for? She joined the church!" I was stunned, dumbfounded, amazed, and elated all at once. The reality of what God had done unfolded in slow but ever-increasing glory as Ms. Kelly became Sis. Kelly with a testimony that has the potential to change the world. It would be an injustice to tell it here; she will speak it in her own voice one day. Sufficient, it is to say that she became involved in several ministries with an enthusiasm that was embarrassing to us, who take our faith for granted. Sis. Abdool soon became an active member of the Allen Prison Ministry, the Security Ministry, and the Allen Grief Share Ministry. She was also an ever-present radiant face among several others.

How profound it is that this bereaved mother would sacrifice time and effort to go to the place where her son's killer was confined and minister without bitterness to young men like him. How awesome that a woman who told me how she "gnawed on the end of the carpet" in her grief is now one called in by the church to console persons with a similar catastrophic loss. More impressive is the fact that Sis. Kelly goes to court with the parents of murdered sons on her own. She prays for them and the families of the perpetrators in the name of Jesus, her son's Savior, now her Savior. She who was lost is now found. We began to pray for her daughter's salvation and daily Sis. Kelly told us of her daughter's interest and encouragement to continue in the faith that saved her mother. We prayed that she would be saved as well. Thank God for the interception that snatched this family from the prison of bitterness and hatred to the Liberty of Christ. My challenge in discipling Kelly helped her walk with patience while running the race before us. Her passion and commitment were often embarrassing.

Many other examples abound as a testimony to the miraculous power God demonstrates to those who care for His flock, especially *the least, the lost,* and *the last,* which brings another experience to mind.

One of the Last

People like Sam Jenkins fell into that "last" category. A young man brash, loud, demanding, and pushy, he came to seek me out. He was in various stages of his addiction and dysfunction when he came to Allen for help. He was a proprietor on Merrick Boulevard selling women's clothing in a small boutique but was spiraling out of control, and he knew it. He was too arrogant to accept the help he needed at that time. He simply wanted us to buy his garments and support his business, or was it his habit? The Lord allowed me to see through his veneer, and I spoke directly and forthrightly to him without fluff but in love. He came daily to see me at the Cathedral and often left disgruntled and dissatisfied.

Sam had to 'hit the wall,' as we say in the addiction community. The hit came when he was on the verge of losing his home, the house his mother had left for him upon her demise. In one of our many sessions, he related that he was incarcerated when she passed and could not attend her funeral. That was hard enough in itself, but worse was discovering documents stating that he was actually adopted. That discovery only intensified his self-loathing because of his prodigal ways in the face of her deep love. He was lost for sure. Not only did he lose the only mother he knew, but Sam also did not know who his real mother or father was and how he came to be adopted. Plus, the one who could have explained it to him was dead. Finally, because of his irresponsible behavior, he faced foreclosure and losing his most valuable asset, the home his adopted mother left to him. Desperate and afraid, Sam decided to sell before the bank auctioned the house.

Fortunately, he could sell it to a Real Estate Agent with whom he entrusted the sale proceeds. He sought my advice on the matter. I expressed my reservations about his decision, especially since he also began working as an agent for the same realtor holding his money. I felt that he had given her too much control and needed to resume responsibility for his own life. He expressed that she had been a recovering addict who understood his plight and was helping him get back on his feet. Having large sums of money was his trigger to get high, so he rationalized that this was a way of staying clean. We continued to meet and discuss his life challenges and how he should apply the word of God in times of temptation to remain a faithful disciple of Christ. Our meetings were never as scheduled; they were in the middle of the night or day, and more so whenever Sam seemed to be having a crisis. They were often at the most inconvenient times and places where I would have to rush to meet him or sit with him and encourage him in the Lord. Meanwhile, He seemed motivated in his new job and tried to earn commission on rentals and sales.

Not long after, however, my worst fears were realized. The agent began to misappropriate Sam's money and to mistreat him. Before long, the situation soon reached a boiling point. Sam threatened to do her bodily harm, so I arranged to meet with Sam and the agent to diffuse the situation. This may have been beyond the normal bounds of Discipleship or Pastoral Care, but I felt that I was the only real help Sam could turn to. He had burnt all his other bridges, and like the prodigal, he was facing a dire famine, and no one gave him anything. I could not turn my back on him though the risks were significant. Much to my disappointment, the agent sent two of her staff to represent her. They promised faithfully to reconcile the accounts and ensure that Sam got his money, but it never happened. The agent started refusing calls and disappeared. Later we learned that Sam's trigger was also hers so that having his money at her disposal proved too much temptation, and she began using illegal drugs again. Sam's money went up in smoke. He was livid, and our sessions were spent trying to encourage a broken man who constantly felt last in the race of life but desperately trying to be in the first place.

This lingering feeling of poor self-esteem and low self-worth confronted him even in times when he was blessed. Yet, inch by inch, he crawled forward on the path of Discipleship, walking with the Lord. Ungrateful of the gains, he always lamented that they were not better, bigger, and faster no matter how significant they were. Then God opened a door. He was offered a scholarship to study for a master's degree at Lincoln University in Social Work. He worked in the field to provide housing assistance to people experiencing difficulties in this area. It was an excellent opportunity given that Sam did not have an undergraduate degree, and it was a chance to acquire a degree from a prestigious college. Sam was pleased to be selected for the program, but he was petrified at the same time. He complained as if he was being resentenced to jail. As usual, I listened and then offered him advice by God's guidance. I told him that I understood his apprehension and agreed that he may be in over his head but that it was an excellent offer, so he should try it at least for one week. After that, if he couldn't handle it, he could quit. He was expecting a fight from me, but instead, I affirmed his reason to fear and even gave him permission to throw in the towel. This was unlike the hundreds of times I had encouraged him to try to overcome at all costs.

Sam attended Lincoln for the first week and returned somewhat surprised at himself. His fear of failure was not as formidable as the demon he had imagined it to be. He called excited but still doubtful. I told him to try another week, then another semester, then another year. This went on until Sam eventually graduated with honors! Despite being adopted, losing his home, losing his children, losing his money, and countless more to drug abuse over the years, through Christ, he moved from last to first at the head of the class.

This success energized Sam; he began looking for his birth mother, his estranged children, and above all, Sam started to seek ways to be of service to others. He who was Discipled wanted to disciple others. Sam joined the Allen Prison Ministry and began visiting and sharing his testimony with the inmates. Sam is planning to write a book, and his thesis on, The Effects of Fatherlessness in the Home is expected to become a program for men, a program he hopes to implement. He desires to help fathers become involved in the lives of their children. Sam proved that the first shall be last and the last shall be first (Mk.10:31).

Lesson from ministering to the least, the lost, and the last

My ministering to the *least,* the *lost,* and the *last* was often not the most desirable area of Christian service. Still, such ministry introduced me to God in profound and unusual ways that I may not have experienced otherwise. I looked back at how this truth was revealed to Jeremiah. He was able to proclaim it to Israel's leaders who abandoned their religious and civic responsibilities for personal indulgences: they built *wide*, elaborate houses with large rooms and aesthetic window views and paneled ceilings of cedar. These vermilion-painted houses stood out against the terrain in contrast to their impoverished neighbors. Still, they stood out in heaven's eyes as well because they were selfishly acquired by exploiting others. Jeremiah's damning words were echoed in their ears:

> Woe unto him that buildeth his house by unrighteousness, and his chambers by wrong; that useth his neighbour's service without wages, and giveth him not for his work; That saith, I will build me a wide house and large chambers, and cutteth him out windows; and it is ceiled with cedar, and painted with vermilion. Shalt thou reign, because thou closest thyself in cedar? did not thy father eat and drink, and do judgment and justice, and then it was well with him? He judged the cause of the poor and needy; then it was well with him: was not this to know me? saith the LORD. But thine eyes and thine heart are not but for thy covetousness, and for to shed innocent blood, and for oppression, and for violence, to do it. Therefore thus saith the LORD concerning Jehoiakim the son of Josiah king of Judah; They shall not lament for him saying, Ah my brother! or, Ah sister! they shall not lament for him, saying, Ah lord! Or, Ah his glory! He shall be buried with the burial of an ass, drawn and cast forth beyond the gates of Jerusalem.
> (Jeremiah 22: 13-19)

God upbraided such covetous, self-indulgent leaders, pointing out that they ought instead to follow the good examples of their predecessor, who *judged the cause of the poor* and the *needy*. As a result of caring for the poor and needy, the former leaders acquired an insightful awareness of God. They had gained wise insights about God due to their work and nature among the most vulnerable people (no doubt widows, orphans, sick, and the infirmed). They acquired a perceptive understanding of how best to live and conduct oneself with humility and grace (Jer. 22:3, 16).

I could have missed such insights into God's nature and attributes had I avoided the least, last, and lost persons of the assembly and community. These tend to be caught in the unattractive, messy circumstances of life. They are the unfortunate ones among us. Reaching and discipling them required my going into the depths of their despair and seeing the ugliness that resided in me as well. This is how we can understand what it is to touch a leper and wade in among the desperate and heal if but one as Jesus did. Such ministry called me away from the more glamorous encounters with pleasant people. It is so much easier to be seduced into the opulence of ivory tower ministry and the pristine quarters of Pastoral office suites, "far from the madding crowd" (Thomas Hardy, 1874).

I found the life of Jacob instructive in this respect. I noted that many a minister (senior and associate alike) have allowed themselves to avoid the ugliness of the spotted, speckled, and ringstraked sheep of their flock, opting to prefer only the pure white or the pure black ones (Gen. 30:31-34). Had I taken an elitist view of shepherding, I would have robbed myself of learning the essential skills and acquiring the more refined art of rearing strong, productive sheep despite their outer appearances. I would have been denied the pleasure of discovering how God prospers those who do. Jacob exemplified this albeit by cunning (Gen. 30:42, 43).

Laban learned the lesson of treating the unattractive sheep as inferior too late as he tried to take advantage of his under-shepherd

Jacob. By the time he realized his error, Jacob was a far more successful shepherd than he. Laban still had the prestige and name recognition in his province, but Jacob had the blessing of God resting upon Him. Laban had the divine privilege of mentoring a young nephew who was entrusted in his care by his sister Rebekah (Gen. 29:12-13). He did not realize the one upon whom the blessings of Abraham, the friend of God, rested upon. Laban was too busy passing off unwanted sheep to Jacob as his wages, but God was not sleeping. Laban's mentality was also manifested in his dealing with his own daughters when he deceptively passed Leah (the tender-eyed, undesirable daughter) on Jacob and held back the more desirable Rachel for whom Jacob had labored seven years. As a result, Laban complicated Jacob's life and subsequently caused a bitter rivalry between his daughters and their sons. However, because of God's faithfulness to His covenants and promises, Jacob emerged as a Prince; He became *Israel,* one who has power with God, a prophetic patriarch of the nation Israel. He ended up with both the wanted and unwanted (Gen. 49; cf. Romans 8:28).

In my case, nothing informed my preaching and teaching more than sitting with broken people in need of the love and salvation of our God: the sometimes nauseating smell of the homeless, the unemptied cat-litter boxes of the once vibrant elderly, the snot of the uncontrollably weeping, the odorous behavior of the porn addict, the repugnant madness of poor mistakes, the rancid smell of unlocked closets of secret sins, the repulsive breath of the chronic alcoholic or smoker, the putrid journey through a life of wanton, sinful indulgence. All these gave realistic weight to the words and theological concepts when I stood before the people of God to minister the Word of the Lord to them in private and public. Such persons mentioned above were in the congregation hidden by their church clothes and decorum.

Messy ministry in the back alleys of life was also helpful at the jails and prisons we ministered to. I could see inmates' eyes well up with tears as we told their stories and accurately identified their pain in the messages we preached from Scripture. It was easier for them to respond to the call to Discipleship from one who preached Jesus, who Himself was convicted, brutalized, falsely incarcerated, and sentenced to death unjustly. I became familiar with that Jesus, Discipling those who had similar experiences.

In other audiences, I saw people light up with familiar agreement when what was presented to them was informed with insight that did not betray their past identities or the confidential information they shared with me. Their faces gave me their approval to expose personal real-life experiences they wanted others to learn from. This vicarious confession helped them feel the touch of the Good Shepherd, that beautiful, loving Shepherd who gave His life for all sheep, including those who strayed from the fold (Jn. 10:10-11).

Also, I learned to hate the path of sin I was often tempted to traverse. I was kept in line by discipling the survivors who lived to tell the horror of the far country. The victims returned without their righteous garments, rings of inheritance, or shoes that bore no tidings of good news or peace but rather ruin, debauchery, and shame. It taught me the reality of Jude's counsel to pull people out of their sinful, carnal wretchedness *hating the very garments* they wear that are *stained with sin* (Jude 23). It taught me to do like the prodigal's father who entered into the celebration of his returned lost son while acknowledging that the inheritance belongs to the faithful son. Often like Daniel, I had to fall to my knees and repent of my and my father's sins and the very latent desires I had secretly harbored in my heart. I turned from fantasizing about some of the very sinful indulgences that had wrecked and ruined those who came pleading for deliverance. Pastoral care and Discipleship taught me to love the clean, holy smell of the new righteous garments that we put upon the prodigals in exchange for their tattered, worldly clothes. They no longer proudly wore even those with the faded and soiled designer labels that emblazoned them; they had no appeal.

CHAPTER 9

Serving in Other Ministries

I quickly learned that Church work never decreases. It only increases without the compensating support services of additional staff, resources of material, time, and finances. Many an Associate Minister can attest that we are often called upon to make bricks without straw, not necessarily because of the Senior Pastor's hardness of heart but because the church and community need often outstrips the limited operating budget. Therefore, we are assigned additional duties well beyond our contractual portfolios. That was the case when I was asked to fill in for the minister at the mid-day service on Wednesdays.

The prior minister was a young, charismatic dynamo. He was an Assistant Pastor, the Youth Minister, a skilled musician, and a prophet. All these gifts in combination made him a beloved and desirable man of God. His mid-day, mid-week sessions were well attended and lasted well beyond their scheduled time of one hour.

His unexpected resignation left a chasm to be filled. I was sent to fill it temporarily. I gladly obliged, not wanting the mid-day faithful to be left in the lurch but kept in the church.

As it turned out, a new Youth Pastor was hired, and she too was dynamic, but the Wednesday mid-day service post wasn't transferred to her. I waited to be relieved but never was. It soon became apparent that this was an additional ministry for which I would be responsible. I did not want to be taken away from Discipleship, but the decision was not mine to make.

The Hour of Power

As I reflected on it, I reconciled this new assignment within my ministry concept. As Discipleship Minister, I held that all ministry was geared to the edifying, equipping, and empowering of God's people, i.e., Discipleship. Therefore, Hour of Power, as it was called, would be a means of discipling those (mainly seniors) who worshipped at that hour.

This approach worked for me in more ways than one. Firstly, it was helpful because it steered me away from trying to be my predecessor. He was known to pray individually for each attendee and prophesy to them, many of whom ended up prostrate on the floor, overwhelmed by the spiritual experience. I felt led by the Lord not to imitate his ministry style or duplicate his gifts that were different from mine. After prayer and soul searching, I decided to function in the Holy Spirit's spiritual endowment. I would focus on teaching the word of God.

Early beginnings at Hour of Power were awkward as the attendees were accustomed to and missed their former leader. Some fiercely loyal to him eyed me with suspicion; others were guarded and related somewhat cautiously with me. After all, I was sent in place of a beloved one who had fallen out of favor with leadership.

Thus, I was in the most tenuous of circumstance in the middle of a polarized situation. Finally, however, those who came to the fellowship hour for that very purpose, more so than respect for a specific personage, embraced me and welcomed me.

In time, Hour of Power became a precious time for the ministry of the Word and fellowship with the special people of God who gathered there weekly. In a short space of time, the attendance grew until it doubled. I borrowed one thing from my predecessor- the study of books as opposed to weekly topical studies. It gave the meeting the desired continuity. Our analysis of the Psalms, which he started, turned out to be one of the wealthiest studies of my life. The Psalms are the inspired, poetic expressions of the people of Israel. They were written by premiere figures that led the nation and featured prominently in their roles as prophets, kings, priests, and musicians. Consequently, these writings exude rich expressions of worship, culture, literature, and emotions that range from aesthetic exuberance to utter despair.

However, Biblical poetry can be more challenging to understand and exegete, unlike narrative texts. Therefore, they often required hermeneutical tools and skills to extract their contextual meaning and contemporary application. Such academic and spiritual exercises plunged me into the depths of Scripture and pulled on all my limited experience to offer the people truth that mattered. In all this, God was faithful.

Another facet of that ministry that proved significant was the members' opportunity to 'testify,' sharing their personal everyday life experiences in the context of their faith. Such private offerings enriched the fellowship among the attendees. We were better able to relate to each other, understand each other's joys and frustrations, sympathize with one another's pain, and better able to celebrate each other's victories, however small. Unfortunately, this hallmark characteristic of Christian corporate worship is increasingly being lost to the detriment of our congregations, becoming more and more impersonal and less and less like the early Church where **koinonia** was practiced routinely.

As the minister over a mostly senior/retired subset of our congregation, I felt like the primary beneficiary. Take, for instance, the deep, heart-wrenching tears of one who was widowed after being married for over fifty years (which at the time was longer than my entire life) and now had to go on alone. In my effort to relate to the grieving widow, I mused that their life together was longer than my earthly existence. It was understandable that she found difficulty doing simple tasks such as shopping without finding herself still picking up his favorite food items or expecting him to chime into a conversation she may be having with herself. Hour of Power became the new family relations where people could come and say what's happening at the doctor, with the children in college, the grandchild that needed help, the housing problem, or life in general.

Hour of Power taught me patience with the elderly as well. Some rose to talk and were delighted to do so with people who patiently listened even to the most meandering stories of seemingly confused persons. I soon saw it necessary to say humorously: "tell us your cares and concerns, your pains and problems we take those too." I watched people age, suffer, lose jobs, start new careers, and retire. I also had the distinct honor of laying many of them to rest who fell asleep in Jesus. In those moments, the attendance at funerals and the fellowship meals after gave the sense of family, caring, love, and belonging to those who needed it most. The fellowship was so rich that members often would schedule their medical appointments around meeting times. Some turned down jobs that precluded them from attending, and others even refused to move away to children's homes because they would be without their Hour of Power Family.

Personally, I was schooled by their individual and collective wisdom, I was taught by their experience, and I grew by my attempts to meet their needs physically, emotionally, and spiritually. They gave me trajectory and acute life perspectives by offering their life spectacles through which I peered as they spoke. I had no fear of growing old if I could do so as graciously and robustly as some of them were. I learned not to treat anyone as dying, specifically those diagnosed with terminal conditions. I watched as many of them led whole and involved lives that bore no hint of their ominous appointment with death. Every day of life was to be celebrated giving new meaning to the familiar Scripture: "this is the day the LORD has made; we will rejoice and be glad in it" (Ps. 118:24 NKJV). Emotionally, therefore, I was broadened by the wealth of experiences shared by beautiful people, some who were well-to-do, some who were poor, and some who were eccentric and somewhat reclusive.

It was not possible to be exposed to such a wide variety of experiences and remain confined to the dictates of my inexperienced, youthfully narrow, individual self. It was, however, in the spiritual self that I grew by leaps and bounds. Many of these precious saints had served the Church for most of their lives. They were past presidents of committees, boards, and ministries. They had sat in Church for collective centuries and heard perhaps all the Scripture texts I presented to them, previously expounded on in several ways from a litany of preachers great and small.

Therefore, my challenge was to offer the Word of God in a meaningful and relevant way to their lives and present circumstances. This meant the astute study of Scripture and effective delivery to a unique audience who deserved more than just an emotional reason to dance and shout. As I endeavored to minister, the mother of the group, Mother Hurst, expressed in her disarming way, "Well, we have been hollered at, spit upon and preached at by lots o' preachers, but

I have learned more from this here son o' mine than all them put together." She may have exaggerated her praise since she claimed me as her adopted grandson, but others shared similar sentiments. I felt in my own self how much I grew as I ministered to God's children, especially those who had grown frail from one condition or another. Many of them could not return for evening services but found an oasis in the mid-week at the Hour of Power, and I felt as though I refreshed my soul there more than they did.

Also, my family was shown much love, especially Lorraine. The girls were lifted up in prayer, and the members were kind with cards and expressions on my birthdays and at Christmas time. When my Dad passed, I returned to Barbados to lay him to rest. The love that the saints of the Hour of Power showered upon us was overwhelming; it made the sorrow of his passing bearable.

Rites of Passage

Almost on the other extreme of the Hour of Power seniors was the ministry to the youth of the church and the community with whom I quickly became deeply involved. Unlike Hour of Power, I was not sent to head this ministry. Instead, I asked to serve The Young Men's Rites of Passage program because there was no official oversight when the minister responsible migrated. Pastors Floyd and Elaine Flake were very concerned with the fate of Black men nationally and locally. Intellectuals such as Juwanja Kunjufu, Dr. Cornell West, Michael Eric Dyson, and Dr. Joy DeGruy Leary were among an avalanche of voices that decried the impact of post-traumatic slave syndrome on the lives of urban youth. Their writings, analyses, lectures, and conferences were conducted with missionary zeal in inner-city communities to stem the tide of destruction, especially in African American neighborhoods such as South Jamaica. Our direct response to their calls to action was to mentor our community's young men and women since this population seemed severely at risk.

The epidemic of illegal drugs, attendant crimes, gangs, failed school systems with failing students along with overly aggressive policing, racial profiling, and prejudicial mal-treatment in the law courts had marched like a merciless army through our communities. Like squadrons of an invading army of occupation, they took out specific assets of our community, especially the men and their sons. Of course, if the men were the targets and consequently victims of these sociological scourges, then the women (mothers, sisters, wives, and daughters) to whom they were connected became infected and affected as well. Those women came to Allen seeking help for their sons and daughters. Mentoring programs were started for both groups. Rev. Dwayne Johnson and Minister Emanuel Haniah were responsible for establishing Rites of Passage. They took the ball and ran like Forest Gump way beyond the touchdown lines. I enrolled my daughters in the girls' **ROP** and looked on with interest at the boys' **ROP**.

ROP, as we affectionately called it, was not considered a cure for all but a beginning, a way of counter-attacking the ravenous societal beasts that sought to devour the hope and future of a people who were the survivors of slavery. The African American Church continues to be the epicenter of the African American community. While it takes a village to raise a child, the African American village typically meets, caucuses, worships, prays, sings, celebrates, weeps, marries, and buries its fallen in its churches. Thus it was not unusual for Allen to take on this challenge. Rev. Johnson pulled me into the fight for the future of our young men.

ROP began with us meeting in the Youth Church's basement with the 13-18 years olds of our congregation and their friends. The Mentors set out to disarm them of the pervasive deviance within and around them. Without programmatic models, scripts, or prior experience, these brothers challenged every ungodly behavior exhibited by their young charges. I was first invited in by Rev. Dwayne and then Bro. Emanuel (now Rev. Emanuel Haniah) as a facilitator to address questions of sexuality and continued to contribute in this way. The young men asked about masturbation, pornography, and sex in general. Issues of premarital sex, addictions, molestation, STDs, adultery and parental indiscretions surfaced like lava to the summits. Our open and honest discussions were unapologetically informed by the Word of God, which was held high before our young protégés. This was another field ripe for Discipleship, and the harvest was plentiful. I signed up to be a laborer among the few.

The young men were hungry for the all-male forums away from the approving/disapproving prudish ears and stares of their parents and guardians. It was a chance to 'get real' on issues without the fluff, and in their terminology, we were able to: 'kick it to them real,' according to age, experience, and maturity. They were engaged on all fronts. For example, they were drilled military-style, taught to memorize and recite Scripture, and mandated to formally dress each Friday evening. Their Mentors took their gang flags, drugs, weapons, music CDs, and DVDs with violent or suggestive content. The Mentors also checked their poor attitudes and behaviors towards themselves, their homework, their academic performances, their friends, and most importantly, their mothers. They were taken to dinner at restaurants to learn proper etiquette when eating out, then to sports arenas to experience live games and other cultural events for their enrichment. They eagerly competed against the Mentors in basketball and other games. Their homes and schools were visited; they were engaged in one-on-one sessions, group sessions, and broader forums. They were taken to Riker's Island to belie the machismo mystique of going to jail by those who try to glorify such a tragic experience to young impressionable minds for 'street credits.' They saw the pain in the eyes of the incarcerated men and boys there and heard their plaintive admonitions to: "stay in school," "respect y'all moms," "do the right thing," and "stay out of trouble."

The program's climax came at the **ROP** Retreat when the young men were taken out of the city to get the *city* out of them. Then, at Mont Lawn Camp in the Poconos mountains, we met with them, ate with them, slept in the same cabins with them, mountain climbed with them, and competed in activities against them. We also conducted intensive workshops with them that got down to the nitty-gritty of personal pain and emotional distress in the presence of the Lord. There they learned to trust each other and us, older men that would not abandon them or hurt them in the ways they had been left and hurt by their fathers and other male figures in their lives. There they became a village of young initiates with their seniors, elders like griots training them to be young lions that will take their place in society for the good of all.

Here I Am, Send Me

Within a year, the first crop of graduates was presented to the congregation. The church beamed, proud of the men who stepped up to serve their sons, proud of the sons who completed the program. Tearful but grateful parents and guardians who attended the special graduation ceremony were appreciative of the changes they saw in their children, often labeled by the social pundits as 'at risk'. Single mothers and grandmothers struggling against the prevailing anti-social forces that tainted their sons were hopeful seeing the new disciplines their sons displayed. To be sure, not all the youth enrolled in the program were terrible. Some were excellent from good Christian homes, well-mannered, good students, well behaved, committed

Christian themselves, and some were the Mentors' own sons. Still, they all needed a wholesome transition into manhood based on sound values, not street values that robbed them of their true self-worth and often their liberty. Through **ROP**, their grades improved, and good character was forged; many avoided drugs and gangs, and the illicit behaviors and activities that would bring them into contact with the police were largely averted. This was Discipleship, a true spiritual transformation, although we may not have recognized it at the time. My daughters often complained that the Boys' **ROP** was better than theirs and wished they were boys to participate.

This process continued unabated for five years, and then the pioneers of the program were gone. It was a sad blow to the circle of Mentors since we had become inseparable friends. 'Revie, Rev,' as we affectionately called Rev. Dwayne Johnson, moved away to Maryland with his wife, Camille. The whole church community experienced loss because Camille was the Guidance Counselor for the Allen Christian School and the primary church counselor. Before we could recover from the Johnson's leaving, Emanuel soon got married and moved away to Texas. These were the innovators and the streetwise Mentors that were the heart of the program. They knew how to tap into the street vibes and speak the language with which the kids identified. They knew the stuff the kids got into that was invisible to parents. They knew how to sass out the ones on drugs or those who began to 'smell themselves' because they became involved with girls. They knew how to negotiate with the gang leaders and neighborhood thugs. This institutional memory was now lost and impossible to replace because it was hard-wired in their personalities; it was not a skill that could be acquired.

Dwayne's daring, spontaneous ideas made us do the most unthinkable things. For example, he marched the boys and their mentors to the subway, lined them up in plain view, made them sing church songs, then preached to the commuters. He took them into a barbershop in full swing, walked up to the TV, turned it off to the owners and patrons' utter shock, and then began to preach to the stunned brothers who didn't even budge or ask who he was and what he was doing. He took the boys to an Italian restaurant on Queens Boulevard, let all 25 or more of them order food, and then tried to figure out how we would pay for it after everyone had eaten. Miraculously, when he told the owner what the program was, the bill was minuscule. He took them to Jones Beach, blindfolded them, and made them trust each other in the dark. He challenged them to walk on water. The Pastor's eldest son, Rasheed, sincerely tried and had to be pulled out, drenched, and covered with sand. No one was given a pass, neither the Pastor's sons nor LL Cool J's son, all enrolled in *ROP*. These fearless lions named Rev. Johnson and Bro. Emmanuel pushed the boundaries and tested the malleable metal of the sons entrusted to their care.

On one occasion, the dreaded Nassau police rolled up and demanded to know what was happening. They had received a report of shouts from the beach from nearby residents. Rev. Johnson stepped up boldly and explained the program, stating emphatically that the boys were being taught values and disciplines so that the police would never have to encounter them. Incredibly, the police told them to carry on and left. As zany and risky as these methods were, they grabbed the boys' attention and gained their respect. These unassuming, well-spoken, well-suited Christian brothers were brave, daring, and unashamed of displaying their faith before anyone. This blew the typical perception of those in the' hood' that men in Church were 'soft,' 'weak,' and 'suckers' to religion. Rev. Johnson and Bro. Emanuel's mystique attracted and kept the boys coming back for more *ROP*. Now was it gone because they were gone?

This loss had a double impact on me. First, my dear friends moved away. Second, the burden of ministry increased. Some of Camille's counseling caseload was soon transferred to me, and Dwayne's baby, **ROP**, was orphaned and flagging. The Mentors left in charge soldiered on, but they missed the ministerial and charismatic presence of the founders and brothers in arms. They had turned an experimental program into one that needed ministerial representation and guidance, which the eyes of the remaining Mentors began to look to me to provide. However, I didn't have the skill set that Rev. Johnson and Bro. Emanuel had instinctively, having grown up themselves in South Jamaica, Queens. I recognized that I could not have that same gravitas they did, given my Caribbean upbringing.

In any case, my plate was full. Yet, the need keep gnawing away at my reasonable refusal. 'How in good conscience could I as a man, a Christian man, a Black, Christian man allow this critical ministry to flop over and die for want of attention?' That was the question I could not evade. Yet, I observed firsthand that this was the ministry that had piloted many young men through high school and into college and careers. It steered many away from or out of court and jail. It taught youth how to handle complex life issues better without resorting to violence or drugs. This ministry helped them navigate the temptations to surrender their virtue and caused many graduates to come back after graduating to repeat the program. Some returned to be peer mentors, while others just wanted to be in *Passage,* as it was soon affectionately called.

Therefore, I approached Rev. Elaine and asked permission to serve as Ministerial Advisor to the Young Men's Rites of Passage. At first, she was hesitant from knowing my workload, and she searched her mind long and hard to think of someone else who could replace Rev. Johnson. Reluctantly, Rev. Elaine allowed me to serve, but with the provision that she would be looking for someone else to replace me as soon as one was identified. With that mutual agreement, I assumed and extended my additional duties to disciple the boys. Thankfully, they were no complex adjustments the mentors needed to make for me as I was already part of the ***ROP*** team. I was well-received, and we stepped forward together.

As we set out to regroup and continue, two difficulties immediately presented themselves. Firstly, there was the need for a more formal structure. ***ROP***, in my view, needed a set format to follow. By now, we had learned how to market to the church body and the wider community, initiate the youth to Godly lifestyles, and what activities were effective and those that were not. Therefore, it was time to streamline the operation so that new Mentors and mentees would tap into the mentoring system physically and intellectually as new mentors and mentees came on board. Rather than being driven by the various personalities who coordinated it, a structured program could be enriched by each coordinators' skill set as he served. In this way, the program would have more continuity and be less impacted by leadership changes. Once again, the lessons I had learned in the Discipleship Model were instructive and adapted to fit here.

Additionally, the structure was necessary because we realized that we were no longer mentoring the children of Allen members alone. We were increasingly attracting referrals from the Probation offices of Queens, Guidance Counseling offices of junior and high schools, and the community members. Without setting out to do so, we had established a reputation of successfully dealing with young men. Many of these professional groups and personnel wanted to see information on the program to guide their decisions and document the youth's progress in their charge. Parents also wanted printed material to know what the program would do for their children to determine its appropriateness, and rightly so. Then there were those suspicious souls who were distrustful of Churches. The Catholic

Priests' scandals with altar boys only tended to make the entire interaction of men and young men in the Church, even our church, appear to be a dirty *off-white* color.

These external demands highlighted the internal need for management and control. We needed to begin to document our best practices and to be able to measure successes and outcomes. Some of our graduates were in excellent career tracks, some had entered outstanding colleges, some were now married, and others returned as Mentors themselves. We must have been doing something right. To know what that something was, we needed to outline our activities and standardize our main approaches so that Mentors and mentees could be on the same page of our manual of operation and codes of conduct.

I realized that removing some of our ministry's subjective guesswork was necessary to make our tasks more objective. This latter point was essential as we rewarded the youth according to their performances. For example, three of them would be President, First Vice President, and Second Vice President of the graduating classes. Others were rewarded as the Most Improved, Highest Academic Achievement, etc. However, objective criteria needed to be set and observed to be fair and avoid any sense of favoritism. Thus, I implemented a point system that, among other things, covered: attendance, the participation of the mentees as well as their parents/guardians, and even bonus points for special activities such as community service and church service attendance.

This new structure needed to be set out in an operations manual, and for that to happen, I would have to write it or hire someone to do so. I had a good sense of what to do, but finding the time to research and study other established mentoring systems and analyze and categorize ours was a major challenge of time and resources. Yet, it had to be done. Moreover, it was embarrassing not to have adequate material to fax, email, or simply copy to a District Attorney's office who wanted to enroll a wayward youth to whom he was extending a second chance by way of community service as an alternative to incarceration. These were excellent compliments but were demands that we were unprepared to meet. Still, we needed to do so. **ROP** evolved beyond the high walls of the Cathedral into the community, which had now had come calling, and we needed to respond well.

In betwixt and between everything else, I began to set down my observations and ideas to capture the essence of *ROP* and its merits. Several Mentors had already done some writing, not towards a manual per se, but as a natural development. For example, a mentee wrote a commitment creed that became our spoken word anthem. Other written aims and objectives were incorporated, along with permission slips and other documents we had used. These were improved to reflect uniformity and to bear the imprimatur of Allen. In his travels, I was also aware that our Pastor talked about the **ROP** program, and a manual would serve as a portfolio document for him once it was finalized.

With these in view, I began the process. My aim was to produce an *ROP* Manual which would comprise of several sections: Administration, listing all the program components, a Mentor section which would serve as a guide for all activities, a Mentee section so that the mentees could anticipate and better participate in the program, and a Parent section so that parents may know what their children were learning and what part they were to play in the process. Of course, this was an enormous undertaking that perhaps required a sabbatical to complete, but that was not feasible given my responsibilities.

Needless to say, while I was preparing the manual, the program was operating and needing the manual simultaneously. In the words of my people, 'while de grass growing de horse starving.' Therefore, I implemented as I went along. I issued parts as I wrote them. As a practical measure, I divided the program into three stages that would form the skeleton of the eight months of mentoring the young men would undergo:

- Part 1. Who am I? (Self-Awareness and Discovery)
- Part 2. How did I get here? (Self-Analysis, familial/societal dynamics and influences)
- Part 3. Where am I going? (Self-projections, perspectives, and pursuits)

Each of these stages had a set of activities that would help the mentees to think through the questions posed, to develop a healthy view of self and society, and the decisions necessary to live well. As the mentees complete exercises in each stage, they would compile a portfolio that would be a personal document folder by their graduation. It would serve as a reference, giving the mentees and families an introspective, retrospective, and prospective view of themselves, the family system of which they are a part, and a trajectory of their future as a result. I also developed the preliminary point system and a Bible study on David titled: *The Boy Who Grew Up to be King*. My excellent assistant, Danielle, made light work of my near illegible rough drafts putting them into print. Soon a folder for each Mentor with our logo as the face of a roaring lion was ready. Although not complete, we were on our way!

The second difficulty I faced in assuming spiritual oversight of **ROP** was a surprising lack of real support and commitment from all concerned. I fully expected that since the problems facing men in general, and Black men particularly, were so blatantly pandemic that measures to correct them would have been at the top of the agenda of pastors and churches, especially African-American ones. I expected the same for Councilmen, Congressmen, Senators, police, judges, men's groups, women's groups, parents' associations, the entire nation, for that matter. From our limited view, it was clear that fathers' physical and emotional absenteeism in the home was the #1 problem in the country across ethnic lines. Several professional studies and sociologists confirmed this fact. The street was the substitute for the homes for far too many un-fathered boys and, increasingly, girls. Gangs became *'fam'* (family), *OG's (Original Gang* leaders), and drug dealers were often the only males that paid concerted attention to young males, albeit harmful and destructive. This was the catalyst for underachievement in education, gang initiation, illegal drug involvement, teenage pregnancy, prostitution, various crimes, and the entrance into the Prison Industrial Complex that was robbing our communities of our fathers and sons.

To all of us involved in mentoring at Allen and everywhere else, it was clear that unless young men and women were fathered, they were severely at risk of being sucked into the vortex of a powerful mechanism. The machine had already vacuumed up their fathers, brothers, cousins, uncles, peers, mothers, sisters, aunts and dumped them into the Criminal *in*Justice System. Our communities were targeted and charges applied with brutal impunity to black and Hispanic minorities for offences that only resulted in DATs (Desk Appearance Tickets) for the same, if not worse, offenses in others' communities, mere streets away. My having gone to the precincts to help distraught parents, negotiating with the DA offices over misdemeanors that were charged as felonies by over-zealous police officers and prosecutors, along with being a Para-chaplain for over 20 years at Riker's Island, confirmed this conclusion. Regrettably, it was well-founded in harsh reality.

Another dynamic bore out our perspective of injustice and our need for male Mentors. We were often told by angry boys who resisted our discipline and our confronting their poor behaviors,

"You are not my father!" We knew from experience that this was more a cry of pain than rejection. In these intense moments of interaction, we recognized that the young men were admitting that we were addressing them as though we were their fathers in the absence of their own and expecting them to respond as if they were our sons. Therefore, we would lovingly but firmly respond: "yes, that's true, but we are going to father you, that we may further you." They had no *comeback* or retort to that! It usually struck their walls of defense and resistance like a Mack truck. The anger of their fathers' absence interfacing with our loving concern was untenable. It was easier to surrender to love than to keep fighting a deep and gnawing need.

We knew that **ROP** was essential! It was not a mere church program; **it was a ministry**! It was the extension of the anointed service of Christ to the fatherless, the motherless, the oppressed, the poor, the abused, the imprisoned, the captive, and the bound (Lk. 4:18, 19). That was my duty to the faithful brothers and mothers who devoted themselves with cultic zeal to their charges and the program forming the ROP Parent Support Group. We could count on them to raise funds, provide refreshments, and help host any activity we planned together. We expected the same commitment from our leaders at every level.

Sadly, I learned that in many cases, the mentoring of young men was not the priority of those who discussed it as if it was on the top of their agenda. Instead, it was all too often merely a hot button issue of discussion and debate, an emotional topic that drove conferences, sold books, CDs, DVDs, and furthered people's political careers. Yet, when it came to addressing the problem hands-on, no money was available, and any attempt to redress such inequities in and out of the Church was met by status quo barriers.

One of the most frustrating barriers was from men themselves. I could have found ten women to every one man who would have come forward to mentor the boys. I studied this anomaly and realized several reasons for this wretched dearth of a 'few good men.' Firstly, the church's good men were stretched thin in every ministry. In Allen, men numbered a third to a quarter of the population. Thus their relatively limited quantity in a mega-church congregation made many of them unavailable to mentor. They were already serving as Choir members, Ushers, Officers, Trustees, and Heads of Ministries. Secondly, many were working jobs that challenged their ability to participate because their schedules conflicted with our meeting times. Many worked for the Sanitation Department, the Metropolitan Transit Authority, the Department of Corrections, etc., and often on the night shift. They were busy earning bread for their families, and it was hard to be there for others. However, I noted that many didn't sign up because they could not give *complete* involvement, but I often told them that *some participation was better than none.* We learned that a few minutes in a young man's life by a man who cared often was what made the difference at the split-second decision point of turning left to negative influences or right to the better way they were advised to take by their mentors whom they did not want to disappoint.

However, the truth is that some men were afraid to sign up for other hidden reasons. Some were never fathered, and subconsciously, they could not see how they could father others. Men don't commit when they feel inadequate. Others were afraid of confronting their past lives and buried behaviors, which were resurrected like zombies when issues the boys presented brought them back to life. If only they knew that in their ministering to the young men's needs, the Lord would minister to theirs and heal them in the process. That happened to us, who stepped up to the plate with our incompetency. We were disappointed when other brothers did not come to help.

In some cases, their own sons turned them over to us to be fixed and returned whole.

Our greatest disappointment of all came from leaders of all stripes, but it hurt worst at Allen, our home base. We were often dumbfounded at the abysmal lack of support when we needed it most. It seemed like we had to pull teeth to get plugs for the program's events and activities. No one seemed to share the passion we had. We went the whole distance for the young men, and when we asked for simple help, we felt relegated to the back of the line. **ROP** Mentors like the audacious Trevor Murrell went to mentees' homes to check their rooms' tidiness, which they were encouraged to maintain as part of the program. Others like Gerald, Trey, and Prince responded to calls from mothers, guidance counselors, and probation officers to deal with youth acting out, cutting classes, disrespecting parents, or being arrested. Bro. Arno, a retired police and corrections officer, served gallantly as our resident griot from his exquisite collection of books that the boys were encouraged to read and educate their minds.

I often had to temper the zeal of one of the **ROP** leaders, Dimas Salaberrios (now a Pastor, Community First Responder, TBN host, and author). He had been a drug dealer, dope addict, incarcerated inmate, etc. His life (well documented in his book, *Street God, Tyndale*) had run the whole gamut of indiscretions. Once he became saved and joined Allen, he approached any ministry where he became involved with the same determination. He was unchurched, unrefined, and unafraid to try anything that he believed would make a difference for the Lord. His 6'4" frame made him stick out like Saul's, head and shoulders above all of us. Like Rev. Johnson, he brought the street culture to Passage, challenging every norm we felt we should maintain for the viability and sustainability of the program. He was not interested in standards and protocols. He wanted results and took every opportunity to get them. Dimas was not an egomaniac.

He was not trying to draw attention to himself. He recognized what we were trying to do with the young men. Dimas knew the dangers to which they were exposed better than any of us church boys, so he took the ball and ran as far as he could with it. The trouble was that while he was well respected by the young men, most of the other mentors could not keep up with him. I was perhaps like a damp towel to his burning passions, but he knew where my heart was. I had to be a responsible steward to keep the program from being shut down for being too radical.

Most of our activities were usually done in the church basement or offsite away from the congregants. Dimas preferred it out in the open to challenge the young men to faith and commitment, so **ROP** activities were more visible. These undertakings raised fears from church officers and trustees. Allen became so huge in the region that people began to seek ways to sue and extract whatever money they thought they could from this 'rich' church. Therefore **ROP** had to exercise restraint in order not to attract any liability. This meant that some of our tactics, considered 'risqué,' had to be curbed. This was too confining for Dimas and others who knew that these threats were attempts to make the program and the Church, in general, ineffective. Thus, we continued to nibble at the edges and keep the periphery from advancing inward as we mentored the young men while giving Dimas as much rope as possible to keep Passage from becoming 'passé.'

Despite these gallant efforts, we struggled to announce activities and meetings published at church services. At times, they were preempted for other ministry priorities and went unannounced. What could have been more important than rescuing the next generation with the gospel? I always had to ask the Pastors to let the young men speak to the congregation, especially near graduation, to attend the ceremony. They were usually persuaded and obliged; after all, both their sons went through the ministry program.

When the young men spoke during the Sunday services, they often moved the congregation to tears on the one hand, and on the other, the congregants rejoiced for the work the men were doing among the youth. However, I always felt that we should not have to jockey for position with the other ministries, all 101 of them. Of course, all ministry was Godly and wholesome, and all my colleagues were equally passionate about their particular focus. Still, our youth, mainly our young men, were in crisis, and a corresponding level of urgency was needed to stem the hemorrhage to Riker's Island and the cemeteries. We never felt that such a critical response was being given except by the women whose sons we were impacting and appreciated the enormous time and effort the Mentors put in to save their sons. We knew deep down that our Pastors supported our efforts, but we wanted more than we were accorded because the boys needed more.

Admittedly they were some people that did come forward to help. Dr. Daniel Laroache, an Ophthalmologist, was an ardent supporter. He was not only one of our regular motivational speakers to the boys, but he also gave a monetary scholarship award to the top academic achiever. A similar distinction was provided by Bill Jones Realty. Bill's sons walked the Passage also. Then, Sis. Eloise Hicks made all the sashes each year for the Mentors and the mentees for graduation. Parents like Sheila Lattimore and Sis. Dennis and brothers like Rev. Alfonzo Wyatt and countless others made sterling contributions. Plus, one of our mentees' fathers donated a genuine African spear used as our symbolic gesture of passing responsibility from the outgoing President to the incoming class President.

I often wondered if perhaps what we perceived as apathy toward *ROP* was prejudiced by the rawness of our immediate contact with the harsh realities of the lives with which we interfaced. We took weapons such as guns, knives, and box cutters from teens. We confiscated marijuana and other illegal drugs. I ended up with a frightening collection of gang paraphernalia, weapons, pornography, etc., in my office. We went to the precincts when our boys were arrested rightfully or, more often, wrongfully. We walked their cases through the court with attorneys and interacted with the DA's office to effect justice. On another front, we saw our men in jails and prisons, many of them fathers of children much like the ones we mentored, with their potential penned up, destinies denied, and ambitions aborted. We cried with some as they were sent upstate to prisons for longer terms and fought successfully for others released by miraculous turns of events. We counseled mothers and sons, and sometimes whole families were reeling from the brutality of one kind of tragedy or another. The worst disasters were the young men's resistance to parents' discipline and unwillingness to submit to the program's rigorous correction. Nothing was more bewildering than seeing our youth fall into obvious traps lying in plain sight. Sometimes they were caught taking a prohibited item to school, hanging out with known troublemakers/gang members, or giving the police probable cause to arrest them by how they dressed and behaved in the streets. Often, they were simply being youth, but when communities are under siege, even that was risqué.

However, despite the indifference of others, scarcity of soldiers, and resistance of the young men themselves, nothing was as dear to our hearts as Passage. The most significant part for me was the retreat. Early in the spring, we would take the young men and mentors for the weekend of their lives to Pennsylvania's Poconos Mountains. Past Passage graduates, Mentors, and other invited facilitators, especially Revs. Johnson, Moutoo, Haniah, and Bro. Max Johnson would join. *ROP* retreats were like none other; they superseded even the men's retreats I attended and facilitated. At Mont Lawn Camp, we dealt with everything we faced as men head-on. No holds barred! Workshops addressed every issue related to our lives from a man's perspective: sex, porn, masturbation, STD's, fathers (present/absent), leadership, responsibility, the role of the man in the home, high school, college, sports, God, Church, Christ, salvation, the Bible, each other, no topic was spared in the pristine scenery around us.

As presenters dug in deep in the reality of any sin/issue in our personal lives or in the societal collective of which we are a part, the Mentors would respond with: "bring it!" With this chant, we submitted ourselves to the lance of the Scriptural scalpels, as painful as they may have been. Like the cowboys in the frontier with an arrowhead or a bullet embedded in his flesh that would cause infection or fever if not removed, we took whatever was dished out like men. Just like in the movies, in the absence of a modern hospital and a skilled surgeon, the commitment of a dear friend with a heated knife was a crude but effective solution. In the act of courage, the suffering cowboy gritted his teeth, saying, "bring it on," mentally anesthetizing himself to the pain. He did it also to dismiss the concern of his 'partner' who would regret having to wound his friend to render him whole (Prov. 27:6). That was the level of love and mutual concern we had for each other and our boys. Thus we gave 'altar calls' after each workshop presentation and dealt with engrained sin concerning a Mentor or mentee. No distinction was made at altar call; repentance was good for all. All of us found a reason to repent, and our openness gave the young men an insight into real men with struggles that were relying on God to deliver us by the power of His Spirit.

I recall a workshop in which the presenter dealt with sexual molestation. I believe it was Reverend Johnson in his bluish army fatigue jumpsuit. He went in deep. He exposed the putrefying tumor. He touched the tender tissues still smarting from the shrapnel left there where no one knew but the one who continued to suffer in silence or the Holy Spirit that wanted it extricated. He went down into the dark basement of minds that had long locked away painful memories and snapped the chains on dusty chests releasing secrets that were not supposed to be ever told. Rev. Johnson, emboldened by the stench of the fetid secrets wafting in the fresh air, followed their musty odors up to the attics of our childhood experiences and opened the toy chests holding the little red Tonka truck with plastic soldiers and our sisters' rag dolls and dusted off memories. Some of us remembered the sisters and cousins we touched inappropriately and the unfortunate carnal knowledge gained in the closets where we hid. As the tears of guilt or compassion for the victims streamed down our faces, others recalled the men who fondled them and threatened them not to tell their mothers. The spirits of fear that had bound and gagged them, robbing them of the ability to trust other men, to have a subconscious resentment towards women because of the evil men they brought into their homes, were now under the spotlight of liberating truth.

It suddenly explained insecurities within ourselves, the fear of intimacy, our predispositions to pornography, and illicit sex without regard for the women we slept with. It made sense why some felt drawn to people of the same sex since the molestations were all too often the first introduction to their sexuality and confused gender identity still growing in innocence by an unwelcomed intrusion. The Revie Rev. went over his time, but we didn't care about structuring the day's program. As long as the Spirit was ministering through whomever, we would not quench His flame.

For the altar call, Rev. Johnson called me to minister to the group that had surged forward with no prodding necessary. Many were visibly shaking, others appeared numb, others stood stone-faced with their lives' videos playing upon the vistas of their minds, others were weeping, snotting, shaking, and crying aloud. Rev. Moutoo, Rev.

Haniah, and I were experienced counselors. Still, in that poignantly charged moment, the catharses, the confessions, the admissions of guilt, the remorse, and the heartfelt cries for forgiveness and deliverance from God was the intervention necessary; clinical sessions could come later. Mentors and mentees alike sought God together; men and young men called out to our heavenly Father for His saving grace. As I prayed, moving through the group, anointing their heads, and embracing the broken, I became the man they could embrace without fear of being hurt. I was the confidant of their hidden secrets, the vicarious victim they needed to apologize to, and from whom they needed forgiveness. I became the minister of hope to men who saw the light of the gospel in the dark alleyways of their minds, where many were emotionally trapped or feared to traverse.

At the end of that session, we all knew we had had a Divine encounter in the mountains, and we were never going to be the same again. For far too many of the mentees, it was the first time they saw men, and Godly men, huddled, conferencing, conversing, showing their vulnerabilities, and praying. To be sure there was much follow-up to take place after we left the mountain: counseling sessions were to be scheduled, confrontations and consultations were to take place, forgiveness was to be sought and given, and new liberties were to be lived responsibly, not as a cloak of maliciousness (I Pet. 2:16). Finally, we went to lunch as brothers, able to look into each other's eyes without cowering and without judgment.

We usually culminated the **ROP** Retreat with an anointing service in the beautiful Baber chapel donated by the Diebold family. I never left there without weeping, seeing visible changes in Mentors' and mentees' lives; both were addressed. We were all younger and older males discovering our proper roles in God's world and how such functions would be played out where we lived. Not even guest ministers/facilitators were spared. We all displayed our vulnerabilities and confessed our faults before God at the Retreat, calling on God to deliver us from our bondages and to give us the power to overcome them on our return. The Lord never failed to answer us because we came home changed for the most part. The young men saw Christian men in strength and human weakness, and we became a band of men ready to change the world or at least our neighborhoods. Weeks after **ROP** Retreat, mothers would come asking bewildered regarding their son, "What did you guys did up there to him? He changed." We would only smile in gratitude to God and be satisfied that we were making a difference. We kept a pact of silence to protect the confidentiality of those men and boys who had bared their souls to allow them time to heal.

In the months that followed, I met with parents and mentees alike to deal with matters that needed redress. One Mentor brought his illegal cable boxes via which he tapped into pornographic channels. Giving them to me was his way of getting rid of his secret sins and the source of them; our subsequent Pastoral Counseling sessions together revealed a cruel rape in his youth by a man while he was on an errand for his mother one fateful evening. He may have been revisiting the pain through the misogynistic pornography he watched without realizing it. Still, another brought his pornography tapes. I had become the repository of rejected, toxic toys from men who had outgrown them, confessing, "God told me to give them to you," which was the usual explanation for their deposits. I believed that this was the first step in the dialogue of healing. I kept them until they had become irrelevant. I was deeply conscious that I had gained their respect and guarded it as a sacred trust. Thus **ROP** became a band of brothers within the Allen family. We returned each week to renew our fellowship. Then every year, to restore our faith in Christ and each other "to the end," as Rev. Johnson would say.

CHAPTER 10

THE GACNY MAP

During my tenure as Discipleship Minister, I was summoned by Rev. Elaine. I went to her office and was given a rather unusual assignment. I was asked to develop a method of screening prospects for ordained ministry; I was to establish criteria that would qualify persons to become Ministers of Allen. At first, I was surprised because I did not expect to be asked to do something so exquisite, especially at Allen, given that both Pastors had earned doctorates and that Rev. Elaine had nurtured Allen Christian School into a thriving institution of learning. She was the educator, and therefore, a screening and selection process of applicants to the ministry was well within her abilities. Then too, I felt that they should want a more hands-on role to determine who enters the excellent ministry they had painstakingly built together. I politely objected, explaining to Rev. Elaine that I saw that task as more of a Pastoral function I was not worthy of. Nonplused, she promptly redirected it back to me to do. I left her office somewhat perturbed and wondering, 'why me'?

A Discipleship Plan for Ministers

I returned to my office, mulling over this massive assignment. It was an enormous task that my mind began to process and contemplate the many components necessary to accomplish it. I had never done anything like this before. Still, I imagined that it would require research to formulate a written process that measured up to Allen's ever-increasing standards of excellence. It would also have to be compatible and interface with the AME denomination (the oldest and one of the largest national and multinational black institutions steeped in rich traditions). It also necessitated developing a track to mentor candidates through metrics to measure outcomes, determine those outcomes regarding applicants, and assign someone to collate, manage, and process the data. But, then, there were other considerations: Who would qualify/disqualify the applicant? What about the time to meet with candidates? What would be the system of processing applicants and application documents? What instructions would the applicants have to have? Would there be a curriculum of study? What would be the curriculum? What would be the resource materials appropriate for neophytes and the more experienced to prepare themselves? All these were the additional questions that were circulating in my mind.

All these concerns seemed overwhelming, and for the first time, I was not willing to do what my boss had requested. I was bewildered on many levels. For one, I was still working my way to finishing seminary, which was interrupted by my wife's illness several times. How then was I to complete this task? In those moments of unwillingness and non-acceptance, I heard the Lord speak quietly to my heart. He impressed me to do as Rev. Elaine asked because of my experience. Somewhere beyond my vision was a bigger picture that I could not see which God had directed via the Pastors to me, the least of the Apostles. With that divine intervention, I sighed, shrugged my shoulders, and resigned myself to work, pondering how all this was to be done.

I was aware of the arduous AME ordination process, having gone through it. I knew from experience what it takes to answer the call and how it feels to present a trial sermon. Therefore, a process was already in practice, but it was not written down in exact, easy steps to follow. I also recalled that a former Assistant Pastor, Rev. Brenda Hazel, used to teach a class for new ministerial candidates. Yet, I never knew the curriculum because she left to pastor a congregation and before I became a candidate and attended her class.

Nevertheless, all the pieces were there somewhere. Then I recalled a colleague in ministry, Rev. Marjorie Nunez, who had become a minister in the United Methodist Church. We often discussed how meticulous, extensive, and detailed the UMC's process was before one was given charge over a congregation and the continual oversight following that appointment. I called Rev. Nunez and asked to discuss her procedures. I also asked to borrow the materials she had on hand. I had a clear sense, though, that the Pastors did not want an elaborate obstacle course but a simple yet effective way of handling the increasing requests of those seeking to serve at Allen. The Pastors loved excellence, but not deadening, inflexible traditions, and unnecessary red tape that hindered rather than helped people. Thus, I prayed to the Lord to give me a process to screen out the wolves in sheep's clothing and help the serious applicants come to terms with their calling. I hoped it would improve how the Pastors made their selections. I also prayed that this format would prepare the selected candidates for the AME Church's demands and ministry at Allen beyond the academic requirements.

It was soon impressed on me by the Lord, no doubt, that the process should not be hostile to the candidates but one that deals with them gently and respectfully. Whatever the outcome of the process, they should all be better for having undergone it. The Lord reminded me that the harvest was plentiful, but the laborers are few; therefore, those who ask to labor in the vineyard were to be given every opportunity to do so. Therefore, even if they were misguided, they should see their way more clearly.

With these tender leanings, I began to write down my thoughts and ideas. In short order, a system began to emerge. I was shocked at how easily my thoughts flowed and how fluidly the structure started to take shape like a figurine from the mass of marble. I would find myself working enthusiastically at the computer, engrossed. At other times I would be vigorously writing down ideas on my legal pads for entry later. Before long, I had a working document to present to Rev. Elaine. First, however, it needed a label, a title. It was there before me almost without much head-scratching: The Greater Allen Cathedral Ministerial Application Process, or in its acronym form, **GACNY MAP**. A *map!* How clever; that should do it.

I presented my Ministerial Application Process to Rev. Elaine for her perusal, and it was promptly forwarded to Ms. London for editing and proofing. It was not rejected outright, so it passed muster thus far. It was returned to me to make the necessary changes and resubmitted again. Eventually, Rev. Elaine approved a final version of GACNY MAP. It was composed of the application form, the criteria of acceptance, stages in the process, a means of advancing fully into ministry at Allen, and referral to the AME District Conference and Institute. These bodies are ultimately responsible for recommending ministerial applicants to the Bishop for ordination. However, it still needed a curriculum for class and the books/source materials to guide the candidates through the process. Again, the Lord was faithful. I prayerfully drew from the academic community, my own academic training and experience, the examples in Scripture, the

Sons of the Prophets motifs, the Jesus' Discipleship model, and the Pauline Practice as documented by Luke and noted in the Epistles. Eventually, I had a straightforward procedure to bring the candidate for ministry to the Pastors' attention for examination and Licensure.

Introduction:
- The General Call of God to All Mankind
- The Believer's Call to Deeper Fellowship

Step 1. Exploration of One's Calling
Step 2. Examination of Persons Called in Scripture
Step 3. Exposition of Scriptures in Calling
- Sermonettes
- Peer evaluation

Step 4. Exposé of Self-Temperament Analysis Profile
Step 5. Engaging in Ministry-Spiritual Formation
Conclusion:
- Analysis
- Recommendation

My rationale for the five-step outline was based on my reasoning that the AME Institute and Seminary would provide formal academic training. GACNY MAP, therefore, would be a process that would enable the candidate to have a personal, introspective examination of their sense of calling in a safe, conducive, non-judgmental environment. The process would allow the applicants to have a profound exploration of the call of God to serve His people through the eyes of prophets, judges, priests, and kings in Scripture, who, at various times and in multiple ways, were called to lead Israel. Then preliminary opportunities to 'preach' in class on given subjects and critique from peers would provide valuable feedback and perspective on content, style, presentation, delivery, time utilization, etc. It was also necessary for Allen and the applicants to have a psycho-graphic view of themselves to determine their suitability for ministry. Temperament Analysis Profiles were helpful indicators of what areas of ministry candidates were more suited and why. It took much of the mystery out of why some people felt driven to particular ministries and why they showed an aversion to others. It also pointed out why persons were adept at being with people (*Sanguine*) or why they seemed passive or indifferent (*phlegmatic*). They no longer had to feel guilty for feeling worn out when meeting with a large group of people because they were more task-oriented (*Melancholy*), nor did they have to think of themselves as vain and arrogant for feeling at their best when in control (*Choleric*). Others were more comfortable giving service (*supine*). These feelings and inclinations could now be explained and put into context. Placing candidates in ministries for their spiritual formation allowed them to continue growing under supervision. The aim was to place them in ministries where needed and where their gifts may be exercised in supervised ministry settings. In this way, they could obtain feedback, and their spiritual development could be kept on track.

With this basic outline and the blessing and oversight of the Pastors, we ventured forth, walking candidates for ministry through the actual *MAP*. As a result, we successfully recommended some 20 ministers to the Pastors for acceptance to function as ministers at Allen throughout my tenure. These preached their inaugural trial sermons and were given licenses to preach by the District Elder and referred to the AME District Conference and Institute for ordination. As a result, most of them are in ministry today.

This was a far different outcome than I envisioned when I was first asked. The joy of seeing new ministers entering into service and the tremendous power of God often demonstrated in the most unlikely of people was deeply humbling. The remarkable beauty of seeing an absolute pearl that God sent to be delicately handled until He was ready to set it among the living stones of His Church was always awe-inspiring. It was clear that the Lord of the Harvest, not us with all our human mechanisms, is the one who calls and sends forth the reapers into the harvest.

The Unlikely Constance Cook

One such laborer was the unlikely Evangelist Constance Cook. Constance was an older member who applied to be a Minister at Allen. This was a bold and daring step in a church bustling with young adults, arguably one of the most contemporary megachurches within the AME fold. Several celebrities and personalities frequented Allen to enjoy its great worship and its cadre of inspirational speakers led by Rev. Flake himself and followed hard by Rev. Elaine's female-focused preaching. Many of the top speakers and preachers around the country came to Allen appreciating the opportunity to do so. Thus a high bar was set for all who wanted to be a part of the ministerial team.

Undaunted by these external optics, Sis. Constance was relentless in her pursuit, and I had no Godly reason to refuse her the opportunity. I gave her the paperwork and treated her with the same courtesies as anyone else. Unfortunately, her age was working against her because the Bishop was increasingly reluctant to appoint ministers beyond their fifties, which Sis. Constance had exceeded. I noticed that she took longer than usual to return the application and occasionally asked about it until she finally confided in me.

Sis. Constance filled out her form, but there were gaps, incomplete sections. When I queried them, Sis. Constance meekly explained that she was yet to complete her High School education. I saw in her a deep sincerity overshadowed by her embarrassment. We both knew that the Bishop would not have accepted her in ministry without a High School Diploma. Against the requirements, I felt compassion for this dear saint who needed the opportunity to serve. She searched my face for some concession, and somehow I could not turn her away. We decided that she would be admitted to the class, but she needed to complete her General Education Diploma (GED) before presenting to the Pastors. Sis. Constance readily agreed, informing me that she had already begun the process.

It was a proud day when Sis. Cook announced that she had successfully written her GED exam. By this time, she attended the classes exploring a calling she had already answered. Already active in several ministries, her life was a testimony to God's healing power. Over the times of our interactions, she relayed how she was diagnosed with MS and had become totally blind and wheelchair-bound. Yet, by the grace of God and her unwavering faith, she recovered in an unimaginable way. Later, she became a source of great strength and a wealth of knowledge in my care for Lorraine, who was also diagnosed with MS.

Once the training was over, and the Pastors accepted her application on my recommendation, Sis. Constance stood proudly before the congregation and preached her trial sermon. Her son and husband expressed deep appreciation for her opportunity to fulfill a dream they knew was a heartfelt desire of one with indomitable faith. At last, she would be listed among the official Evangelists at the annual Conference and participate in the Pastors' ministerial meetings among her peers. Most importantly, she was now officially authorized to carry the message to all under the banner of Allen.

The Case of Sis. Debbye Turner-Bell

What a pearl of great price was Debbye Turner-Belle, who went from being a volunteer in the Discipleship Ministry to navigating the GACNY MAP. I was first introduced to her as Pastor Flake called her out of the assembly one Sunday morning. He identified her as a former Miss America and called her upfront along with her mentor, another Miss America, with whom she had come to attend the worship service. In his usual charming way, he gave them the most gracious welcome and invited her to continue to worship with us more, and she did. Sometime after, I was summoned to Rev. Elaine's office, and there she was radiant and beautiful but not pretentious. I was asked to sit with them when Rev. Elaine explained that she was transferring from another assembly and wanted to serve in some capacity at Allen. The Flakes knew her pastor well and obviously had received an excellent report regarding her. Rev. Elaine felt that the Discipleship Ministry had the scope to utilize her skills, given the enormity of its task. With that, she turned over Sis. Debbye to find the appropriate placement within the Discipleship Ministry.

I was unsure where to place her so that her well-honed skills could be best utilized. Admittedly, given her Curriculum Vitae, it was somewhat intimidating. At the time, Sis. Debbye was a CBS Correspondent and appeared on television as part of the news broadcast quite often. Additionally, she was also a qualified Veterinarian, a motivational speaker, and among other things, an uncompromising believer. After some consideration, I decided to place her in a Discipleship class as a Teacher. We always needed good competent teachers to keep the congregation motivated to study the Word and grow.

After meeting with her, I suggested that she teach the class on the book of John. This was our first class and designed to excite the students' appetites to continue studying the Scriptures. After John, they were guided into the DFD series (Books 1-7). I usually taught John, but with Sis. Debbye teaching, I was allowed a rare opportunity to monitor the other classes to see firsthand how the other teachers and classes were fairing. Surprisingly, Sis. Debbye declined to teach John: "Oh no, she said, I am not teaching your class. No, no, no." I had already assigned a teacher for the other classes, so we agreed that she would teach along with me and then, at some time, take over the course. We started in earnest, and she was punctual and diligent. I would invite her comments, include her in the discussions, and let the class get a feel for her as a teacher. For the most part, she did very well and even had disagreements with some of my theological positions. They were nothing major, just peripheral issues that were neither here nor there. Since we invited questions and comments, these differences encouraged discussion.

Over time we became terrific friends and Sis. Debbye retained her genuinely humble demeanor, even as she excelled in ministry. As we became ministerial colleagues, she even confided in me of her love interest in Gerald Bell, a wonderful man who later became her husband and the father of their beloved daughter, Lynlee.

Before long, she, too, went through the GACNY MAP. Sis. Debbye could have used her persona to get around the requirements; her name and status would have made any ministerial portfolio look better. She could have used her connection with the esteemed Rev. Kirby John Colwell, her former Pastor, brother-in-Law, and friend of the Flakes, to circumvent the process, as others sought to do, to be ushered into the Allen ministry team, but she did not. None of these attributes or privileges were ever on display, only her sincere desire to serve God's people, and she was competent in doing so. Sis. Debbye went through the GACNY MAP demands and became ordained as a Local Itinerant Elder, serving humbly, dutifully, and beautifully at Allen.

The Lessons of Serving Under Difficult Circumstances

I often wondered what would have happened had I not accepted the difficult task assigned to me. What did my Pastors see in me that I did not recognize in myself? Why did they give me this honorable role of preparing God's people to serve at this nationally recognized church? I don't have answers to these questions yet, but I did learn valuable lessons. I pray they prove helpful to others in similar positions of ministry. As Associate Ministers, we are often placed in positions we may resent or with which we are disgruntled, albeit for a good reason. It may be that we are embarrassed by a sense of incompetence or the fear that our inexperience may cause us to look stupid swimming at the deep end where we are thrown in. There may also be times when we believe we are being given an unfair share of the workload or set up for failure. Often, the Associate Minister endures the ministry's grind and gory while the leader enjoys the glamour and glory. In such cases, we may feel discouraged toiling in their shadows. However, as I discovered from the opportunity afforded me, such undesirable tasks yield a tremendous experience that cannot be gained anywhere else. Their worth may not be appreciated at first, but in time the wealth of toiling in the vineyard in the heat of the day will be priceless. Eventually, we will forever remain indebted to those who pressed us into the crucibles of service, whether they were led of the Spirit or driven by their own ulterior motives. These ideas are further hashed out in the *Shadow Minister Devotional*.

CHAPTER 11

OUT OF THE SHADOW – INTO THE LIGHT

Becoming a Pastor is a question I faced as an Associate Minister, mainly since I often functioned in that capacity when the Pastors were absent or delegated 'pastoral' duties. I reconciled such times through Scripture reading, which showed many junior ministers functioning in place of their seniors in the Biblical record. I noted how Gehazi was sent by Elisha to act on his behalf on specific occasions (II Kings 4:29, 31). The *sons of the prophets* often ran with the word as dispatched by their *father* in ministry, burdened with the oracles of God (II Kings 9:1-3). It was pretty natural for me to ask myself what I would do in this situation or if I were the Pastor. Alternatively, as an Associate Minister, it was also natural to review a case, to evaluate it by asking other questions. Would I have done such things this way or that way, and why?

Pastoring: Holding the Reins of Power

These points of introspection are healthy parts of the growth stages I underwent serving under the Reverends Floyd and Elaine Flake. They were fitting questions for serious contemplation because they were not prompted by a quest to wrest power or assume positions inappropriately. Instead, these were sincere self-examinations, cautioning one to be careful how one conducts oneself in the service of another selflessly and without ulterior motives.

The Associate Minister's temptations to think of themself more highly than they should be is disastrous. Such was Absalom's case as he served as a provincial Prince under his father, King David. He used his position to mount a *coup de tat* against his father because of his bitterness and anger towards King David's handling or mishandling of the rape of his sister Tamar by their half-brother Ammon. It is vital for Associate Ministers not to harbor such subversive thoughts because too many divisive elements feed such egotistical musings. Satan himself feeds the heart fire of envy, malice, covetousness, and prideful ambitions that are not ordained by God (Isa. 14:12-20; Ezek. 28:12-19). I found that such serpentine thinking is un-Christian and must be dismissed from the Associate Minister's mind as soon as it is conjured. As an Associate Minister, it is more important to keep a sound, Christian perspective, especially if there is the aspiration to lead.

Considering Leadership

In contemplating leadership, I observed how many aspiring leaders worldwide beat a path to Allen clamoring to sit at the Flakes' feet to learn their successful community development and ministry model. Many were ambitious, forward-looking ministers aspiring to occupy future leadership roles and striving to learn how to be as successful as Allen was in their own context. Being a minister on Allen's staff, I inevitably met several of them and listened to their comments at the Community Empowerment Seminars Allen staged. I saw the wonder in their eyes and heard the admiration in their voices as they were guided around the Allen campus. At the end of the tours and presentations, I went away realizing how important it was not to seek to duplicate the success of another or occupy their space but to be guided to fulfill one's own unique calling. Missing from the seminars was the bitter struggle that produced the glowing results they saw. It was easy to desire the glory shimmering above and overlook the gore hidden from us beneath the surface and the backstory of bitter struggle behind beautiful accomplishments. I learned that clamor for leadership was not the desired goal for those who serve in the shadows of great men and women; service was the better goal to aspire to.

I found wisdom for this principle in the servant attitude of Jesus. He addressed this issue of private ambitions of leadership and power with His Disciples. The Gospel accounts tell us that they entertained thoughts of who was the greatest among them *in the kingdom.* Obviously, the King was the greatest, especially since He was among them and demonstrated His power before them. To that, they all agreed; therefore, the tussle was more likely who was the greatest *among themselves*, the Apostles (Mt. 18:1-6). It reached a sore point when James and John's mother actually made a bold, direct request that her sons sit as co-regents with Jesus on both sides of his throne. She left no room for anyone else (Mt. 20: 20-28). Sensing the outrage among them, Jesus quickly established the principles by which they should view greatness. I sorted them into three rules I had to observe for my own sake lest I fell into the same snare:

1. The Rule *for* the Great – The Mega Rule

The one who desires to be **mega** must take the place of the minor. In the exact words of Jesus:

> ...whosoever will be great among you, shall be your minister (Mark 10:43 NKJV)

Here the one who wants to be great (***mega*** in the Greek) has the idea of being preeminent. Such a one desires to be seen as the elder over others, having the noble virtues, as more substantial, more excellent, more suitable or stately, more blessed and favored by God to so lead. On one level, such ambition is not all bad or satanic in nature, necessarily. Those who are more spiritually endowed, educated, experienced, and equipped, ought to lead. However, the point here is not a qualification but an attitude and mindset. When the desire to lead goes beyond the well-being and welfare of others to be served by that leadership, it is no longer Christian. It is arrogance, presumption, and "derogatory to the majesty of God" (Enhanced Strong's Lexicon 3173).

2. The *Role of* the Great – The Mega Role

The one who desires to be deemed chief must expect to be **diakanos** (deacon)

In other words, they must strive to be the *deacon* of the group. They must recognize that they are under the authority of a Greater Master (Christ, the Lord) and must willingly follow His commands to act in the best interest of their fellows.

3. The Reed for the Great – The Measuring Rule

In case the feuding Apostles did not understand how to be Christian leaders, Jesus used two measures by which they could estimate it: a child and Himself. His instruction to His Disciples was most insightful to me as well. It is an excellent reed, a yardstick by which I could measure my own motives and attitudes in any aspiration upward.

On one occasion, Jesus set a child among His Disciples and used that child to instruct them. He taught those jockeying for a future position in His kingdom to become like the child. They were to be as humble, equitable, trusting, uncomplicated, and sincere as children were (Mt. 18:1-4). They were not to be simplistic and childish in their intellectual capacities, but innocent and free from evil desires.

In another passage, Jesus established His example to measure leadership ambitions against. They were to be servants who desire to lead:

> Just as the Son of Man did not come to be served, but to serve, and to give His life a ransom for many.
> (Matthew 20:28 NKJV)

His quest was to liberate others from bondage, even at the expense of His own life. This standard was maintained throughout His life before He passed on the baton of leadership to His Apostles. At the *Last Supper,* where He shared a final meal with them, He got up from His place as Chief among them, in rank, place, position, character, power, influence, and need and washed their feet as a house slave would have done, were there one present. He did so intentionally! He told His befuddled, embarrassed Disciples:

> You call Me Teacher and Lord, and you say well, for so I am. If I then, your Lord and Teacher, have washed your feet, you also ought to wash one another's feet. For I have given you an example, that you should do as I have done to you. Most assuredly, I say to you, a servant is not greater than his master; nor is he who is sent greater than

he who sent him. If you know these things, blessed are
you if you do them. (John 13:13-17 NKJV)

Interestingly I noted that the Christian leadership model of Jesus has an additional benefit patently missing in the secular leadership model. Christian servant leadership rewards the leader with happiness or blessedness when he acts Christ-like as a servant. Secular leadership has no such graciousness; it rewards those served at the top with bonuses, stock options, exquisite benefits, plush offices, adulation and acclaim, even golden parachutes when things go south. It's no wonder people clamor for the top spots with the corner offices in a quest for power, dominance, and notoriety. Jesus condemned such worldly ambition:

> Ye know that the princes of the Gentiles [nations] exercise dominion over them, and they that are great exercise authority upon them. But it shall not be so among you; but whosoever will be great among you, let him be your minister. (Matthew 20: 25, 26)

Unfortunately, like James, John, and their mother, even ministers of the gospel can allow the world's conditioning to shape their perspective of leadership and ministry. However, I understood not to be seduced into thinking that I was in an insignificant subordinate position because I was an Associate Minister. I didn't need to strive to be my own boss, as is done in the corporate world. Being the Pastor, Senior Pastor, Bishop, etc., was not the quest. What mattered most was being a servant leader.

I was privileged that my Pastors exemplified servant leadership. In every sense, Pastors Floyd and Elaine Flake presided over more extensive operations and funds than many Wall Street CEOs of major corporations. They entertained, engaged, and interacted with Presidents, mayors, senators, congressmen, the rich, and the famous. They walked with kings but never lost the common touch. In our Pastors, we saw people who gave themselves in enormous ways publicly and personally. Their lives of service are well documented and can be found in any serious urban development study or thriving faith-based initiatives country-wide.

However, their example of Christian leadership went far beyond public perception. I personally saw that it was not unusual for the Flakes to forego personal benefits for the good of the assembly and more often for the good of the Jamaica community, even when some misinformed members of that community spoke negatively about them. Their individual and collective skills would have served them well in corporate America, which often invited them to their board rooms and corporate suites. Many companies came seeking their expertise. Daily there were calls from all and sundry for endorsements of ideas and business ventures. Many opportunists saw Allen's membership and community as a prime cash cow or the Pastors as their ticket to somewhere. I was often privy to such discussions or allowed to meet with persons and groups with glossy, attractive business proposal packages or new ideas from film scripts to health products for African Americans to be passed on to the Pastors for their buy-in.

Many of these business ideas/proposals were well thought out, researched, and financed. Some of them could easily have netted personal profits for the Flakes by simply endorsing a product or giving access to their coveted flock. However, they often placed the Lord, His work, His people, and His call on their lives to serve His cause above the lure of personal greatness and gain. I can recount numerous examples of their generosity that were never publicly declared. I vividly remember Rev. Elaine taking out her personal checkbook to sponsor a child or underwrite some impoverished soul's expense. Their service encouraged mine in turn and prepared me for the opportunity if and when it presented itself beyond Allen. If nothing else, I knew not to be pompous and self-centered with a large entourage of armor-bearers, all of us dressed in expensive suits and inaccessible to the people as some ministers have done to their detriment and that of the people they lead. Our Pastors advised us by precept and example to avoid such leadership styles as we looked beyond Allen.

CHAPTER 12

Looking Beyond Allen

As shadows shift when the light moves, so do the circumstances of those in others' shadows. Sooner or later, as our Pastors encouraged, it was inevitable that their Associates step into the light. Moving beyond Allen required maturity and a strong personal sense of calling because it is such an excellent place to learn and practice ministry that one is tempted to stay. Wherever I went and mentioned that I was a minister of Allen, I was always met with enthusiastic, wide-eyed responses such as: 'Floyd Flake's Church? Wow!' Many envied the Associate Ministers who had the privilege of being under these luminaries' wings among America's megachurches. However, it was easy to become too comfortable and forget about personal growth and development. Pastor Flake never encouraged this mentality. He always made it clear that we ought to grow and move on. Our members had difficulty leaving the fellowship and dynamic ministries of Allen. How much more those of us who were immersed in making such fellowship and ministry happen by God's grace.

To maintain perspective, I had developed a personal philosophy of keeping my head above the Cathedral walls. It was easy to become so immersed in Allen's activities and new exciting changes that one can forget that there is a broader world beyond our beloved community. Such a philosophy was critical for several reasons. Chiefly, it served to remind me that should the Bishop assign me to pastor an assembly, I should be able to cope without Allen's well-developed systems and infrastructure. Secondly, I had to remain cognizant that the Lord could call me to go anywhere, and I, therefore, needed to stay in touch with the realities of ministry in the global context.

Although I was not actively pursuing moving beyond Allen, I received numerous requests to speak at several congregations. Because I needed to manage the altar call at Allen and give my service to the Prison Ministry, I could not accept many Sunday morning invitations, but they kept coming. Therefore, I tended to go where the need was most. In this respect, I got an invitation to minister at Grace Reform Church, Brooklyn, NY. I was moved to go because they had no Pastor and needed to be served until they could appoint someone.

Grace was a quaint, well-established congregation within the Reform group of Churches. It was a predominantly West Indian/Caribbean congregation with a vibrant group of teenagers, first-generation Caribbean Americans. I felt pretty at home there, even though the liturgy was slightly different and more structured than Allen's. Of course, at one time, Allen had a very structured liturgy set out in its Book of Discipline until Pastor Flake began introducing a more contemporary praise and worship format, with fewer hymns and without reciting the Decalogue or 10 Commandments. Therefore, I was familiar with the style, but I had to be more attentive as I was the minister leading them at Grace. It reminded me of my primary school days in Barbados, where we were taken on specific holy days in the Christian Calendar to the Anglican Church. We would watch, intrigued as the priest went through the rituals from processional to the recessional.

It was not long before I was invited back repeatedly to minister. I utilized my familiarity with Caribbean customs and mores in my sermons and soon found resonance among the members who relished the nostalgic moments and comic relief they brought. I mainly focused on the youth and drew on my Rites of Passage experience to speak to their issues and challenges as Christians among their peers. Such approaches endeared me to the congregation. For example, Sis. Pearl insisted that I sing every time I came to minister.

I was not surprised when members of the Consistory offered the position of Pastor to me. It was an excellent, tempting offer for several reasons: the congregation was responsive to the word of God in my mouth, the youth were ready to go to the next level of spiritual development, and although I did not venture to discuss remuneration, I had a sense that the benefits were excellent. The fact that I loved Brooklyn, the stately parsonage next door, and the opportunities to minister among the Caribbean emigrant community was very tempting.

Nevertheless, as I consulted the Lord and discussed it with my wife, I was not moved to accept; I did not feel led by the Lord to do so. As much as I personally could see myself filling the role there, I knew that it would have been selfish and detrimental to the good people of Grace to fill the position and not be the one God sent. My wife was characteristically cautious and indifferent, deferring to my sense of God's leading. I wondered at the displacement of our children from school and my need to finish seminary, although Grace was willing to pay for it at New Brunswick Theological. However, as I prayed, I felt the familiar leading of the Lord to *stay at Allen.* Grace was understandably quite disappointed that I had turned down their offer and attributed it to my unwillingness to leave Allen with all its grandeur. The truth was, I respected them and the Lord too much to make a career move rather than a response to a Macedonian call. I, therefore, declined.

Then there was St. Paul's Community Church in Harlem, New York. Like Brooklyn, the rich history and the mystique of Harlem were appealing. I attended their services as a guest speaker on several occasions at the invitation of my friends and colleagues, the late Rev. Elliot Hobbs and his wife, Rev. Eleanor. They were laboring in the vineyard on 135 Street and Malcolm X Boulevard across the street from a massive apartment complex. The growth potential was enormous in the small but roomy church building that was initially a theatre. It harkened back to the great days of the Harlem Renaissance when music and the arts held sway.

The congregation was small but growing mainly because Pastor Hobbs was no slough, and neither was his wife. They were both competent professionals in their secular careers and sincere, passionate ministers of the gospel. However, Harlem was marred with drug addiction, economic depression, and political neglect for all its grandeur. It was hard labor extracting souls from the soils soaked with worldly pleasures and overindulgence. Several other churches in the area cast their nets at the same elusive fish. Nevertheless, the Hobbs soldiered on, and the congregation was slowly growing. I sat enthralled on the platform looking into the empty balcony, imagining it full and the joy it would bring when it happened. I was willing to help in the effort, so I was there to lend my words of exhortation to the saints assembled.

Curiously, St. Paul's was a break-away assembly from the AME Church but had kept its worship format, including its hymnals and liturgy. Therefore we were quite at home, and besides a few exceptions, it was easy to follow the style and flow of the worship service. The worship was beautiful, and the singing breathtaking. I was spiritually and culturally moved as the choir sang. The Negro Spirituals were rendered flawlessly with a proficiency that explained why we would often see tourists and visitors to the city come in to sit through services to experience them. I was told of the tour buses that routinely visited some historic churches; I was unsure if I liked being seen by curious onlookers as part of a tourist attraction in the middle of service as if it were some staged minstrel show. Yet, if those who came in heard the gospel, I guess there was some benefit. I saw some degree of sadness in Rev. Eleanor's eyes, though. It had been over the congregation's men, some of whom indulged in alcohol and other carnal behaviors and thus needed deliverance; she was burdened by this.

I was content to visit and minister, but a situation developed and changed all of that. I received an urgent call from Rev. Elliot one Wednesday afternoon in my office at Allen. He requested that I would minister that coming Sunday morning. I was prepared to do so, but he explained why he would be absent; it was sobering. He stated that he would not be returning to St. Paul's! I reeled at the impact and fallout on the congregation, sympathizing with my brother over this sudden shift.

Apparently, that same week after the Sunday service, the AME Bishop called and summarily assigned Rev. Elliot to St. Paul's AME Church in Long Island, where he was to report by the following Sunday. He was given no time to prepare or to transition. His position at St. Paul's, Harlem, was not the Bishop's priority; filling an empty pulpit in his district was, and thus the people of St. Paul's Congregation would be left in a free fall without their beloved Pastor.

I wondered if the Bishop's decision was a Godly one, a kingdom decision, a proper apostolic edict that considered the entire body of Christ, including the assembly of St. Paul's Community Church.

Perhaps it was a narrower, parochial determination that gave no assessment to the whole body. I surmised, too, that Rev. Hobbs was caught in the dictates of the protocol. As an ordained Elder, he was sworn and duty-bound to serve at the Bishop's pleasure. Outside the denomination, his current pastoral position was insufficient to delay or deny the appointment issued with immediate effect. Ironically, he was assigned to another St. Paul's, but in Long Island. Deeply perturbed, he stated that he could not think of anyone else he could ask to go to his bereaved former congregants at such a time. It was into this egregious circumstance I was to go and fill in for my brother and sister.

As expected, I walked into the sanctuary, and it felt like a funeral was about to occur. It was as if Elliot or Eleanor had died. I don't know how many in the congregation knew he was removed, but the attendance was sparse. To make matters worse, the musician decided to go with Rev. Hobbs to the new assembly. That was a double blow to this church's growing aspirations struggling to survive in ever-changing Harlem compliments of the state-sponsored gentrification programs. The church musician was a music lecturer at New York University and brought his students to the worship services; no wonder the singing was exquisite. Now he, too, was gone along with the preacher. These are two essential elements for a good church in the African American and any Christian community.

As I pondered this in the hushed, melancholic atmosphere, I wondered how my sermon that morning could have made any difference in the face of such loss. My musings were interrupted by the head Elder who called me into the vacated pastoral office where Rev. Hobbs had sat last Sunday. I expected the usual courtesies to a visiting minister, but there was something else on his heart that caught me off guard. After exchanging pleasantries, he came straight to the point. He stated that the congregation was impressed with my ministry and that if I could guarantee them five years, "the church is yours." I, of course, knew he meant that the church would be mine to pastor, not to own. Moreover, he also added that he was contemplating moving down South shortly but wanted to ensure that the church was on sound footing before doing so. I told him that I would consider it and communicate back to him. What else could I say? I was dumbfounded.

I, then, turned my attention to the grave task at hand- ministering to troubled people whose hopes of growing and establishing a viable ministry in their neighborhood seemed dashed violently against the rocks of disappointment and despair. I met with one of the church mothers, a stately elderly lady, one of two who served as liturgists. She was her usual calm self, exhibiting a dignity that suggested that she had thread these turbulent waters before or perhaps that she was confident that God's work will continue despite the decisions of men. I did not ascertain the source of her quiet resolve, but her unshakeable faith was evident. I don't recall the sermon I preached that Sunday, but I am sure that it could not assuage the deep sorrow felt by those who gathered for worship. It was better to weep with them in the ashes than to try to help them overcome it. After the service, the question was whether I would step into Rev. Elliot's shoes and pastor St. Paul's Community Church in Harlem.

It was a tempting offer for some of the reasons mentioned earlier, but I was chiefly drawn to the fact that this congregation was shepherd-less and in need of a leader. Such situations have always been more noteworthy to me than those where the ground is fertile and additional help is just that, merely additional. I think I picked up that tendency from my mother. She always wanted to minister to people in need and where her gifts were better utilized instead of where there were more beneficial to herself. Clearly, there was no rich reward at St. Paul's Congregational given the tiny congregation that seemed to be about fifty people in a sanctuary that could probably seat 1,000. I was moved by their need. However, I still felt that my tenure at Allen was not over, and I should not leave yet. It was clear that my premature departure would unravel all the structure I worked hard to put in place. I was still training the ministry participants to command the post to bring Discipleship at the center of all our ministry as I was mandated to do. We were not there yet.

I discussed the matter with Lorraine, and we thought through the feasibility of remaining at Allen but filling the pulpit at St. Paul's on Sundays. I could serve at Allen's 6:30am service and easily reach Harlem at 11:00am. That seemed doable, but I was not happy with the divided loyalty this scenario presented. How would the congregation grow if I am only acting as Pastor, not being one, a hireling? I was willing to serve, but it seemed fitting to give all or nothing at all. What about funerals and sick visitation? How and when would they be given, and which ministry should be given preference in conflicting circumstances? I approached Pastor Flake for his advice to help me decide; he was always fair and objective in these matters, even when it didn't benefit him directly. He readily agreed that I could and probably should go, and I was surprised at his freedom in doing so. However, I wondered if he gave enough thought to the conflicts that could result and the ministries I may have to sacrifice as I served there. I would not be able to give myself to Allen Prison Ministry or perhaps to Rites of Passage, and who knows what else as I went along. Principally, I would be missing from the Chapel after the 11:15am services when most of our prospects joined. There, we saw the most fascinating scenarios of need and bondage, and we needed the most pastoral support. Whether these were weighed or not, he was willing to see me go serve at St. Paul's and continue as Discipleship Minister.

However, with each passing day, I did not find the peace of God to straddle these ministry fences. I had to regretfully and respectfully decline the offer. I recalled that one Sunday, Rev. Flake looked across and saw me at my post among the ministers at the 11:15am service and with a puzzled look on his face mouthed to me, 'What are you doing here? Go; get out of here', but I could not go in good conscience, even with such encouragement. I was to stay within the walls because my time had not yet come. I had to be sure when it did.

Discerning When to Assume the Mantle of Leadership

I needed to discern God's will for myself as an Associate Minister. At times the test to go or stay may have come through those I looked up to most such as my Senior Pastors/mentors in ministry, but in the final analysis, I was personally responsible to the Lord to move as led by His Spirit. I consulted the Word and recognized this truth in the life of Elisha. He was anointed to succeed Elijah. His mentor, Elijah, had asked him what he desired as he would assume his new role. Wisely, Elisha asked for a double portion of the Spirit that rested on Elijah. Elijah was prepared to impart such a blessing but warned Elisha that he must observe the very time that Elijah was taken up to receive his request. At Elijah's translation, Elisha would automatically become his successor. I did not want to be knee-jerked into a position, however beneficial or spiritual. I wanted to be sure of what God commanded me and not to defer from it if, indeed, I was to transfer to a more significant leadership position.

Interestingly, Elijah often urged Elisha to stay at certain places while he went here or there, but wisely Elisha refused. The power he would minister with would depend on his obedience to the One he would be totally reliant on in his mentor's absence. Elisha remained so focused that when his peers would advise him, he would concur with them but ask them to withhold further comment. Elisha prevailed because of his dogged resolve to remain focused on the Word God spoke to him. It was so cemented in his heart that hearing it again from someone else was superfluous and distracting. He was the picture of concentration that resulted in his prayer being realized. He saw the ascent of Elijah; he saw the mantle fall, and as a result, Elisha was able to exercise the power with which he was immediately endowed (II Kings 2:12-14).

Even after this, the sons of the prophets tried to persuade him to ascertain Elijah's rapture by searching for Elijah in case he was not fully taken up but simply transported elsewhere. This was an incredible imposition on Elisha since it was evident that he was anointed with the same Spirit of God, which was operative on Elijah. They even bowed to him. In effect, they were submitting to his leadership among the prophets. Still, they prevailed upon him to the point of embarrassment to send out a search party to look for the Elijah, who they had earlier concurred would be translated. Elisha satisfied their lack of faith but remained resolute in his own.

I considered this a lesson on resolve and laser point focus on God's revealed will. I equated this scenario to a newly appointed pastor coming into a ministry and finding a preexisting team of strong associates gifted and opinionated. Elisha maintained his mantle of leadership and cooperated with the request without capitulating to their reticence. In the end, his knowledge and confidence in God's Word regarding his ministry proved to be the greatest strength. He was never questioned after that. Therefore, knowing what God said regarding assuming leadership and acting unwaveringly according to it was the very means of maintaining leadership among other anointed, strong prophets. I gathered from the Elisha account that if one is unsure about God's specific leading into new ministry areas, it would be difficult to lead a solid concerted group of persons who may have been in ministry longer.

The Call to Taiwan

In the early summer of 2007, I received a call from Sis. Ouida Duncan, a member of Allen. She sounded excited. She explained that she had attended a series of healing services in Flushing, Queens, led by a Pastor, Dr. Ezekiel Chung, and she felt that I should meet him with the view of inviting him to Allen to minister in the future. I had no authority to do so and thought that the purpose of meeting this man was somewhat futile, such that I was inclined not to meet. However, I have always tried to be careful not to extinguish the flame of zeal among God's people. I would rather inform zeal than extinguish it, so I reluctantly agreed to meet.

The appointed day was a holiday, and we went to a restaurant where I was introduced to a very humble and demurred Dr. Ezekiel Chung and two local female associates. Sis. Ouida assured me that she had checked him out on the internet and that he was legit. He hardly said a word as we ordered the Jamaican cuisine. The two Asian women talked giddily about their experiences in the meetings. Of particular note was that a disinterested relative was now suddenly willing to attend church and accept Christ as Savior. Then they both began to talk about *tefa* (gold). Apparently, when Pastor Ezekiel ministers, a phenomenon occurs- specs of gold dust appear on people's skin, face, and hands in the congregation. I was immediately skeptical and watched with guarded curiosity as they search their hands and excitedly showed tiny specs of this *tefa*. At first, I felt there were no more than specs of glitter left behind from a girls' night out. Dr. Chung showed only little acknowledgment of this spectacle before him.

Then I responded to a question posed to me involving the end-time. I referred to Israel and the current developments in the Holy Land. Suddenly, Dr. Chung spoke, lifting his head. He stated that he had not heard anyone articulate the end-time prophesies regarding Israel as I had. In the next breath looking at me, he said, "You need to come to Taiwan with me to minister in revival services there." I was flabbergasted. Here I was supposedly sassing out this minister for possible recommendation to Allen. Then, in a dramatic turnaround, he invited me to Asia to minister with him in revival services. He had never heard me preach; he did not know me personally; he did not interview me to determine my suitability for the mission. I was speechless, stammering, lost for words. I was barely able to spatter out, "Well, let me look at that and see if it's possible."

Dr. Chung was undeterred by my ambivalence and insisted that I come to Taiwan. He proceeded to plan and strategize how I could be brought in to get around the Chinese government's anti-religious red tape exercising its control over Taiwan's affairs. Before I could object, Pastor Chung had mapped out with his associates sitting with us how to package the information for a flyer to be sent to him with info on Allen and my three-week missions trip! When I interjected that I could foresee a week but not three, he dismissed it, stating that a week was too short and three weeks was best. I sat stumped and astonished as the conversation continued. Then to cap it off, Dr. Chung was scheduled to leave for Asia the next day, giving me little room to liaise with him on the issue.

I left thinking that I had not discussed this possibility with my wife, with my Pastors, plus, I hadn't thought through the matter or even prayed over it! Questions flooded my mind: Did I have the vacation time? Who would take care of my wife while I was away? Would I be going as a minister from Allen? What implications would that have? What of the risks involved in going into territory hostile to Christianity? What about the language and the culture I was unfamiliar with, and how would the trip be financed? Who do I liaise with to answer these questions? Where is God in all this? Was this a Macedonian call to Taiwan?

I returned home and related the difficulty to Lorraine, who was equally intrigued. In days I was receiving calls from Ouida and then from Sis. Edna. She was from an Asian assembly in Flushing, who called on Pastor Chung's behalf for information about myself and Allen. I began to pray that the Lord would guide and direct my steps into this new and unknown territory way beyond the Cathedral walls. My prayer was meek but sincere: 'if it is indeed of the Lord, then open the doors, and if not, close them.' I have always prayed this way in times of uncertainty, using Psalm 16:8 and 119:105 as my guiding light to my feet and path. Of course, the Lord alone opens the doors to ministry as we pray (Eph. 6:18-20; Col. 4:3; II Cor. 2:12; I Cor. 1:9; cf. Rev. 3:7, 8).

I discussed the matter with my new Administrative Assistant, Stacey, who was also receiving requests for information. I needed to control the flow of the material passed on. In a few weeks, I found myself reading up on Taiwan and then applying to the Taiwanese visa center for permission to travel there. It was an exciting experience to walk into the Taiwanese visa center and fill out the necessary paperwork. As I waited, I watched the staff encounters with the clientele. I noticed that I was the only non-Asian that day. The security person directing applicants to the windows to be processed was a Latino. I found that strange, but then again, we were in New York. He was quite helpful and helped me negotiate the application protocol. Noticing that the numbers weren't being called despite a number system, he instructed me to stand in line before the booths. I was a little reluctant since I did not want to appear forward or pushy, but he assured me that it was okay advising, "If they don't push you, you push them." On his advice, which seemed sincere, I gingerly stepped forward until I was too obvious to ignore and was called. The advice worked. I later realized upon my exiting that the security officer was a believer.

After a few awkward conversations and an interview, I turned in my documents as directed and was told to return the following week. The interviewer was very dissatisfied with the letter sent from Dr. Chung's ministry in Taiwan. She mulled over it quizzically, and I heard her mutter that it was *rude*. It was very terse, but I thought it was brief to avoid complications. It simply stated that I was invited to attend Taipei's business conferences. I was careful to explain that I was going on business.

Dr. Chung had explained that giving a religious reason for going to Taiwan would undoubtedly lead to rejection. I used my personal company that I had formed and a letter from my Congressman to support my motivation to go to Taiwan to explore business opportunities. I had two products with pending patents I could research in Taiwan for sale in the USA market. Dr. Chung would have a business seminar as part of the outreach to the business community. However, I was a little uncomfortable with this because it felt somewhat deceptive since my primary reason for going was to minister the gospel. My only solace was the counsel of Jesus to be as *wise as serpents and harmless as doves* as we are sent forth to spread the gospel as sheep among wolves (Mt. 10:16).

As I waited for the outcome, I remained prayerful and limited my discussion of the trip to very few people. I did not inform the Pastors, sensing that the lack of information on Dr. Chung and the unusual way the trip came about was too tricky to explain. I did tell my brother in ministry, Rev. Dwayne Johnson, who insisted that I inform my hosts that I could not travel alone; he was coming with me as added safety and protection. However, if I was to go into supposedly dangerous terrain, I did not want to be responsible for my brother being harmed in any way, so I opted not to do as he insisted. I knew I would not be focused on ministry if I felt responsible for someone else in that way.

The wait and silence were shattered not long after a Taiwanese visa center call that I may return to pick up my passport and visa. I was surprised at the speed at which the documents were processed. I returned to the visa center, and sure enough, my passport was returned to me with a visa stamped into it, allowing for 30 days with specific dates. I thanked the visa personnel and the security, of course, and left saying within myself, "Well Lord, the time has come. The door is opened to go beyond the Cathedral wall, but what a distance to go!'

Taiwan was a far cry from Brooklyn and Harlem; it was not on the other side of town; it was on the other side of the world! On my return to the office, I informed Stacey that my calendar could be cleared and my vacation time could be filed. I hated to miss a renewal of vows since I had given my word to the couple to perform it. They were celebrating their golden anniversary, but it could not be avoided. At home, Lorraine and I began plans to have her mom come to stay with her and the girls while I would be away. Confident that my Pastors would be supportive, I was now ready to inform them of my mission to Taiwan. As expected, Pastor Floyd was quite supportive. Rev. Elaine offered no objection except that it presented a problem for the vacation schedule. She asked preliminary questions but left me to make the final decisions. I finalized my arrangements with Sis. Edna, and in a matter of weeks, I was due to leave for Taiwan.

Taiwan Bound

I had no itinerary and little information to go on, but I was assured that I would go forward into the unknown beyond the Cathedral walls. I called key brethren and requested prayer. I told my Hour of Power family, and they were excited and committed to praying for me. Braced against those prayers, I ventured forth on the long 18-hour trip halfway around the world where I would spend three weeks ministering. Exactly how and where was still to be determined. Nevertheless, I packed my bags and left. The flight was long but pleasant. I sat beside a man going to Taiwan on business and picked his brains on the country, and he gave me some pointers. I wanted to discuss Christ with him, but he was not very interested, so I sowed a few seeds and refrained, less I offered gospel pearls to one that could not appreciate them.

On arrival, I was surely a stranger in a strange land. I negotiated my way through customs without much difficulty, claimed my baggage, and exited, not knowing who would be awaiting me but not worried in the least. As I emerged from the terminal, I met the usual line of people awaiting their guests, but of course, I recognized no one. Then I heard what sounded like: 'Pastor Paul from New York,' and I turned to see Sis. Doris and another sister waving at me. I was easy to find being the only Black man among the emerging passengers. Sis. Doris and the party took my luggage, and soon we were in an awaiting taxi heading for the Army Hotel in Taipei. Sis. Doris was a charming woman conversant in English and Chinese, so I answered the preliminary questions. They, of course, asked about the flight and welcomed me to Taiwan.

As we drove along the highway, I glanced at the topography with its mountains rising in the distance and the buildings with distinctive designs that differed from the Western and European styles to which I was more accustomed. I looked with curiosity at the vegetation, particularly those familiar to me. It was harder to get a sense of the climate because the windows were closed, but they explained that it was the height of summer and could be very hot. My immediate impression was that Taiwan was a tropical island with lush vegetation. It bore much resemblance to the more mountainous islands of the Caribbean. My contemplation was broken by Sis. Doris's question. She wanted to know what my ministry specialty was. "Ministry specialty?" I asked, "What exactly do you mean?" No one had ever posed such a question to me, although we have taught and been aware of what gifts of the Spirit are operative in our lives. Sis Doris explained that some ministers could exorcise demons, others healed, and others prophesied. She was curious which of these or others I was operative in. I responded that I did not see myself as specializing in any ministry area, which was somewhat braggadocios; instead, I believed that believers ought to be available to the Holy Spirit so that however He wanted to utilize His vessel that they were so amenable. I could see that she was not impressed with my answer, but I was not prepared to go against my conscience at that point to satisfy a curiosity.

What struck me as we drove along was the prolific amount of motorcycle traffic that flanked the cars like official, escorting entourages everywhere. I marveled at the daring skill of the mass of women and men that rode on these scooters. They were in front of the cars, behind the cars, and beside the cars, darting in and out fearlessly like a weaver's needle between strands of thread. I had a new admiration for the drivers, especially the cab drivers I immediately rated above those in New York City known to be daredevils on the road. However, they didn't have this added factor to contend with. I had to also relinquish my personal prejudice for drivers in the Caribbean who have to perform feats with nerves of steel on tiny narrow roads in two-way traffic, plus pedestrians and the occasional sheep, goat, or cow all at once. Those challenges paled compared to the convergence of modes of transportation, all competing for the same travel space and time.

I watched with rapt attention as our taxi driver navigated with a heightened awareness of the other riders and drivers as they made their unpredictable, spontaneous maneuvers along the way. I asked if they were many accidents, but my guest assured me that they were not as many as I imagined. I resolved that the commuters had some collective sense of each other as a column of ants instinctively moving in either direction. That experience was instructive, indicating harmony, discipline, and mutual respect; necessary parts of this nation of 23, 061, 689 million people on an island 394 km long and 144 km wide. Yet, there was so much more to learn as we pulled up to the Army Hotel, in the shadow of the Royal Palace, the President's official residence, and government headquarters.

Inside, I met Dr. Chung and his associates preparing for the evening evangelical session on its second night. The hotel was simple and austere. The lobby had ample open space with a balcony overlooking it. Off to the left was a small café and gift shop adjacent to the general office. Across from the office, the corridors led to the elevators and stair access to upper and lower floors. A huge oil painting of a battle scene depicting a historic battle of the armed forces hung prominently above those doorways. I learned later that the hotel was more or less the barracks for the troops that served Taipei close to the seat of power. After checking in, we went to dinner, where Dr. Chung began to sketch the service strategy. He suggested that I rest given my long travel but should expect to be the main speaker starting the following evening. Strangely, I was not feeling fatigued but felt his counsel wise. Sis. Doris was assigned to translate for me in the services and during social interactions.

Into the Fray

The evening service was held on the lower floor of the Army Hotel. It was a big room that seated about 250 people. I was escorted to the service by Sis. Doris, who sat with me and translated for me. The service began with praise and worship lead by the Fountain of Joy Ministry youth and their guests. The music was refreshing and engaging; clearly, they were serious and sincere about their faith; they set a good tone for the entire service, which was turned over to Pastor Ezekiel Chung after the announcements. He reinforced that I would be speaking the following night and brought much awe from the crowd when he mentioned that I was from a church of some 15,000 members. In such moments, I realized how globally influential a mega-church was. At Allen, we never really played up our size or influence even though we were nationally and more so internationally known. Instead, our successes were taken in stride and often for granted.

However, having many believers in one church was impressive in a country of millions where the 95% majority are Buddha worshipers. I began to see how large churches in the USA, where Christianity was the mainstream religion, encouraged and emboldened the struggling saints and suppressed minorities among the non-Christian masses. Furthermore, it dawned on me that we were grown to that size by the Lord, not simply to be the who-is-who among large churches in America. Plus, our size was an effective tool that may reach the international arenas with significant credibility and resource capacity to win the lost for Christ. Unfortunately, my being from Allen may also have heightened the audience's expectations, which had come desperately looking for help and answers for a myriad of problems. Such expectations were to be presented shortly.

No sooner than Pastor Chung was finished preaching, he made an altar call, and almost all of the audience came forward, saints and sinners! Pastor Chung had spoken a simple message on the end time and called people to be saved, healed, delivered of demonic control, and for God's blessing in their businesses. I watched to observe how he would minister to do accordingly. Suddenly I was pressed into service. Pastor Chung mentioned that he would deal with those who needed prophecy in the rear and that those needing prayer should remain in front so that I could pray for them.

I was taken by utter surprise, given that I was not to minister that night, but I was soon to learn that Pastor Chung was very flexible. Praying for those at the 'altar' was well within my ability as an integral part of the Discipleship Ministry in New York. So, I stepped up front, ready to pray. As I panned the faces of those lined before me in eager anticipation, I instinctively realized that they were not expecting a generalized prayer of goodwill. They really wanted to experience God's power in their individual lives.

Led, I believe of the Lord, I began praying for the respondents before me individually. Sis. Doris was glued to my side, translating my every word with startling results. As I went down the line of respondents touching and praying, some people fell helplessly to the floor, others became overwhelmed with emotion and began to weep, others began to vomit and were given cellophane bags for their vomitus, others began praising God vigorously. At the same time, some showed little to no reaction at all. A few responses caught my attention because they indicated demonic forces.

Taipei or Gadara?

One man, in particular, fell down on his back as soon he was touched and began barking like a dog incessantly. I needed no translation for that! In almost a fetal position, he was yelping as a dog would. I leaned over, and placing my hands on his stomach, I began interceding for his deliverance. He immediately began grimacing as if in intense pain and would fall back into his barking routine. I relented when he seemed relieved and the pressure of others desperately waiting precluded more ministry to him, who was consuming the time and my attention.

Another woman was having violent reactions and constantly spewed as we prayed. I was convinced that she was clearly manifesting demonic possession as well. However, we could not continue because we had exhausted our time allotted for the leased space and the hotel personnel began to lock up, motioning for us to dismiss. We had unfinished business, but we had to leave. We were already incurring additional expenses by overstaying our time; it was not far from midnight. The remnant of the audience followed us in the lobby, determined not to leave until we prayed with them before they left for home. We quietly prayed for them and sent them on their way until the following night.

Later that evening, I reflected on the service with deep contemplation. This was not the conventional evangelical outreach I was accustomed to and undoubtedly expecting. Typically, in my experience, the service would begin with praise and worship, followed by preliminaries such as announcements, introducing the speaker, who would then preach the word of God. Following the message, the opportunity would be extended to attendees to accept Christ as Savior. Periodically special prayer would be given to the sick and those oppressed by the devil. This was different. I realized that I had become lulled into a convenient salon-style ministry where people came in for spiritual beautification treatments. We would fluff their hair but never examine the scalp for serious conditions hidden beneath. We would buff their nails and polish them, overlooking the fungus growing underneath. We would do facials and makeovers, but the heart's deeper conditions that were not skin deep were left masked and unaddressed. It seems we spruced up but never pruned. I felt a sense of shame and embarrassment at how we were ministering back in the USA. I felt as though we were cosmetic and superficial compared to what I saw in Taipei.

Pastor Chung's ministry was striking at the heart of the kingdom of Satan in a land where the devil was given full license to operate. I had the stark realization that there was no room for window dressing. Christian ministry was a demonstration of the power of the Holy Ghost, or I should go home. I was particularly disturbed by those under the influence of demons; they seemed to be so many. Nevertheless, I was determined to represent Christ well and minister to every need presented before us for relief.

At the same time, I needed to be careful to unify myself with The Fountain of Joy Ministry's brethren and not see myself as the 'American Missionary' who had come to save the people of Taiwan. The thought of seeing myself as the one with the answer was judged in my mind as ludicrous, condescending, and utterly bankrupt. There was no time for ego-tripping; we were in a war for souls, and I needed to apply all my faith, experience, and knowledge to the task, but with wisdom.

The next day I consulted with Sis. Doris and spoke at length about the people we were ministering to. She explained that China and Taiwan were under the demonic influence of Buddhist temples. For example, she relayed what many businessmen did when their businesses began to fail because of the economic downturn precipitated by the American shift to China away from Taiwan. In desperation, many went and borrowed large sums of money not to pay their debts but to give the Buddhist priest to pray for their economic prosperity. She said, sadly, others who became insolvent committed suicide, ashamed to face their inability to pay their debts and take care of their families.

Doris explained that many families were hard-pressed due to the prevailing economic conditions as factories closed and businesses shifted to Mainland China to pursue the American dollars to be earned there. People are prone to be manipulated and fall under ungodly cultural and traditional trappings in such circumstances. As a result, many turned to the gods of their fathers, and consequently, they became bound by the spiritual forces to which they surrendered their lives.

Everywhere I looked as we walked or drove, I saw the temples and symbols of Buddhism: off the main highways, at the sides of major causeways, on the main streets, and in every village, on official buildings and cultural sites. It seemed as though they were everywhere with the ominous image of dragons coiled around the pillars, etched into the walls, and looming dominantly on the temple roofs' peaks. Dragons were even delicately carved in the beautiful jade jewelry on display. I felt as though I was on enemy territory, and his subjects would have to be liberated with a power greater than his own.

After two nights of intense ministry and prayer, I realized that some of the people we prayed for were returning, manifesting the same bondages they did the night before. Obviously, the work was incomplete, and that to me was misrepresentative of the Jesus Christ we preached. Back in the USA, I always resented when this happened. A visiting minister explained the failure away, saying that the undelivered lacked faith or had another sinful element in their lives that precluded their freedom. While there may be some truth here, I felt those excuses were more cop-outs than reasoned fact. Thus I went before the Lord for guidance. My issue presented before the Lord was whether there was real deliverance for those who had come faithfully each night in distress.

Like Joshua before the Lord at the failure to take the city of Ai, I was jerked off my face with a stern rebuke. The Spirit of the Lord spoke impatiently to me, reminding me of the words of Jesus to his frustrated Disciples: *this kind can come forth by nothing but prayer and fasting (Mark 9:28, 29)*. I felt as stupefied as the beleaguered Disciples in their futile attempt to remedy a demonic child. Without hesitation, I went into a three-day fast to prepare myself to meet the forces of darkness that appeared to be mocking our preaching and prayers. Additionally, I began to read every case of Jesus' exorcism of demons again in the gospels to refresh myself of His exercise of power over the enemy.

As my bodily yearning surrendered to the denial of food that abounded and the natural man gave way to the spiritual man, my mind began to gain some spiritual insights as soul and spirit became intertwined. First, I needed to divest myself of any carnal or worldly attachments to which my self-concept was hitched and therefore defined. It couldn't matter that I was the Discipleship Minister of the Greater Allen Cathedral of New York or that some people were impressed with my being a minister from New York. Such superficial status was not relevant to the demons that possessed the victims' bodies and did not want to leave them; these vain credentials had no currency in the spiritual realm. I, therefore, had to dismiss any vanity or pride that such accolades held or could bring. I also realized that it was unusual for Black Ministers to be operative where I was. While I appreciated the enormous respect being shown to me, it was not to be wallowed in. Instead, it was more important to remember that I had come as one under authority both of the Greater Allen Cathedral and, more importantly, of Jesus Christ. Everything else was vain glory to be sent like to the dunghill like the Apostle Paul said.

In addition, fasting to be prepared for service opened up my understanding of fasting more. I realized that God honored the prayers of those who fasted for the deliverance of others. I found what could be considered a Divine rationale why God responds to those who fast. Here was a frail human being dependent on food for sustenance, willing to forego that need on behalf of someone else; in this case, a perfect stranger, all to God's glory. Surely that attracted God's attention. Such personal sacrifice was reflective of His own as exemplified by His Son, our Lord, and Savior Jesus Christ, who gave Himself on Calvary at the Father's will.

I also learned what significance food held in the culture of the Taiwanese. My hosts were seriously concerned that I was not eating. From my perspective, my fasting denied them one of their principal ways of bonding and socializing. Secondly, it hindered them from showing hospitality to their honored guest by serving and sharing meals together. My conclusions were drawn from my noticing that several people paid for our lunch or dinner. They wanted to have a private sit down with the ministers (Rev. Chung and I) to ask questions, make our acquaintance, and show their deep appreciation for the blessing that the ministry was to them. Thirdly, those responsible for our well-being were somewhat concerned that my not eating was not good, given the hours we spent ministering to hundreds. "Mousa Paul" (Pastor Paul- my rough translation) they would ask worriedly, "No food?" "No food," I would respond. "How about lunch? How about dinner?" they pressed. I politely refused, careful not to offend my hosts. Generally speaking, though, they understood.

Each night I marched into the auditorium with a greater and greater expectancy and a more transparent focus, ready for the Lord to honor His word; He did just that. I surveyed the line before me, looking for the barking man and the women not yet entirely free. As I came to them, I placed my hands on their stomachs, the areas where the reactions were often centered in such cases. The most violent reactions began to occur as I did so: people began quivering, eyes bulging, convulsing and vomiting, falling and flailing, crying and screaming. I paid particular attention to the barking man, and as he fell, I knelt beside him and began fervent intercession. His barking increased, and he started acting like a monkey; then, a voice came out of him different from his own. It was the principal demon, the strong man. It communicated that he was an old man who had inhabited that body for a long time and did not want to leave. It was as though he was protesting my unreasonable demand.

Without engaging in the dialogue and following the example of Jesus, I commanded him to cease and desist and leave. Then, after a struggle, a subtle change came. We checked him, proving the spirit by the confession of faith in Christ and acknowledging His Lordship. Once satisfied that the demons were gone, we moved on and did the same to several others until the whole line of people was served. I returned to the hotel, drenched in sweat and soaked to the skin but rejoicing in what victories the Lord had won. It was clear that we had experienced a breakthrough.

The following night I returned to minister, and at the altar call, I panned the line of respondents for those exceptional cases looking for the evidence of God's salvation. The barker was not on the line as he was every night I went down the line praying as I was accustomed. Then suddenly, I saw him ministering to others who were being prayed for, catching them as they fell! What a dramatic turnaround for him. He went from a captive to a liberator! I learned later from members of the organizing team that he had traveled from another town night after night. Thank God that his visits were not in vain. Likewise, the other women and men I was monitoring were smiling; there was a visible difference in their demeanor and physical well-being. Some were demonstrative in their praise and worship. The Lord had prevailed.

Of course, they were those who needed further intervention that was beyond the immediate scope of the meetings, but at least the process had begun, and their obedience would lead to complete healing. I took comfort in this conclusion from my reading during my times of meditation; all healing was not always either instant or permanent. Instead, some recoveries required the obedience of the sick/sinner. This was evident in accounts recorded in Scripture, especially the gospels. In several cases, we observed that Jesus instructed some who requested His healing to do various things to obtain that salvation: "go wash," "go show yourself to the priest," "stretch forth your hand," "get up, take up your bed, and walk," "go, your son lives," and so on. In each of these cases, the healing was conditioned on their obedience to the instruction given. Thus, some recovery is progressive rather than instantaneous.

It was vital for me to recognize this fact as I ministered to various people with diverse conditions and different life circumstances in which this situation did occur. On one of the earliest nights I ministered, I came to a woman with what I would describe as a very soft and subdued demeanor. As I laid my hands on her head, I was impressed to ask her a question. It was not a comfortable one, but at that moment, there was little time to gauge political correctness or even cultural sensitivities. I had to trust that I was being led by the Holy Spirit because I had no other reason to conjure that question. Thankfully I did not hesitate or refuse to ask. "Is your husband faithful to you?" I questioned, sensing in my spirit that this was the source of her problem. She opened her eyes and looked at me, somewhat startled. Then, in staccato, she paused and replied that she did not know. After a few more minutes, she collected herself and asked me why I had asked that question. I told her that this is what the Lord had impressed me to ask her. After praying for her, I asked her to call her husband, who happened to be present, to pray for him. I encourage him to love his wife as we are admonished in Scripture (Eph. 5:21-33; I Pet. 3:7). He looked disturbed but simply acknowledged my warning. As a result of their reaction, I felt a little unsure, hoping that I had spoken prophetically and moved on to the next person.

Later that evening, I conferred with Sis. Esther, who had translated for me instead of Sis. Doris. Amazingly, Esther confided that she knew the woman I had spoken to and that she was amazed that I could discern her situation so accurately. Esther related that the woman's spouse was a bigamist; he was married with three children in China but came to Taiwan seeking better opportunities. He had met and married the woman to whom we had ministered, and they had one daughter in common. However, he was in daily conflict, torn between loyalty to his Chinese and Taiwanese homes. Without knowing any of these details, the Lord demonstrated his power revealing a hidden sin. Sis. Esther regretted that the Taiwanese wife did not admit a serious problem in her marriage. Naturally, then, their obedience to God's word would bring about their healing, and their continued disobedience in bigamy and denial would keep them and their family in the bondage from which they were seeking deliverance.

As I processed this situation, it was even more remarkable that unbeknownst to both parents (and I did not confide this to Esther), a teenage girl who turned out to be their daughter had confessed to being sexually active with her boyfriend. Similarly, the Holy Spirit prompted me to caution her about spiritual purity without knowing anything about her. Therefore her parents' behavior may have affected the moral status of their home. The spirit of immorality was being given room to kill, steal, and destroy. Only their obedience to heed the voice of the Good Shepherd and become His sheep would free them from the clutches of the wolves in their lives. The Lord gave them the opportunity to have life and to have it more abundantly (John 10:10, 11). That family did not need prayer more than they required obedience at all levels.

Not only had the people seen the delivering, revealing power of God, but I could have seen in the eyes of the local missionary team and visiting Christian Ministers who attended the events that we had won new respect. Many of them now joined the line for prayer after the respondents had been prayed for with dramatic results. God opened my mouth to prophesy to them and expose areas in their lives that needed to be brought under the power of the Lordship of Christ with poignant accuracy. As He had done for Samuel, He did not let any of the words of my mouth fall to the ground (I Sam. 3:19). Therefore, as I had explained to Sis. Doris, several gifts of the Spirit became operative as I ministered. Prophesy by telling God's word to the collective group and individuals, the expulsion of demons, spiritual discernment, the word of knowledge, and the word of wisdom were all spiritual endowments that the Holy Spirit bestowed as the need arose. The gifts of the Holy Spirit were also manifested when I met individuals in one-on-one encounters and in small groups when I met with people in private counsel. Many of these persons had questions and concerns best addressed in this way, but the Lord was faithful to His servant and did amazingly to all who sought direction in every situation. Such encounters were so extraordinary that I had to diarize them for future reflection.

Also, the Lord blessed in other ways. He provided so that all our hotel expenses were met by persons who contributed from their own resources. This blessing made it possible for the mission to be continued in other places, churches, and cities beyond Taipei. I was invited to minister to students in a Seminary and even the Royal Palace's official staff. The latter of the two opportunities were particularly notable.

In both cases, Sis. Doris had made the arrangements, and I readily agreed. The Palace was within walking distance of the Army Hotel, so Sis. Doris and I walked there comfortably. En route, Sis. Doris explained about a Bible Study group among the Official staff, and we were invited to minister to them during their lunch break. We accessed the first gate to very somber army soldiers who never once smiled or exchange pleasantries. Our host contact, a charming man, met us at the second checkpoint and lightened the mood of the very austere admission into the well-manicured buildings and beautiful grounds. Unsure of the outcomes, I could feel my body rigid and tense, given the hostility against the gospel that we were briefed about back in New York. Now were we going into the very center of power to conduct Bible Study? I ran several scenarios in my head in preparation for the event, and these raised questions: What if the study got out of control and we broke some protocol? Would we be arrested? Will the President be there? What if God so allows us to minister to him? How would that turn out? All kinds of possibilities played out upon the stage of my mind, which alerted me to be ready for anything, including jail.

While my inside turmoil continued, we continued to follow our hosts through pristine grounds and buildings. I took in all the sights, amazed at the opportunities I was accorded without any actual significant diplomatic status but an Ambassador of the King of Kings. I needed to bear my colors well, I thought. Soon, we were ushered into a large conference room; it had an air of prominence. The extra-large black leather chairs were arranged in an oval, each with a microphone situated before them. I felt dwarfed and somewhat intimidated as we sat there waiting for the group to assemble. I appreciated this quietness because it gave me time to pray and collect my thoughts. I was awed by the mere fact that I was invited to minister at the seat of power, contrary to the apprehensive view expressed in New York about China's anti-Christian policies and its imposition of rule over Taiwan. I centered myself and tried to rehearse my brief meditation for the day, given the time allotted.

I needed to be quick, but I wanted to be effective since those who would attend may be the ones who influence policy and the rule of law. I couldn't help asking, 'who knows if I had come to the Kingdom "for such as a time as this?" (Esther 4:14).

At the appointed time, several people came in precisely on time. They greeted us politely and took their seats around the table. One of the brothers had brought along a guitar, and soon we were singing praise songs. Sis. Doris would often pause as she did in the evangelical services to interpret the words for me. I appreciated her care, but I enjoyed listening to the saints praising in their vernacular. I even tried to learn the songs as they sang them, some of which were familiar to me, but certainly not the language in which they sang them.

Shortly after, I was presented to speak. I rose to accomplish my task, careful and conscious of the sensitivities of politics and the hostile environment often meted out to those who would be sincere in their faith. Nevertheless, the gospel of the Kingdom had to be proclaimed, and so it was. I felt led to speak to the staff about *The Christian Perspective of Government* based on Romans 13:1-7 and 1 Tim. 2:1-6. I proposed that:

1. Government is of God – the ultimate authority
2. Government is to be respected
3. Government is responsible for the good in society (as God's servant)
4. Government should be prayed for

The examples of Mordecai, Daniel, Nehemiah, and other Biblical public officials were cited to strengthen my premise.

After concluding, I turned the meeting back into our hostess's hands. However, I was surprised that the government executives there requested prayer as enthusiastically as those we had met in the evangelical services at the hotel. Once again, we relied on the Holy Spirit to pray on our behalf as we presented each participant's various infirmities before the throne of grace.

Then, Sis. Doris was led to pray for one who complained about backaches. I watched as she seated him and had him extend both feet forward. As both of his feet were matched together, it was visibly evident that one of his legs was longer than the other by 2-4 inches. It seemed apparent that this inequity was the source of the back pains. I could not fathom at the time why she had done this and revealed this condition. It seems as though the brother seemed unaware of the situation himself. Sis. Doris began her intercession for him, and before our very eyes, his shortened leg began slowly to stretch to match the other. I began to pray for her, recognizing that the Lord had reversed our roles. I was in the subordinate support position. It did not matter who Mousa was and who was sister; the operation of the gifts of the Spirit was dictating our places.

Thankfully, having been an Assistant to pastors, I resumed the supportive role as the Spirit led me. I became Mordecai and Doris was now Queen Esther. As the man's foot stretched to the entire length of the other, Sis. Doris now asked him to stand, and from all appearances, his pain was diminished if not gone. Others were so excited by what they saw that they too requested to be checked, and sure enough, some had unproportionate foot lengths. Visibly we continued to see feet move, and audibly we heard the sound of one shoe rubbing against the other as it elongated forward. I had heard of such miracles, now I was seeing it with my own eyes.

I was instantly reminded of one of the miracles of Jesus when He restored the man's hand, which was withered and drawn. "Stretch forth your hand," He commanded, and the man's hand was restored to the amazement of the congregation in the synagogue that day (Mark 3:3-5). Here we were in the state's Royal house and witnessing a similar scenario. I was careful to mentally equate any phenomena I experienced with what I saw in the Word of God. This was my way of authenticating the action I saw. I never wanted to be carried away with emotionalism or other strange activity, which may be pseudo-Christian. As unusual as the experience was, I felt at peace in heart and mind, even as our session ended and the staff reported back to their posts. This was an unusual Bible Study that included healing.

Honestly, the Royal Palace staff could return to work saying, "We have seen strange things today" (Luke 5:26); so had we. As we exited the Palace, I breathed a deep sigh of relief that nothing untoward happened. We were not censored or even interrupted by the very stern, stoic guards at the entrance or the officials who observed us or attended. Interestingly, in the West, we would have been denied access or escorted off the premises. Still, here in a non-Christian society, we conducted a Bible study/prayer meeting/healing service with government workers during working hours without anyone raising an eyelash. It wasn't that we came in incognito. How more visible can an African American visitor and a female be in an official government building? Gratefully, without hindrance, the burden of ministry was discharged.

At the end of the day, Doris and I were a team that ministered to some of Taipei's Royal Officials, which I could not have anticipated when the trip was planned in New York. Whether we were officially recognized at court was irrelevant; we were recognized by the court of Heaven, which was enough for me. Interestingly, before I left the USA, I packed a tuxedo because I felt guided to do so. The thought was if I was invited to some official function, I would need to dress appropriately. I didn't wear the tux, but the garments of righteousness and the armor of the LORD proved necessary.

Given what actually happened, I could only say that it may be that the Lord was spiritually preparing me to serve his people in the Palace. It was not a formal occasion such as a dinner, but our noon-day ministry was far more significant than a high-brow affair that would give little opportunity to witness beyond a few rubbed elbows. Our less than official invitation allowed Doris and me to do more than hobnob. We were able to freely speak the Word of the Lord to His people, lay hands on them, imploring the Lord to relieve their sicknesses, and give them the wisdom and power to serve people in crisis. Our ministry was a refreshment to their souls, empowering them to wrestle against principalities and ungodly forces in high places.

I reflected how such influences confronted the Godly and righteous who have the charge of serving in the halls of power throughout the world from time immemorial from Joseph's Egypt to our brethren in Taipei. Doris had spoken to me with a deep concern for her country. She mentioned that the Taiwanese government had paid great homage to the Dali Lama when he visited sometime before. Many business persons lavished the celebrated Buddhists' Monastic head with substantial financial gifts. I wondered if that gesture may have been political posturing to China's leadership due to its claim on Tibet and Taiwan. The Dali Lama is the primary religiopolitical leader of Tibet. However, to Taiwanese Christians like Doris, working among the masses ravaged by Buddhism's demonic forces, Taiwan's official reverence and homage of the Dali Lama represented the leaders' yielding to darkness instead of the liberty of the Lordship of Christ. It was no wonder then that those who labored both physically and spiritually for their country's salvation like the one we ministered to would experience spiritual and physical afflictions. Thank God for the refreshing that we were able to administer to them. I hope to see the Palace staff again and hear their personal testimonies one day.

However, before we could fully savor such blessings, Doris reminded me of the next assignment the following day. I was scheduled to minister to a Theological Seminary for the entire day! I was somewhat off-put by the invitation because I could not envision what to speak on for the whole day to satisfy the Seminary. I had never spoken that long before at the Seminary level. To my mind, such a task required enormous preparation. I had to be academically sound and theologically balanced to satisfy the necessary exegetical and hermeneutical challenges of any subject raised. Plus, address textual difficulties that may be resolved in the meaningful study of Scripture. I wanted to be a responsible expositor of the Scripture and offer the students truth just as I was careful to receive when I was in Seminary. These various concerns troubled me, so I tried to ascertain exactly how I was expected to minister. However, Doris kept assuring me that I need not worry as the school president and founder had attended our services at the Army Hotel and was satisfied that I could speak to his students.

Before the event, I had the opportunity to speak to the Seminary's president, Dr. Thomas Lee Yic-Mun. He earned his Doctorate in Ministry in the USA and returned to Taiwan to start his school, Global Chinese Bible Institute. I was all the more impressed not simply by his scholarship but with the fact that amid hostility without official and corporate funds, he had raised up a theological institution to train ministers! Wow! He assured me that any subject of my choosing was acceptable, and I was scheduled to address the entire student body.

Unworthy of this high honor, I turned to the Lord who had brought me thus far and was putting me in places and spaces on the other side of the globe I never imagined. I was not long in prayer when I was impressed to structure the end-time Scriptures that I was studying and preaching in the seminary's general services. The topic had sparked deep curiosity on Israel, the fig tree as Jesus had described her, and I was exploring the Scriptures on the subject with much delight and new insight in my private study. I actually began preparing notes on the subject, not knowing that those very notes would be used here now at the Global Chinese Bible Institute in Taipei.

Thus Israel, the proverbial fig tree, the seasons it will endure, and the implications of these prophetic developments to the Church and the world became my thesis for the day-long workshop/lecture. Less concerned about myself and the novelty of the experience, I was now absorbed in the material's structuring so it would be clearly understood. However, there was still the language barrier to overcome, and I needed to be as simple and straightforward as possible to translate it easier.

On arrival at the Seminary, we were greeted by Dr. Thomas Lee Yic-Mun with a huge smile that reflected his joy in our being there to impart to his student body. The school was small but well laid out; the external building façade made it stand out from the rest of the row. Inside was thoughtfully structured. The main entrance opened up to a main lecture hall/meeting room with additional rooms attached. The décor conveyed a sense of sobriety but not stiffness, more of reverence. Perhaps studiousness is a better description. President Yic-Mun received us enthusiastically and seated us. He explained that I would give my lecture in four parts; two before lunch and the remainder to follow the recess with a brief break in the middle. Given the gaps in between, I could better lay my lecture out even though I was still concerned about the students' ability to remain focused. Maybe this way, I could keep them engaged.

My lecture notes on - 'Israel: The Prophetic Fig Tree to Observe' were subdivided. I settled into my thoughts to ready my mind and vocabulary to be as simple as possible for translation. My challenge was the numerous theological concepts with cultural connotations or western expressions that may be difficult to convey over the language barrier. Some theological ideas I took for granted are often without dynamic equivalence in other languages as I was learning. However, Doris reminded me that Dr. Yic-Mun would be the lecture's translator. Given his USA theological education and familiarity with his students, my concerns were alleviated.

The first lecture followed a session of praise and worship conducted by the President. I learned that he also used that same space for church service with a congregation he pastored. The worship session was passionate and sincere with beautiful piano accompaniment; it was uplifting. After the first session, I realized that I was imposing and projecting my fears regarding the students based on my experience. Unlike students at home, these were like the noble Bereans: keen, conscientious, and for want of a better term, hungry for the Word. They appeared to be far more serious about their learning, seminary education, and Christian service to follow than those I had observed in the US. I also had a more professional, detached approach to my seminary education and to Biblical instruction as a whole. Here the students recognized that they were in a fight for their faith, for the souls of millions of their compatriots lost and suffering under the merciless hands of demonic forces evident all around them. No such challenge was recognized in the West under the deceptive Christian nation veneers. Could it be that we don't realize that we are no less ravaged by Satan, who has anesthetized believers and deceived the masses with a form of godliness but that denies its power? The Global Chinese Bible Institute students wanted everything I had and more to better prepare them for the war against the kingdom of darkness.

In turn, I found this motivating and energizing as a teacher/preacher. Because of the devout interest on the students' part, I was moved to share without reservation. In my tradition and experience as an Afro-Caribbean American minister, the audience-speaker connection is a crucial dynamic of our communication. Sensing that that dynamic was present by the look of the faces and the translation's enthusiasm, I poured forth.

At the end of the day-long presentation (of course, there were breaks for lunch, etc.), the subject was well covered, although I felt I could have communicated it better. Further study would have given me a better grasp of the subject matter, but all in all, the pertinent facts were shared. The president and his student body were both pleased as well as Sis. Doris. Then unexpectedly, it happened! President Yic-Mun asked us to pray for his students. Again this was no meager prayer of dismissal for general grace, but they wanted effectual, fervent prayer that ministered explicitly to any and all conditions of their individual selves.

Having learned that it was not by our might or power but by the Spirit of the Lord, we interceded on behalf of the column of students assembled before us. This suggested an immediacy in response to the Word among these Taiwanese believers. There was an evident marriage of Word and application, a meeting between the material preached and its material inculcation in the hearer. There was a congruity between the preacher and the people to whom he preached such that the people wanted the preacher to pray that the truths proclaimed are realized in their lives right away. Much like sinners would submit to the gospel for salvation, there was surrender to the Lord's will among believers. This was wonderful.

It was clear that what was proclaimed by the speaker was not considered mere scholarly discourse to be admired for its erudition or elocution. Rather, the knowledge imparted was to be experienced. The power of the God it declared was likewise manifested in the charged moment when faith in His Word was exhibited. What a departure from our sterile method of allowing these moments to pass when the power of the Lord is present to heal (Luke 5:17). Over and over, the Asian audiences taught me that far too much of our ministry in the West was mere words, without the commensurate works: form without function and shadow without substance. In Taiwan, I was expected to demonstrate that what I had spoken were not mere words of human wisdom but in the power and demonstration of the Holy Spirit. In this way, their faith was not grounded in the understanding of men but in the power of God experienced among them (I Cor. 2: 4).

As I thought about this while I was ministering and reflected subsequently in my journal, I realized that this demand for the immediacy of the manifestation of God's power was very Biblical. After Jesus taught, He healed those who listened to Him and desired the life of which He spoke. He did not finish at times but was interrupted by some desperate soul yearning to receive the power that His words declared (Luke 5:18-20; Mark 1:1-34; 5:23; Mt. 4:23). The Apostles experienced this same immediacy when sent forth to minister (Luke 9; 10).

I reflected later that this practice is our commission and our heritage which we have abdicated by capitulating to the gods of culture, customs, and conventions that have nothing to do with God's will and the guidance of His Spirit. I realized that we have lost the vitality of our faith in action in our westernized Christianity. We are comfortable in our salon-type churches where we indulge in religious therapeutic exercises with no actual application to the harsh realities confronting the real world. We are willing to pray for healing at a particular prayer service planned and convened by the Church Board or the Pastor. Deliverance will occur when the ministry specialist comes to town in the summer. Such sophisticated Christianity was not in evidence here in Taipei. Even in the Seminary, the students wanted to experience the authentic, immediate power of the Lord. They wanted to know the incarnated Living Word, not dead religious commentaries on living truth.

I could not imagine such ministry taking place at a US Evangelical Seminary. God forbid that a Seminary Professor should pray after lecturing under the power of the Spirit for their class that they may be healed, filled, or delivered. Such behavior is generally regarded as unprofessional and unfit for academia. Yet, in the sacred halls of intelligencia, the very ministers trained to do such ministry are taught. How absurd! I began pondering whether we were denying our pastors the effect they could have after preaching penetrating sermons on their sitting congregations? Were we denying our congregants the breakthroughs they yearn for by having them sit passively in the face of struggle and pain? Instead, we have allowed our schedules to hurry us to the benediction so we may leave church on time for lunch, dinner, or supper where we intellectualize on the preacher's sermon that now hangs stiff with rigor mortis in the air—what a departure from Biblical experience.

As an Associate Pastor, I learned in Taiwan to be ready to preach the gospel of the Kingdom, heal the sick, and deliver those oppressed by demons as the need arose. I learned to plan for its arrival immediately. One thing became evident. If the Word of God was spoken in Spirit and in truth, then ministry to the hearers will be necessary. The light of the gospel would expose hidden devils, motivate the sick to press for healing, and move the sinful to desire salvation (Luke 4:33-36; Acts 5:12-16). Seeing God's power affecting people's lives from the Palace to the Seminary ignited my faith and passions. I wanted to see more, learn more, experience more, and be more. That opportunity was to quickly follow as we turned to the coastal cities to share the gospel message.

On to the Other Cities

Having concluded our special services, the Fountain of Joy team leaders redirected our efforts to several churches in Taipei, and more importantly, to those in the coastal cities. Pastor Chung left to return to Australia, leaving a Sis. Tian in charge. I felt uneasy, as though my primary contact, who insisted I join him in ministry in Taiwan, would now up and leave me somewhat in the deep end. I couldn't quite figure it out. I felt like the proverbial Boy Wonder of Batman fame, and like him in his moments of crime-fighting, I had little time for explanations because the next day, we were headed to the coastal cities via train to the other side of the island.

Sis. Esther had joined us as an additional interpreter, and we had some stimulating discussions. Esther related how she had lived in the USA for a considerable period, and I discovered some common experiences we shared. She had many questions about the Bible in general and some about herself. It was clear that Esther respected my Biblical perspectives, and at times I felt as though I was counseling more than discussing. As we journeyed, she pointed out that the coastal cities were areas where the tourist frequented and, therefore, where most hotels and other attractions were found. Sis. Esther brought two other matters to my attention that she felt I needed to be aware of; the first had to do with the people to whom we would minister and the second had to do with some changes within the ministry team.

Among the Aborigines

According to Sis. Esther, regard for Christianity was highest among the more indigenous Taiwanese in the coastal cities. She educated me that the indigenous Taiwanese were Aborigines and had embraced Christianity more devoutly than the general population that continued to be loyal to traditional religions such as the worship of ancestors and Buddhism. I was genuinely ignorant that there were Aborigines among the Taiwanese. Instead, I associated Aborigines with the original natives of Australia. She further explained how like Australia's original peoples, they were mistreated and discriminated against at times in the nation's history.

My being a black man, these revelations resonated deeply with me and engendered empathy for these precious brethren that were holding up the blood-stained banner of the cross highly. To add to my emotional identification with this minority group, I learned that they were exceptionally musically gifted and whose dances and cultural expression best portrayed Taiwan to visitors. They were the people of the "sweet potato," as they affectionately refer to themselves because of the island's shape. Sis. Esther also revealed that some of our team members were Aborigines, and as a matter of fact, we were going to the same regions where they were born before they had left for college in Taipei and became part of the Fountain of Joy Ministry. Their subtle, distinct features soon became more apparent and pronounced to me as I began to pay closer attention.

Mei Lun Baptist Church, Huan Lien

One of the first churches where we ministered was the Mei Lun Baptist Church. This was a curious situation for me, being raised a Baptist. I wanted to see how this denomination had accepted and practiced their faith. Traditionally, Baptists were not open to charismatic expressions of faith like laying hands to heal the sick and casting out demons that had characterized the entire trip. This church was apparently founded by Baptist missionaries but was autonomous. However, I approached the ministry of the Word cautiously and carefully so I wouldn't offend the Pastors who were not apt to show their disapproval directly out of respect for their guests by my reading of the culture.

As I contemplated and prayed about what the Lord would have me to preach of in this region, I was drawn to the book of Revelation's seven letters to the Churches. However, I was unwilling to preach on these Churches in the text because I was uncomfortable about whether I could deliver the severe rebukes of the Lord Himself. I did not want to convey the wrong impression that I was being judgmental of the brethren of the coastal cities. However, as I resisted the Holy Spirit, I was not spared the LORD's rebuke, which said: "Read the beginning of the book!" I believe I heard that strong directive three times. As I did, I was driven to my knees in repentance. The Scriptures clearly read:

John to the seven churches which are in Asia... (Rev. 1:4)

The Holy Spirit then gently asked, "Where are you?" Without answering, I suddenly realized that I was in Asia. Words cannot express the sense of purpose and Divine destiny that overwhelmed me. Still, I remained humble and approached my task with fear and trembling not because of my own personal timidity but because of the seriousness of the Lord's burden, which He wanted me to discharge to His people. Furthermore, as I counted the engagements to be fulfilled on the preaching schedule, they numbered exactly seven, one letter to match each church event on the agenda. I could not have planned it any more precisely. Thus, I burrowed into the task of preparation with a renewed sense of purpose.

In each service at Mei Lun Baptist, the Lord was faithful. Sis. Esther (my translator) and I became a team and preached forth the word of God as best we could with our shoes off, as was their custom for persons ministering on the platform. As we had seen at the Army

Hotel, the Palace, the Seminary, and wherever else we ministered prior, people streamed forward for prayer from the audience. They kept coming until we had to leave because the church building had to be closed. I was still concerned about how the leadership perceived the ministry. Feedback from one of the Assistant Pastors allayed my fears. In his prayer time, the Spirit confirmed his perception of me as "a pure vessel" the Lord was ministering through. I was embarrassed at this relatively high enormous compliment but relieved that the word of God was well received as I was directed to give it.

Bethel

We said a fond farewell to Mei Lun Baptist Church and moved next to Prayer Mountain. I was told that Christians of all denominations met periodically for fellowship and prayer at the mountain top fellowship facility. I first met the brothers who blew the Shofars there, a whole choir of them! Spontaneously in the worship service, different elders would stand up and blow their Shofars and then in chorus, about seven more would join in and fill the air with blasts from their rams' horns! This was different. By now, I had acclimatized to differences in food, customs, culture, and churches, but this was wholly unexpected. It forced me to think through the use of the Shofar in Scripture and how that use was contextualized here in this indigenous Asian church's corporate worship.

However, my mental flights were curtailed by the burden I had to discharge. Once again, among these elders who were passionate for the Lord and the original launching pad for Christianity in Taiwan, my sermon was on the corrupt church of Thyatira where the false prophetess Jezebel was contaminating the church with sexual immorality. Despite the lessons of the previous inertia, I was uncomfortable preaching this rather scolding message of indictment to the elders I had the greatest admiration for. Their record of service was to be commended. How many of us in our lifetime can say that we introduced Christianity to a country or that we are the children (physical/spiritual) of those who have?

Nevertheless, as John was not to determine the tenor or tone of Christ's message for each Church, it was not in my place to do so. I was simply to express it accurately without censure. Thus respectfully, I preached with a sense of mission as I was directed. The sermon, despite my concerns, was well received. I studied the response to observe, learn, and discern God's move among His people, praying that I had done as He would have me. Throughout, the Pastor gave a reassuring smile as he translated for me. I loved his translations; they were done with the same intensity, pitch, tone, and passion, which I expressed as if my words flowed from his own mind.

Any lingering concerns I had were soon dismissed. We were invited to continue our ministry at this church that Sunday morning and evening services in Mati Tu, Tai Chun, by the Pastor who attended Bethel Baptist services. Those services were a delight. The vibrancy and passion for the Lord were evident in the choir and among the youth. I was privileged to be asked to dedicate a service to the youth and gear the message accordingly. This was somewhat of a challenge because I still felt that I should continue to minister from the letters to the Churches. On the other hand, Sis. Esther was worried that the content I was preaching may be inappropriate or irrelevant to the youth's issues.

As in every place, the brethren here were concerned for their youth adapting foreign lifestyles, premarital sex, teenage pregnancy, drugs, and a general increase in lawlessness. I assured Esther that I will not deviate from the Revelation texts but will continue to speak as directed and make the message relevant to the youth. Esther reluctantly relented. I did not bother to reassure her of my experience in dealing with youth in the Rites of Passage program, directing programs for inner-city youth in Brooklyn, or my years of being a youth minister in Barbados before immigrating to the USA.

I could have told Esther that I observed that Taiwanese youth, like most worldwide, were all heavily influenced by the Hip Hop culture of the U.S. It was evident in some of their mannerisms, mode of dress, and how they greeted me after the services with some of the *homeboy* handshakes they no doubt had seen on American TV and movies. All these factors became instantly relevant and helpful even here in Taiwan. The young people here were no different than those I had seen in Barbados, Brooklyn, Queens, or the UK. Thus, I applied the letter to the Church at Sardis to them with the admonition: *Choose Life Not Death*. I found the words of Jesus in the text instructive to encourage them:

1. be Careful/Watchful
2. be Strong
3. be Mindful
4. be Undefiled
5. be Overcomers

These five admonitions were reinforced with true-life stories of other youth who were pleasing or displeasing to Christ, as expressed in the text. I got *real* with them as I shared the story of one of my own daughters, a Sardian in behavior. I shared her Christian upbringing and devotion to God, her giftedness, and her straying from the faith when she went to college, which resulted in her pre-marital pregnancy. This self-effacing story from the one who was the preacher and whose family ought to have been paragons of virtue gripped the youth. As embarrassing as it may have been, I spoke about the flaw in my family. In the eyes of some of the teens and adults present, I saw that they identified with me and the path my daughter chose. As we made the call for discipleship, many surged forward, some weeping, some solemn and penitent at the end of the session. Others seemed to be making decisions to follow the Lord. Generally, it was a stirring move among the youth, especially the males. As the Lord led, I waded in among them, praying and speaking words of warning. Of all the times I ministered after preaching, this was undoubtedly the most dramatic in how strongly I felt the Holy Spirit moving among the congregation. My discernment was heightened to the degree that I could call some people forward and pray for them specifically regarding their needs and struggles with accuracy and no prior knowledge. Many of them fell to the floor, overcome and overwhelmed in that charismatic moment.

By the end of the night, it was clear that the elders were pleased with our ministry and embraced us warmly. The Pastor was delighted that we addressed a growing need among his lambs. Sis. Esther and the Fountain of Joy missionary team were pleased, but all was not well. The enemy was mounting a counter offense in our very midst, and I had to be careful not to be a tool of his as he did so.

The Enemy's Counterattack

Satan soon tried to destroy the successive invasions into his territory. The first casualty was Sis. Doris, whom I now considered a friend, and translator. However, it would appear that the team was not satisfied with her translation. It would appear that the audience was not benefiting fully from what I spoke, and some things were being lost in translation. I tried to be simple and use the most common words like I had done in the prisons when we used translators to speak to our Latino brothers and sisters in the USA. Therefore, translation and speaking through a translator was not totally new to me, although the culture and, consequently, some colloquial expressions would be.

One of the most significant challenges was in translating the Scriptures themselves. I learned that their meaning was sometimes the hardest to convey, especially when I inserted and quoted them in my discourses. I also realize that I needed to give complete thoughts rather than phrases so that the translator could understand for themself what they needed to say to express what was said. I had noticed that when Pastor Chung left, his translator was switched to me one night. Later, Sis. Esther told me that someone remarked that they were now hearing me well for the first time. Because I was not bi-lingual, I did not know. This meant that the Holy Spirit was operating over and above our inadequacies! It was not the wonderful words we thought we were saying but what He was doing. How humbling!

Nevertheless, Sis. Doris had accompanied us to the coastal cities but as Sis. Esther tried to explain to me, she was not to translate. I felt sad about this but understood. The somewhat gnawing and disparaging feeling I had felt from the Team Leader before we left Taipei was even more awkward. The matter came to a head when we reached Huan Lien. We met to discuss the services, and I sat with the team as they discussed the details, but they did so in Chinese. I felt this was odd since I was always granted translation and accorded much respect. I became frustrated as they talked on, and it was clear that they were deciding on Sis. Doris, but I needed to know details on the services to better prepare.

Eventually, I turned to Doris to ask what was going on and what the intense discussion was about. It seemed somewhat tricky for her. She did not want to speak on whatever was said, which made me more frustrated. I should have just retired to my room until the meeting was over, but I felt that would appear rude, so I tried to stick it out. At one point, Sis. Esther paused to tell me a few details, and then when I wanted to discuss them, she jumped back into the fray. It was clear that something was afoot.

As the situation dragged on, I became more irritated. I simply wanted to know when and where we were ministering next to begin my preparation, but that information was not forthcoming, and time was running out. Preparation was of the essence. I developed the idea of forming a sermon outline for the interpreters to better think through and know how best to convey any complex Scripture text in advance. Besides, I soon realized that the decision to replace Sis. Doris was a foregone conclusion and my trying to enter the discussion was moot. It seemed that she was allowed to come along because she was responsible for making connections with the churches in this region.

As my efforts to break into the conversation were rebuffed, I muttered that the situation was ridiculous and turned to Sis. Doris to ask her what was going on. The team leader or other interpreters did not appreciate this, who were in constant dialogue and had shut us out of the discussion. Eventually, after tensed and exasperating moments ticked by, I was told that the team leader was upset because I failed to turn a service over to her back in Taipei. She was apparently angry because it would have allowed her to speak, make announcements, and raise the offering after the message to make an appeal for financial support. I did not recall those instructions and therefore turned over the service to the Pastor of the Church. My out-of-hand treatment of this matter was not well received by the team leader, who may have been upset about it for a while. I questioned why it was not brought up before and dealt with then. Without knowing it, I had offended the team leader. Later, I was told she considered my response disingenuous and inappropriate for my position as a Pastor. She withdrew, refusing to speak to me, but continued to function as a leader. I clearly miscalculated the depth of the sentiments here, preferring to deal with the current matters at hand. Perhaps her own remuneration was tied to the offerings, or

I overlooked some cultural norm in my preoccupation with ministering the Word and the current matters at hand. One thing was sure: the enemy had penetrated our ranks and caused a division among us. The division was apparent when Sis. Doris packed and left before we had begun ministering because she felt pushed aside and insulted. I regretted seeing her go. She was indeed a woman of God, and her ministry would have added to our efforts.

It was painfully uncomfortable discharging my responsibilities in such a disunited climate. I felt we were compromised because the team leader's responsibility was to introduce me as their speaker from New York each time I spoke, yet she was not conversing with me. As if this was not bad enough, Sis. Esther relayed that she had disagreed strongly with Pastor Chung about me staying for three weeks and scheduling other engagements at churches to extend our work beyond the Army Hotel. I was somewhat disturbed because the invitation letter came from her for the visa issued in New York and specified the dates.

Additionally, Pastor Chung insisted that I would serve three weeks which we had not yet exceeded. His not being present made the situation more untenable. I felt like a house guest that had overstayed his welcome. Suddenly, I began to question whether the ministry in the churches was contrived or of God.

Nevertheless, I soldiered on. I resisted the urge to call Pastor Ezekiel Chung and instead prayed and tried to explain the matter to Sis. Esther. It did not help, but at times aggravated the issue. Suddenly, my team, the only people I knew, my hosts, the ones I relied on, my fellow laborers in Christ became a thorn in my side. However, His grace was sufficient for me, and His strength was made perfect in my weakness. Other team members, our young Aborigines, who comprised the Praise Team, continued to show respect and appreciation to me. I was in their home territory, and they sang and performed with even more exuberance. Later, they conveyed that their people "liked me". Sis. Esther felt that they identified with me. I spoke with an understanding of their standing and status as a people, me being a Black man in the United States of America with all its discrimination and prejudices to which they could identify.

I may not have realized it then, but my having served in subordinate positions as an Associate Minister at Allen had well prepared me for this unpleasant part of my ministry in Taiwan. I drew heavily on those prior experiences and remained humble, refusing to allow the enemy to use me in any way. Instead, I committed myself to pray particularly for the team leader and for the mission as a whole. During the services, I lavished her with praise, not mere flatteries but commendations for all the coordination she had done and the team's maintenance. By so doing, I was determined to overcome evil with good. I had come from too far and had endured too much to allow the enemy to have any glory! We ended the mission earning the team's respect even though we may not have resolved the misunderstandings. I was given tokens from the brethren in the coastal cities. I was given traditional headdress pieces and other gifts, even some for my wife. Above all, I was invited to return. That request to come back meant more to me than any other thing I received.

The next day we took the train back to Taipei to pack and take my flight home to New York, leaving new friends and associates in ministry behind, hoping for a return in the future. We bid each other a fond farewell, sharing our last meal at the airport. Even there, Sis. Esther bought a present for Lorraine, and another sister called to say that she was on her way with gifts that I should wait for. There was no way I could add anything else to my luggage. I was already carrying an extra bag which Sis. Esther tried to have the airline wave the cost, and when they didn't, she refused my paying and paid for it from her own resources.

As I made the long journey home back to America, back to Jamaica Queens, back to the Cathedral, and back to being the Discipleship Minister there, I realized that I was changed, transformed, and knew I would never be the same again. How would I return to Allen and continue what I was doing without my missionary experience manifesting in my work? One thing was sure; I could not preach the same way; my sermons must be fully oriented to the return of Christ and preparing His people for Him. I could not simply preach homilies and feel-good messages; the urgency of the Bride's need to prepare for the marriage supper of her Lord was paramount, and to do less was now unconscionable.

Secondly, I saw upfront and close the havoc Satan was causing in people's lives, and I was not passive about this anymore. Too many were in the congregation living through pain and suffering unnecessarily without our intervention. I knew I would have to use my new honed skills to confront sickness and demonic oppression and possession, however they manifested themselves in the lives of our people. Broken marriages, rebellious children, drug addiction, gang warfare, rampant violence, lust, pornography, teenage pregnancy, risky sexual behaviors, homelessness, and mendicant welfare mentalities are all under the auspices of evil spirits. They influence those given to the lust of the flesh, the lust of the eye, and the pride of life. Those who are disobedient to the Word of God don't realize that they fall unsuspectingly under the sway of Satan himself. Their paths tread down well-beaten tracks on Broadway, Main Street, under the glamorous lights of Sin City in every borough. Unless we can deliver the enemy's victims with the power of the gospel of Jesus Christ and bring them under the rule of the Lord of heaven, what was the relevance and purpose of our ministries? As a result of my mission abroad, I returned to Allen with a new mindset. I surmised that a church of some 15-20,000 members must be able to change the city, the borough, the region, at least the neighborhood in which we live. Taiwan admired Allen's accomplishments from afar, but New York should be feeling its ecclesiastical power near.

As I reflected on my total experience, my only concern was whether I had fallen out of favor with Dr. Chung, given the impasse with his local team leader. I also reasoned that the Apostles had experienced the same joys and sorrows, successes and challenges as they preached the gospel. My experience could be no different. To have ministered without the enemy's backlash was naïve, totally un-Biblical, and unrealistic, I supposed (Matt. 24:9-14). However, while I expected attacks from the enemy's camp, I was not prepared to experience them from within. The friendly fire attacks were the worst of all because they were unexpected and painful coming from people I regarded as co-laborers whom I came to respect for their work for the Lord. I recalled that several Biblical characters had friendly-fire experiences: Moses had his from Aaron and Miriam, Joseph from his own brothers, Jacob from his father-in-law Laban, David from his own son Absalom, Nehemiah from priests within his leadership circles, Paul from false brethren, and of course Christ Himself from his most trusted disciple, Judas.

My minor situation, painful though it was, may have been the essence that made the Taiwanese mission consummate and complete. A preacher I heard on the radio put it in perspective for me as he spoke on surviving the fires of life, which ultimately refine us. He illustrated that if one tastes vanilla essence alone, it is bitter and unpleasant to the palate. Still, ice cream, coffee, cake, and pastries flavored with vanilla are delightful to the taste. Somehow the bitterness is lost among the ingredients, and the full flavor is enhanced considerably. His punch line stated that a bitter experience is God's added flavor to enrich our lives. Such was my Asian experience beyond the Cathedral walls.

Asia, USA

I returned to the Cathedral to a warm reception from beloved friends, mothers, and fathers in the ministry. However, it was not long before calls to go beyond the walls would come again. To assure me that I was not out of favor with the ministry after my return, I was contacted by Pastor Chung to go to California to minister with him among the Chinese Americans there, where he had special services. I accepted, and once again, was blessed to be among excellent saints reaching out to the lost, proclaiming the gospel, and praying for the sick. I met new wonderful friends and brethren who extended my experience and enriched my life with their lives and ministries. One such person was Pastor Deborah. Once we met, I made an instant connection with her. A retired financial executive, she was now the director of a private junior high school in her upscale Asian community. We toured the school and met some of her teachers and administrators who were fully engaged in educating young, eager minds in a very Christian environment. However, her passion was not there. She had a burden driving her into unchartered territory and wanted support to accomplish it. She invited me to partake in the project.

Asia Meets Africa in California

Pastor Deborah drove me to her other ministry work, and I soon understood her burden and the challenges it presented to her. It also offered a challenge to me, causing me to question whether that was where the Lord was directing me beyond the Cathedral walls. A forty-five-minute drive from her community brought us into a less upscale part of town where Latinos and African Americans lived. Pastor Deborah had used family funds to purchase a large church from a Caucasian assembly that had largely moved out of the community in the usual 'white flight' manner. The youngest of them attending the flagging group may have been in his sixties. Pastor Deborah was able to purchase the property in a precarious move. It included a sizeable beautiful sanctuary, an attached chapel, a large fellowship hall, an auditorium, classrooms, and a large backyard that made any expansion very possible. Unfortunately, land and property in this community were scarce and becoming increasingly expensive.

Pastor Deborah was convinced that the Lord had called her to establish a ministry in this Afro-Latino neighborhood with a similar school she had established among her own people. The plan was fraught with difficulties. Her own family had sacrificed over a million dollars into the property, making it difficult to recover if the mission failed. She was already running a very successful school in her community among middle and upper-class Asians who spared no expense on their children's education, including music lessons after school. The Afro-Latino community to which she was coming would be suspicious of her motives to serve them; they could not pay the private tuition to attend the school and make its operation profitable. Also, an African American assembly was renting the chapel from the former body, and a Latino assembly was renting from the same group in the afternoon. I was saddened that neither of these had the foresight to acquire the property themselves. The Lord called a Deborah from another town to minister to their people spiritually and educationally with a burning passion she could not shake.

As we toured the complex, she shared her heart, and I was moved by her compassion and sense of mission for the city's people. By American norms, these were not her people. From a secular perspective, they would be considered more mine than hers. To hold such views was as much bigotry as it was prejudice. Rather than seeing from a non-Christian worldview, we spoke as brethren in Christ with the mission field before us white and ripe for harvest and in desperate need of workers to cultivate the seeds so generously sown. I relayed to her how my church saw similar blight, went against detractors and the conventional wisdom, and provided education for our people from pre-K to junior high school. She listened with keen attention and then asked a difficult question that required much careful thought. "Why don't you come here to California and work with me to help get it off the ground?" Now that was a staggering offer that was hard to ignore.

As I thought about it, the magnitude and scope of the mission and the excellent prospects it entailed touched every part of my core. It was hard to restrain myself from not saying, 'Yes, I will.' It was a new church-planting project in a growing mixed neighborhood that increasingly integrated as more Asians moved in because of the lower housing cost. It was an opportunity to pastor in such an exciting field, uniting several ethnicities in one Christian church. The church would provide educational resources to more impoverished underserved communities, with excellent support from the Asian parent church. If there was a chance to make a difference in people's lives spiritually, economically, and socially it was being presented to me by one of the most humble persons I had ever met. The possibilities were endless, yet I knew that I had to seek the Lord before making this commitment. I had too much respect for this saint of God to capitalize on an opportunity for personal gain. This would have to be the expressed will of the Lord for my doing so.

For the moment, I turned the discussion towards funding for charter schools and the possibility of networking with representatives in the area. They would gladly support new money and ventures coming into their neighborhoods when others left. Faith-based programs proved effective, and I believe that the support would be given. Pastor Deborah informed me how well connected to the local political machinery she was, and this only added to the wellspring

I was trying to contain within myself. She stated that she did not desire to be Pastor, only to see the project succeed, and relayed how broken her life was after her divorce and the near mental breakdown it brought. Then in a series of dramatic Divine interventions, she was led to do the missions she was now seeing prosper and bloom. The move to this part of town was the latest unshakable vision God had relentlessly impressed upon her despite her resistance and protest. As we spoke, I began to spark with ideas of what could be done, all of which had led to the phenomenal growth our ministry in Queens achieved with national recognition and status. My thoughts were met with her admission that she did not know how to do all the suggested things. Again to buy time, I recommended that Pastor Deborah attend Allen's upcoming Economic Development Conference in Queens. She agreed to come.

We ended our tour with a visit to a mall under reconstruction. Pastor Deborah's brother was the construction engineer, and another brother owned a pharmacy in the complex, so the mall was actually theirs! The meeting was pleasant, and I invited them to come to the Economic Conference to inform the ideas we discussed to turn their sister's dream into reality. They promised that they would try to attend. Pastor Deborah had another motive for meeting her brothers; the builder was unsaved, and the pharmacist was a believer but somewhat inactive. She perhaps hoped the meeting of her brothers with Pastor Chung and me would lead to their commitment to the Lord. We prayed for them before we parted, but the opportunity to share the gospel was not fully there. We planted seeds and trusted God to water them.

After the meeting, Pastor Chung headed for the airport en route to Thailand, where he was scheduled to conduct evangelical services. He wished that I could accompany him. Instead, he left me once again to finish the special services. As in Taiwan, people were not shy about coming forward for prayer, and we obliged, interceding to the Lord on their behalf.

Once the services were ended, I returned to Allen with my perspective widened and broadened by another opportunity to minister beyond the Cathedral walls. Again, I was challenged whether I was to stay and continue serving as an Associate Minister/Assistant Pastor or go beyond those walls and assume a pastoral position in my own right. In light of excellent ministry opportunities, it was necessary to examine where I should serve and why. I needed thorough self-examination. Perhaps it may have been helpful for a mentor to probe me.

Several questions challenged me. Had I avoided serious consideration of Pastor Deborah's fantastic offer out of fear? What were possible worries there? Was going out of my familiar context to another unfamiliar one the stumbling block? I reasoned not since I was prepared to go outside my cultural and geographical box to attain more outstanding achievements for my family and myself. My studies in England, then the USA were far more significant leaps than changing to another state. Although it would mean uprooting my family, I had already done so and was prepared to do so again as long as it was the Lord's will. Was it the cultural challenges that the scenario presented? This was a legitimate fear given the USA's sociological landscape, but I had transcended these biases because of my studies in multi-cultural contexts.

Additionally, my DNA was not inherent in the historical and systemic prejudice in which American children of all ethnic groups are tragically bred and breastfed. Although I lived with it daily, it was more an external sociological dynamic than an internalized psychological determinant of my behavior. Of course, whether my wife and children had reconciled these issues within themselves was another matter that needed to be considered since any move to the West Coast from the East was one that would involve the entire family.

Another question that merited attention was the financial factors. Was the mission sustainable? Could I maintain my family while trying to save those at risk? Unfortunately, I did not discuss these matters with Pastor Deborah since I was not prepared for her offer on the spot. Therefore, I did not have any information on which to weigh that factor. Yet, it was clear that there was considerable support for this bold and atypical Godly woman who had reached across the cultural divide to serve with the help of her God-fearing brothers.

Most importantly, however, any decision to go beyond the Cathedral anywhere had to be by the Holy Spirit's direction. The Apostle Paul and the missionary team he led discovered this essential factor when they desired to evangelize Bithynia. However, Luke documented that they were restrained by the Holy Spirit from doing so, the very Spirit who identified them and called them to those same missionary campaigns. Nevertheless, they were to go where he directed them, not where they preferred to go:

> Now when they had gone through Phrygia and the region of Galatia, they were forbidden by the Holy Spirit to preach the word in Asia. After they had come to Mysia, they tried to go into Bithynia, but the Spirit did not permit them. So passing by Mysia, they came down to Troas. And a vision appeared to Paul in the night. A man of Macedonia stood and pleaded with him, saying, "Come over to Macedonia and help us." Now after he had seen the vision, immediately we sought to go to Macedonia, concluding that the Lord had called us to preach the gospel to them. (Acts 16:6-10 cf. 13:1-3 NKJV)

Clearly, the Holy Spirit was the ultimate overshadowing presence under which the Apostles and all disciples were to serve. Paul and his team were eager and willing to share the gospel as called, but they did where and when the Spirit orchestrated the efforts. What if they had resisted and gone against the Spirit? Would they have received the vision of the Macedonian man where the help was needed and the cities ready for the gospel? I recognized then that I also needed to be governed by such spiritual discernment. Once again, I heard the restraining voice of the Spirit saying as He had done often before, "Stay at Allen; everything you need will be provided there." That settled the matter and put all doubts and questions to rest.

Thus, I returned to my role in the shadow of the Bootstrapper, ministering to the youth in the Rites of Passage program and the seniors in the Hour of Power, discipling the membership, training new applicants for ministry. I counseled members, visited the penal institutions, and even handled the additional task of Housing Manager in an HPD project that the Pastor asked me to assist. Bro. Edwin Reed, the CEO, was responsible for the project, which was flagging badly, but my role was not long. Nevertheless, my horizons were about to be broadened again.

CHAPTER 13

GOING FULL CIRCLE

Interestingly, life has a way of revolving. The whole world moves in cyclical patterns, and so do our life experiences. This reality became more apparent because of experiences that opened a new season in my life and ministry. First was my return to my alma mater, York College. I had left Barbados to come there as a student; now, I returned to York as a Lecturer. I applied to York because I needed to supplement my income. Unfortunately, my fixed mortgage rate moved to an adjustable one, and there was an immediate increase by my bank on my monthly payments. Efforts to refinance to a fixed mortgage proved futile in the then increasingly tightening credit market.

Sis. Daisy Bernard, one of my spiritual mothers, encouraged my considering applying to teach at York. Sis. Bernard even hinted that she knew the President and would give a reference on my behalf. My application was successful, and I was hired by my former speech professor, Dr. James Cuomo. I taught Speech 101 to three sections and enjoyed it in short order. I was almost reduced to tears as I sat at my desk in my office at York and recalled the trying years I endured working my way through my undergraduate degree, including the mandatory speech class I was now teaching. Tears welled up in my eyes when I looked down at the first paycheck I received. I was amazed at the grace of God that provided through those years of successive tuition hikes that made my student loan inadequate. What was calculated to be enough for four years suddenly was only good enough for one. I had to work however and wherever I could to make ends meet. I recalled finishing but could not receive my diploma because I had a balance to settle before accepting it. At the same time, I could not get a job to pay the credit because I needed to show my diploma. The college where I had to stand in line at the Bursar's office to pay, was now paying me! I was overwhelmed by how the grace of God had brought me full circle.

I was, however, not totally happy because I wished I were teaching theology in a Bible college. I was glad that I was not instructing Business because I did not want to lend my skills, honed in the vineyard of the Lord, to worldly affairs. I took comfort in the fact that Speech was a part of my craft. It sharpened my ability to think more critically, speak more competently, listen with acuity, and be generally more analytical. I was aware that though the Lord had opened this door, I could not settle here. I did not belong to the world of academia. I was the Lord's, and all that I was and had become was undeniably a result of His grace alone.

Another consolation was how the classes opened a door for me to witness subtly. I realized that Dr. Cuomo had incorporated the word **logos** in his book, the main text for the course. I was pleasantly surprised. As a student, I recalled that he had given us a list of words and asked us to provide a conceptual speech on the word we choose. We were to show its etymology and essential characteristic to bring its abstract concept within the audience's mental grasp. I chose the word '*word.*' It stuck out to me. I wanted to avoid it and could not. I felt the Holy Spirit challenging me to speak on it not simply as a verbal expression but as the WORD, Christ. I was reluctant and resistant, but He was relentless. I was made to see the evangelical opportunity I had to present Christ uniquely and creatively before a class of sharp minds. I had been active in the Intervarsity Christian Fellowship (IVCF) at York, so I would be a hypocrite if I failed to witness when I could. Many of these students and professors paid the Christian students scant respect when we made our public outreaches in the common areas and invited them to our presentations.

Consequently, I went to work, exploring the concept entirely. My speech was divided into three parts of a typical homiletical discourse: the spoken word, the written word, and the living word. I was careful to fulfill all the academic requirements of my task, but also to state firmly that the Word was so profound that it is the embodiment of thought, the reason that explains every mystery. The Apostle John even used it to describe the incarnate Jesus as the Word, the full expression of God. I recall the rapt attention of the class and Professor Cuomo, himself, on whom I had obviously left an indelible impression of the concept of logos. Even that reference to the Apostle John was in the current edition of Dr. Cuomo's book. Whether that inclusion resulted from my presentation or not, I would not dare suggest, but I was glad it was there because I had a legitimate reason to speak on it.

Other opportunities came when students made their presentations in class. They often invariably spoke on religious topics or made references to the Bible, sometimes supporting their views or denying its claims. All these were fertile ground for my witness, which was done skillfully and wily. I never wanted them to know that I was a minister because I wanted them to come to truth objectively via their reasoning engaged in this setting. Also, I did not want to give the enemy occasion to accuse me of proselytizing in the class or for students to presume upon my generosity. So I always left them guessing and wondering, sometimes asking what I did apart from lecturing until the very last class.

My end-of-the-semester pep talks in the last class were the times I capitalized on their curiosity and seized the moment, my best moment. I simply did as eloquently and passionately as I could. I did what I had taught them; I gave a speech. In it, I encouraged them to graduate, to finish. I advised the young women not to be sidelined by misguided romances, premature pregnancies out of wedlock, and immature, insecure males incapable of being good husbands. I encouraged the men to make sure that they finished well and assume their leadership roles in their homes and society. I particularly pressed the African American men to go against the prevailing expectation of low performance and not conform to the stereotypes. Several students expressed appreciation for my encouraging them afterward and often greeted me respectfully in the hallways.

Return to my High School – Ellerslie Secondary (Barbados)

My second circuit came when I was invited by my high school alma mater, Ellerslie Secondary, to be the featured speaker for the school's fortieth anniversary. I was utterly flabbergasted and humbled by this invitation, given that I was away for so long and that there were many noble graduates of Ellerslie in Barbados that could have filled the role. Finally, however, the honor was accorded me. After speaking directly to my former French teacher, Mrs. Porte, the Assistant Principal, I accepted the invite. I made the arrangements to travel home for the celebrations, but not without asking why I was chosen. Mrs. Porte explained that they had short-listed three persons, but my name kept emerging as the primary choice. I was even more humbled and driven to worship the Lord for such favor.

As I sought the Lord on what I should say, I could not help thanking Him for keeping me from sin throughout my fragile youthful years at Ellerslie. I recalled the temptations to become involved with girls who liked me for one reason or another. I thought of those I was attracted to and those all the boys desired. I saw in retrospect how the Lord placed His mark on me and set me apart as a Christian, preaching on the school grounds before the body of students. I was unable to hide after that. Such a declaration eliminated some friends, their influences, and their vices. It also made it nigh impossible for me to venture into some behaviors because of my peers' constant expectations of Christian deportment. Of course, some tried to overcome prohibitions of my faith (with my willingness to comply at times), but the Lord was always there to shield and protect me. One way He did so was to place teachers in our lives who attended the Inter-School Christian Fellowship session we held on campus and motivated us to serve the Lord unashamedly. Mrs. Porte was one such teacher. Their presence made an enormous difference because it represented authoritative endorsement among those we looked up to and respected.

The fact that some teachers were Christians themselves, willing to declare it above their professions and among their peers, gave us credence and hope. It bolstered our witness, often stymied or mocked, especially by some science teachers who wanted to belittle and embarrass us. Take, for instance, Mr. Mark Stoute. He was tall and handsome, and the girls drooled over him. He was also reasonably competent and effective as a teacher. Therefore, you can imagine him stating in class that the Bible could not be correct, referring to the account about Joshua's commanding the sun to stand still because, as he pontificated, the earth revolves around the sun, not the sun around the planet. The young impressionable minds all smiled and nodded in agreement, and I sat there stung by this assault on my faith and incompetent to defend it with other scientific counter-claims to prove him wrong other than 'but God can do all things.'

Another teacher was more direct with me. He spoke to me directly and asked, 'Why don't you Christians tell the people the truth!' At first, I was surprised and unsure what he was talking about. He was apparently alluding to the theories that Blacks were the true Jews and whites had corrupted Scripture for their colonial imperialistic ends and so on. These theories were new to me and foreign. Was he asserting that we were preaching lies? I had always believed that Christians were the purveyors of the truth! These and other such encounters made our witness among the student body more difficult. It gave the students excuses to doubt; after all, there were different views to consider and other persons of higher authority who questioned our claims back then.

Given this invitation to address former peers, teachers, and the current student body, I wondered how they would now receive my message as the school paused to offer thanksgiving to our Lord for its continuance thus far over the past forty years. My task was made stress-free because I was the speaker at a scheduled church service. Accordingly, I neither had to defend or affirm any theological issue but simply to demonstrate the grace of God that evidently benefitted Ellerslie thus far. Therefore, I sought the Lord about the Scripture to present the faculty and student body with a sense of triumph. The text came quickly. Psalms 124 was to be lifted.

On the day of celebration, the Western Light Church of the Nazarene's sanctuary in Husbands, Barbados, was packed with students, parents, alumni, teachers (past and present), government officials from the Ministry of Education, and others. The Governor-General,

Sir Clifford Husbands, was to be in attendance but was unable to do so, and thus I was elevated to do what he was invited to do: inspect the honor guard of the school's cadet core! Could it get any more splendid than this? I attended to my task as diligently as I could, drawing on all my training and relying on the power of the Holy Spirit to execute the task. Without apology, I delivered my sermon, careful to make it relevant to the young students present. From all accounts, it was received well. Upon my conclusion, I could see those who had invited me sitting back in their seats as though they were vindicated in their decision to send for me. Their sentiments were, however, echoed in the vote of thanks.

After the service, the sanctuary became a reunion hall as old friends became reacquainted. We stared into each other faces, laughing sometimes and almost crying as we tried to update the images of each other in our minds. We taxed our memories to recall experiences that had long been mentally archived by the sheer necessity of growing and maturing into whom we had become. In the days that followed, I attended the official banquet where several honors were bestowed on teachers who had served the school's entire life and others who had made valuable contributions to the school's development. I was asked to participate in the awards ceremony, overwhelmed that those I received tuition from were now receiving service tokens from my hands. God was kind and gracious beyond measure to give me such honor.

As I mingled with the audience made up of many Ellerslie alumni, I could not help being grateful to the Lord for the narrow paths on which He had led me. I kept asking myself, 'What if the Lord had not kept me when I was a teen at times not so willing to be kept from foolish and unwise decisions?' Without God's providential hand, there was no way that I would have been so honored, and if perchance I was, it would have had a hollow ring to all those who constantly asked, "Do you remember me?" These would be the ones whose words would have brought me down from the pedestal to which I may have been unduly elevated. I could not imagine that I would be there at that time in my life over 30 years later. What teenager thinks, 'I will live well now so that should I be called upon later in my life, I will have the commensurate respect to qualify for honor?' None that I have met, and indeed, I like my peers, was too consumed with enjoying life to think so deeply and philosophically. Nevertheless, I was glad that I was respected by my peers, teachers, and officials before, whom my life as a young man and now a more mature Christian was lived out as a witness for the Lord.

To crown my experience, the principal invited me to address the young men of the upper forms (grades), the juniors, and seniors at an assembly during the school week. The principal was unsure what he wanted me to do, but he felt it might influence his students to strive for excellence in their careers if I addressed the young men from a testimonial perspective. Thus I was thrown into the packed auditorium with hundreds of students required to listen to my speech. I knew from experience that I would have their attention for all of 20 minutes maximum if I merely speak. This sized audience of young men needed dramatic presentations to keep their attention long enough to convey a value or two. This crowd was ripe for pranks and cranks. This was the platform for gamesters and jesters to unnerve the speaker, unravel the fragile structure, and disrupt the entire room into chaos. I had to think quickly, but I had met this scenario before.

My years of Rites of Passage work and assembly presentations in schools in Brooklyn with Mr. Arno were not in vain. Thus, rather than mount the platform, I walked the floor. Rather than a dry speech, I asked provocative questions and obliterated every Smart Alec answer with 'comebacks' that made them the laughing stock.

I picked on those who were talking and brought them out front to be my props, and I turned all the informal leaders, whom I spotted, into my aides. I made them compete for money if they could answer my questions, and I totally disarmed those who wanted to be incorrigible. At the end of the session, I shared my Ellerslie story and saw them in rapt attention. We dismissed the session to relieved teachers worried they would be embarrassed by their charges acting out or the session falling short of their intentions. Again, I was grateful to the Lord for my years of working in the shadows, behind the Allen Cathedral walls, and in the trenches of Queens and Brooklyn that could be effectively employed on foreign soil.

Following the Hall presentation, I was immediately asked to stay and attend the Interschool Christian Fellowship (ISCF) meeting. I could not refuse. I walked with students who escorted me to the room designated for the meeting. While they asked me questions about myself or my presentation, I was catapulted back in time in those surreal moments. I was walking down the same corridor I had walked as a student. I peered into the same classrooms where I sat, and memories flooded into my mind. Faces, places, and spaces where past experiences happened were now a photo album turning its pages on my mind's screen. I was moved to worship inwardly, thanking the Lord for every act of His Divine providence and preservation that made this poignant moment possible for me and now for the present Christian teens who gathered to hear me. I was glad that mine was not a testimony of how badly I behaved at school before the Lord arrested me. I was delighted that I did not have to confess how many girl's lives I had ruined with deception, illicit sex, and abortions as many of my peers had done. Mine was less eventful, less scintillating, and saucy. It was a story of my standing embarrassed before the students lined up at the outdoor cafeteria and preaching to incredulous stares. It was one of struggling to overcome the deficit of being one year older than my class chronologically but two years behind them academically. It was an anecdotal tale of hard work and long hours of study through sleepless nights that led to becoming Head Boy of the school and among the top three students of my class. It was a recall of being among the first to take advanced level classes in Art, representing the school as football captain, and winning nationally televised competitions to make our school proud. It was my testimony about being a Christian when it was unpopular, at times unpleasant, and even undesirable. It was a confession of being thankful to God, of having no regret but respect. I left Ellerslie and Barbados knowing that they were others that the Lord would bring through their turbulent teens to be witnesses for His cause as he had done for me.

Return to First Baptist Church (Barbados)

Life returned to normal as I continued to provide for my family and take care of Lorraine, whose ability to climb the stairs was now slowly eroding as her legs grew increasingly weak. We soldiered on with therapy and the best nutrition we could afford while juggling my seemingly increasing duties at Allen. However, all this was to be interrupted again by my third circuit. A letter came from the Pastor of the First Baptist Church, Barbados inviting me to be the speaker for the 50th Anniversary of the church in Bridgetown. This was a tremendous request that resonated uniquely between myself and my wife, who was the only other person who could have appreciated the importance of such an invitation. First Baptist was the church we grew up in and from which we left as married young adults immigrating to the USA.

Consequently, to be asked to be the speaker for its golden anniversary and its subsequent week of services was staggering. We felt so honored given that the Baptist work in Barbados was started by white southern missionaries over 100 years prior. We had been accustomed to receiving evangelists and speakers from their missionary organizations over the years, coming to Barbados and ministering there. Although the work was now in local hands and the stream of missionaries had long stopped flowing, I expected that the Church Board would have invited some of those who played significant roles to speak on such a monumental occasion instead of myself. I would have been away for some 20 years by then. Unable to deny our beloved church, which we constantly prayed for, Lorraine and I accepted the gracious invitation and traveled back to step up to the task.

The services went well. I was moved to use the example of Nehemiah's experience in rebuilding the walls of Jerusalem as our theme for the week. The congregation responded well to the messages and the evening services were better attended than expected. As we greeted the folk after services, many of the older folk that knew Lorraine and me as children looked us in the eyes with piercing authority and asked, "When are you coming back?" The younger ones, less discreet and more impetuous, asked, "Why don't you come back and pastor this church?" We politely moved them along and ducked such loaded questions. Later, it became apparent that all was not well at First Baptist between the Board and the then-current pastor, Pastor Ezra Crichlow. I noticed some unusual responses during the services but was not sure why they were as such. We stayed above the fray and returned to New York, amazed at what the Lord had done. Reflecting on the state of the church since we left, this time, there was no comfort in returning to my previous tasks. I was restless; the comfort of the shadow was gone with no effort on my part. The sun was shifting more directly overhead, causing me to stand in my own shadow.

Two years later, the pastor resigned from First Baptist and became the Superintendent of the Fundamental Baptist Churches of Barbados, including First Baptist. During this time, I was in Barbados attending a friend's wedding and was asked to meet with the Church's Board. I obliged and was confronted with their interest in me as Pastor of First Baptist, should I return. It was more of a feeling-out session than a firm offer to be considered because I realized that much needed to be in place to accommodate a new pastor. Pastor Chrichlow had labored without any financial reward and had suspended the church services' formal collection of monies. The church's budget was not dealing with the maintenance of a pastor, nor was it growing because the usual manner of collecting steady income was interrupted. There was no parsonage, no transportation allowance, no medical benefits, and no pension plan. These were standard parts of the pastoral compensation packages I was familiar with. I gently pointed these out as objectively as possible without appearing to be self-serving. The meeting ended without any firm decisions made on anyone's part, and I returned to the US and continued my service to Allen.

The restless heart murmur was becoming heaviness within me and would not relent. First Baptist continued to present itself before me. Lorraine and I prayed about the burden we both began to feel given the vacated position and the division that Pastor Chrichlow's sudden, unexpected resignation had caused among the brethren. For the time being, however, I had to pay attention to the upcoming AME Church conference at which I was to receive a second and highest ordination. As an ordained elder, I would be eligible to be transferred from Allen to pastor an assembly in or out of New York at the Bishop's discretion. Many of my peers began speculating that I would be appointed to an assembly given the outstanding vacancies. Somehow, I was not worried because my heart had an abiding peace concerning the entire process. When the conference's final day came, all the ministers sat together nervously as the Bishop read out reappointments and new appointments. Several of my fellow 'Allenites' kept eyeing me, telling me that I will be appointed like the sons of the prophet to Elisha, but like him, I would advise them, "Hold your peace." At the end of the day, there were some surprising announcements and appointments. I was omitted. Again, several persons expressed that I should have been assigned a church instead of other appointees, but I knew in my heart that the Lord had not so prepared me. There was something else; I could sense it. I just had to keep serving faithfully in the shadows until it manifested itself.

Stepping into the Light

Every minister who serves as an associate will not necessarily become the pastor of a church, let alone a Senior Pastor. God will keep some of us in what would seem a subordinate position indefinitely. It is our task wherever He leads to follow and to be good shepherds whether we are the ones with the primary responsibility or not. Remember, those with greater responsibility will face greater condemnation (James 3:1). Many of God's best servants went unnamed in Scripture, but their names are written in heaven (Heb. 11:35-40). Jesus, the Chief Shepherd, who will appear to reward us all for our labors bestowed on His behalf, admonishes us not to rejoice at the exercise of spiritual authority. We function as agents of the Kingdom (Lk. 9:1-2; 10:1-2, 17-20). Nevertheless, The Good Shepherd will at times call some of us out of the shadows of others to stand in the whole light where we must face Him alone and cast a shadow of our own.

There are times when the call comes suddenly and unexpectedly, as in the case of Nehemiah. He was the lowly cupbearer of the king that conquered his own people, the Jews, until one day, the news of their welfare and his desire to alleviate their wretched condition converged to motivate him to action. Soon, he was governor of the very city of Jerusalem and supervising the rebuilding of the city's walls to shut out the enemies that frustrated the temple's reconstruction. What a dramatic turn of events. Clearly, Nehemiah was not trying to advance his career, as Haman was (Esther 2:6-9). Rather, he sought to advance the cause of God's people and was thrust into the light as a result.

At other times the call into the light is more anticipated as perhaps it was in Joshua's case. He knew that Moses was denied leading the people of Israel into the Promised Land. This great honor was to be given to someone else! As Moses' minister, he was privileged to lead Israel several times but only temporarily as Moses instructed Him. He was one of two forty-plus-year-olds who would be allowed into the land of Canaan. Everyone else from the generation that left Egypt would die out, except Caleb and Joshua (Num. 14:24; Deut. 1:38). Therefore Caleb could have been chosen, or Phineas, the priest, for the bravery he showed and the moral stand he took at one of Israel's darkest moments (Num. 25:6-13). However, Moses was instructed to lay his hand on Joshua to transfer the leadership position. The Spirit of the Lord that had empowered Moses to lead the fretful, fitful masses of Israel now strengthened and encouraged Joshua to conquer and divide up the land among the tribes of Israel (Deut. 34:9; Joshua 1:1-8).

My call was sudden. One morning, we were told that Pastor Chrichlow had deceased. The news struck like a lightning bolt. It was not only sad that a significant leader in whose shadow we had served was dead, but it meant that his two offices (Superintendent and Pastor) had to be filled. Instantly, there was a gnawing uneasiness within me. Lorraine and I thought of attending the funeral, but circumstances precluded us from doing so. Instead, we committed ourselves to prayer for First Baptist and the Fundamental Baptist Churches, which had now come to a major junction in its existence as they sought to fill those vacant positions. As a result, the Board's discussions of interest with me took on a different tone and weight. As I reflected on the situation, I remembered the Scripture that the Lord impressed on my heart about five years before. It was Joshua chapter one, verses one through eight. The second verse was particularly jolting then as now:

> Moses my servant is dead; now therefore arise, go over this Jordan, thou, and all this people, unto the land which I do give to them, even to the children of Israel.
>
> (Joshua 1:2)

I recalled then that I had questioned why this verse was impressed so forcefully on my mind while I was in prayer. There was no doubt in my mind that the Lord was referencing First Baptist, but I was doubtful of the meaning at the time. I even responded, "But Bro. Chrichlow is not dead." It was as if I was fact-checking my spiritual receptivity, but nothing more was received. So I put it at the back of my mind and continued serving, not knowing what to do about it. Now it was foremost in my mind.

I did not want to appear like an opportunist, but I could feel the firm hand of the Lord directing me to reopen the dialogue with the Deacon Board beyond expressing sympathy on the passing of their leader. I wrote them a letter of thanks for meeting me over a year before, but I never mailed it for some reason. Finally, the Lord reminded me of the letter. I now had to find it and send it. At their request, it included some ideas for the church's future, which I had been thinking through ever since I left Barbados over 20 years ago. I was uncomfortable sending such correspondence at that time, lest I was misunderstood. However, the Lord's strong leading was unmistakable clear. As I got ready to mail the letter, I heard Him say to me, "Don't mail it; take it!" Take it? I questioned. Now that was a far cry from mailing it. I struggled with this idea until it became unbearable, so I booked a flight to Barbados. I informed Lorraine, who sternly warned me not to make any hasty decisions there but consented to my going, and in short order, I left for a week in Barbados. I called ahead to request a meeting with the Board to present my letter to them, and they convened an extraordinary meeting to meet with me.

As I prayed and prepared for the meeting, I couldn't help reflecting on what was happening within me. I felt as though I was going through a metamorphosis. I began to realize that I was at the zenith of my career at Allen; there was nowhere else to go. There was no other ministry that held out any new territory for me, and I had worked in the corporate side of the church in more than one capacity. I felt that I was given a consummate education at the 'University of Allen.' I could hear Bro. Charles Jenkins echoing in my mind, "Boy, when you leave here, there will be nothing you will not be able to do." I couldn't shake this growing feeling that the time to 'leave here' was here. Without desiring it for the past year, I felt readied to go forth. All kinds of thoughts had begun to converge in my head, creating discomfort with my present circumstances. I had started to see changes in our world that prompted me to take my place in the kingdom and began to affect change in the world. It seems as though Barbados was where I was to begin.

Global Change

I also perceived a global change, and I had begun to keep an informal score. By my observation, I noted that a new political party had swept into power in Barbados, throwing out a very stable and prosperous regime that had served for over 14 years. I also saw changes coming to America. Actually, I was already proclaiming to Allen that the USA was headed for a significant fall because of imperialistic policies in the Gulf and at home. In Latin America, there was a growing change away from a pro-American to an anti-American stance from Bolivia to Venezuela. Additionally, the EU was strengthening. The Asian Pacific (particularly China and India) flexed new financial and military muscle, and Arab and Israeli-Western relations were a tinder box leaning to the apocalyptic. All these developments were colored by the preemptive war in Iraq. I felt as though my time at Allen was up, and it was time to move on. Now it seemed as though God was driving me back to Barbados.

In Barbados, the Board was receptive and anticipatory, eager to hear what I had to say. Basically, I reiterated what I had articulated in the letter. I did not intend to be prophetic, but I could not help saying what I had traveled from so far with the burden to say. I made a presentation to the church stating my willingness to serve in whatever capacity. I knew within my heart that God was prompting me to return to Barbados to do ministry. If First Baptist was willing to offer the Pastorate, I was spiritually obligated to accept. However, I was returning even if that was not the case. I was prepared to do para-church ministry and serve in whatever capacity because of the undeniable conviction within my soul. More than ever, I felt and expressed that the church, the country, and the world at large were on the verge of significant change, and the Board needed to recognize it and navigate it carefully for the future well-being of the assembly. Having made my presentation, I sat back to hear the Board's response. It was a poignant moment; it was heavy. Clearly, the Board had undergone a period of struggle with the former pastor; therefore, they were cautious as they spoke with me.

Eventually, the questions came. One Board member requested that I elaborate on my vision for First Baptist, and another questioned my expectation of remuneration. This latter question recognized that my current pay was way beyond what they could afford. At Allen, each minister on staff was given a housing allowance, medical benefits, and an insurance pension scheme on par with many corporations in the mainstream. None of these were in place at First Baptist, and this Board member was somewhat embarrassed as he discussed this lack on their part. He didn't think the church could pay me according to my qualifications and experience, given my present position at Allen. I could see the acknowledgment in the heads that lowered to their notes in silent assent. We had reached the breaking point of the entire decision. As tensed seconds ticked by, I felt that gentle prodding to say what I was led to say should this issue come up. It was not what I would have preferred to say. Under normal circumstances, I would negotiate for the benefits, including transitional costs, to help with my family's relocation, but this was not normal. Reluctantly I eased the tension as led by the Spirit. I expressed to the Board that I would be prepared to stay with a relative until I was settled and accept 10% of tithes and offerings as my total compensation.

The moment the words exited my mouth, I felt a strange release and relief in my Spirit. My rational mind recognized that I had put myself into a very vulnerable position without even knowing what the church collected in income or held in accounts. I had no idea whether there was adequate room at any relative to accommodate my family and me, especially Lorraine, given her particular needs. The Board stared at me incredulously. The specific Board member who had posed the question stared at me, mouth agape. Then responding to my incredible statement, he remarked that I had encouraged his faith. At that moment, it was as if the tension was broken. Others weighed in on the discussion stating that my generous offer would not preclude them from offering more if they agreed as a Board. I could hear Lorraine in my ears saying, "Don't do anything stupid or rush." I was not sure if I hadn't, but I was doing what I dearly believed to be right in the sight of God.

From If to When

Like water released after a blockage is removed, the conversation flowed freely, moving from 'if" I would fill the position to 'when' time frames. The pertinent issue was now when might I begin. I felt confident that I could do so at the beginning of the ensuing year and boldly said so. However, there was much to do on both sides to make the transition possible. I left the meeting with a somewhat surreal feeling. I had made the most outstanding commitment of my life. I had accepted a position to pastor a church but not just any church: one which was outside the AME denomination, outside the United States, my home for the past 20 years, a church that was broken, demoralized, and one that did not even have a secretary on staff. The aged janitor was the lone employee. Nevertheless, this was the path set before me beyond the shadow of the Bootstrapper, beyond the walls of Allen Cathedral.

Upon returning to the US and Allen, I needed to be highly strategic in announcing my departure for several reasons. I needed to plan my resignation to allow me sufficient time to take care of financial obligations, my family's health care (since they were still on my medical plan), and ensure minimal disruption in the Discipleship Ministry. Besides, I had to be very careful with Lorraine's medical benefits, which could be lost with a move to Barbados. I also had to inform my Chairman of the Fine Arts Department at York College that I would be unavailable to teach the winter semester. Despite these very pressing concerns, there was an urgency to push forward. My decision consumed my waking and some sleeping moments. My cover in the shelter of my Pastor was no longer a place to stay.

I was like Andrew and the other unnamed disciple who heard John the Baptist announce Jesus and then pointed Him out in the crowd. Immediately Andrew and his companion left off following John and followed Jesus. They realized that John was preparatory. His ministry pointed to One mightier than himself, with a baptism of fire and the Holy Spirit that superseded the water Baptism John offered for the repentance of sins (John 1:29-50). I paused to wonder why others stayed with John even when he made it clear to them that he was not the Messiah. Jesus was. He told those who remained that he was like the best man pleased that Israel (the bride) was now turning to Jesus (the bridegroom) as determined by heaven (John 3:22-36). Like Andrew, I was compelled to pursue beyond where I was to the ministry I was now called to lead.

After prayer and much soul searching, I told my Pastors that I had a firm offer from the First Baptist Church Barbados. The Pastor was characteristically happy for me, responding with, "Praise the Lord!" His eyes probed my face to learn details and hear my response and my next moves, affecting Allen. He asked about Lorraine and her feelings regarding the position, which involved moving back to a different climate given her condition and her need for ongoing care. He asked whether our girls would go with us or stay. Many of the details were still being worked out, but I confirmed that I would accept the offer and, therefore, would tender my resignation. Rev. Elaine was more forthright in her response. "Good!" she said, and we briefly discussed the possibilities of the offer from First Baptist Barbados. We parted with the understanding that we needed to come together in a formal meeting to plan exit strategies. Once I had informed the Pastors, I entered into a new relationship with myself, my family, and Allen, with First Baptist and mainly with the Lord, fresh, unknown, and unsettling.

My first observation was what began to take place within myself. I said yes to pastoring a church. For me, that was a huge commitment that I took seriously. My past experiences, but especially my understudy of the Flakes, demonstrated the rigors and demands of pastoring. It was a life-consuming responsibility that required the shepherd to extended care from the womb to the tomb. One has to meet needs in the lives of all placed under one's care, including their families, friends, and community. Discharging that responsibility was a mammoth undertaking that would demand all the intestinal fortitude one can muster, given the nature of ministry. It is one thing to be a secular firm manager concerned with strictly business operations. It is quite another to be managing the lives of people who depend on a spiritual guide to advise them how to live as Christians daily, which may include handling their businesses/careers in a secular world that may not operate according to Biblical standards. As a Pastor, I would not have the convenience of the older, more experienced Senior Pastors like Flake over me to whom I may defer some responsibilities and decisions. Any that arises at First Baptist would now be mine, submitted to me by others. The reality of such a position slowly sank in, and my mind needed to be oriented to it.

A Sacred Trust

Having been raised in a Christian home and seeing ministry through my parents' eyes, and having served in the various capacities at home and abroad, I had a deep sense of the sacred trust which a Pastor was given. There was a sobering realization that the vocation was not simply about one's competence but more about one's character. It became apparent now that I began to consider myself in that role. The moral authority necessary to pastor a church does not come from one's seminary degree as conferred by some renowned institution, nor does it emanate from any personal achievements, however grand and outstanding. Rather, moral authority comes from one's walk with the LORD. The consistent pattern of uprightness that characterizes one's life has a spiritual power that compels others to emulate and respect those who walk uprightly. The honest character also predisposes one to leadership. One who lives morally will take a principle position on issues and inevitably oppose unethical policies and people perpetrating them on others, like the vulnerable and disadvantaged. This often leads such persons and people, in general, to look up to such principled persons for help and advice. Of course, uprightness of character is commendable in God's sight. It is the Lord who bestows the favor and graciously chooses to appoint the upright as faithful stewards over His beloved household (Mt. 24:43-54 cf. I Sam. 16:1).

However, that spiritual authority could so easily be lost by human fallibilities. Many a Pastor regrettably have fallen, and I did not want to be among the casualties of castaways (I Cor. 9:27). This deep expectation was all the more impressed upon me, given First Baptist's history. It was beset by the mistakes of too many who had fallen prey to severe lapses of judgment of which I was personally painfully aware as they had impacted my own family immeasurably.

All these musings were obviously the working of the Holy Spirit within me as He had previously done when I was called into Pastor Flake's shadow under whom I had served now for ten years. However, unlike being appointed as Discipleship Minister, the Spirit of the Lord was not gearing my mind to function under a Pastor understanding his vision and person, people, and mission. Instead, the Holy Spirit was now at work, tooling me to see the revelation He wanted to be realized in the First Baptist Church Barbados ministry. That was now mine to grasp, communicate to the Lord's people, and execute it per His directions. The words of Joshua chapter one kept resonating in my head as the Lord began to communicate that revelation. Before long, I had written out a five-year plan for First Baptist.

Interestingly, some of the writing was already done without knowing why I was directed to write it. For example, my preparation of sermons in Taiwan was periodically interrupted by sudden spurts of thoughts and ideas. I was moved to record them with the sense that they were for First Baptist, Barbados. When they came, I questioned their validity. Why are these thoughts coming to me now? Why am I writing 'ideas' for First Baptist when I am immersed in ministry in Taiwan halfway around the world? Was this a distraction from the enemy to throw me off track and hinder my sermon preparation? On reflection, I evidently received the vision for an appointed time and place now unfolding before me.

As I contemplated pastoring First Baptist, my second observation was my attitude towards my Allen ministry. As if I had undergone some supernatural operation, I no longer had the zeal to serve. It was not burn-out because I was not mentally or physically tired per se. On the contrary, I loved my job, my brethren in Christ, my Pastors, and the ministry as a whole. I could spend the entire day and night at the church, but my passion for my duties began to wane. It was as if my job at Allen was ended, and I needed to pull the tent pegs and journey to where I was being led. This was a most discomforting feeling because my job demanded passion and personal application. I could not teach Hour of Power dispassionately nor mentor in Rites of Passage indifferently. I could not serve in the Prison Ministry disheartened. I could not teach Discipleship classes, serve in the Chapel, or host New Member Receptions out of duty alone. How could I counsel, fill in for the Pastors, preach, or whatever else I was asked to do without the commensurate fervor in Spirit that these tasks demanded (Roms.12:11)? Yet, I found that I had to muster that effervescence which once came so naturally and easily. I now had to fan into flame gifts that once burned incandescently. It was disturbing as I had never experienced this at Allen before.

The Shift

This shift also meant that I had to begin to scale down projections and set plans for a year in advance, and consider training persons to step up to positions to man the ministry until a successor was in place. That person would come into office with a church intact, a ministry that would need their oversight and management, not building a new ministry as I had the privilege to do. Consequently, I began to discuss with my secretary not to schedule any counselling appointments beyond the ensuing year and to refuse those that may extend into my transitional period without telling her why. It was too soon to convey the information of my leaving even to one I trusted implicitly, but because of the ramifications and impact premature information could cause in the ministry. More importantly, it was the Pastors' prerogative to make the necessary announcement at the appropriate time, and hence I had to maintain my silence and composure. That was hard, given my growing passion for First Baptist and my diminishing passion at Allen. Also, I needed to introduce key persons to more of the office's day-to-day operations without alerting them totally about why except to give the impression that it was a spiritual formation exercise to improve their ministry skills.

We had already done some such training on a limited basis. Some of the team members were even allowed system access passwords to enter attendance and new membership data as they monitored classes as a matter of expediency. Now it was a matter of necessity. Lorraine and I began to pray for the Lord's guidance about who I may suggest to our leadership as suitable replacements. Then there were so many I respected at Allen that I was obligated to tell, but I needed to do so at the appropriate time. In the face of all these inner and outer conflicts, I soldiered on working tactfully by initiating the steps to formalize procedures with First Baptist and those necessary to close the doors at Allen. I had not done so soon enough before one last assignment.

After tendering my official letter of resignation in the fall of 2006, effective January of 2007, I obviously avoided any assignments that would require my management beyond this date. This meant that I was far less vocal at executive meetings and more transitional as I spoke to the Discipleship Ministry team in our monthly sessions. All seemed on course for my departure when Feed the Children and the NBA Players Association came calling at Allen's door. They wanted Allen to host a Christmas event to give away 10,000 food and gift hampers to the people of Queens and the neighboring boroughs. Before long, discussions commenced in the Conference room as leaders assessed the feasibility of that gigantic operation. Its success would require Mayoral approval to close city streets, rerouting of traffic, and police presence. We needed local City Council approval, adherence to district regulations, and Fire Department approval. Federal, State, and local representatives had to support it and the neighborhood churches and the community. Plus, we would require an enormous outlay of resources, including thousands of dollars on Allen's part alone. I kept my nose out of the meetings, thankful that I was not invited to attend.

My low profile strategy did not last long as the Pastor walked into my office one morning and told me that he wanted me to sit in. As I had three or more months before my term of office ended, I was obligated to comply, but I tried my hardest not to become too involved. This was new because I usually undertook every assignment with full gusto to serve my leaders and congregation well. So I went to the Board Room and was introduced to the professional advance team that was hammering away at the impossibility of pulling together a city-wide event in months that should have been planned in no less than a year's lead time. Nevertheless, according to its reputation, Allen took on the task fearlessly and moved full steam ahead, with all systems operating at maximum capacity.

The meeting was a bevy of task assignments: political liaisons for official approvals, marketing to advertise the events in the media, logistics to determine how the distribution would take place, tickets for the recipients, recruiting, training, and coordinating the hundreds of volunteers needed, scheduling the 18 wheelers to drop their loads where and at what times of the evening, security to man posts and manage people, considerations to the elderly, the disabled, press passes, celebrities on hand to make donations and to see firsthand how their generous gifts would be distributed, all under Allen's management and control of the entire process. The list extended like cashier's tape tallying an unending stream of grocery items for an endless stream of customers much the same way we would serve the thousands that were bound to come ticketed or not.

I sat and listened quietly until Mr. Mew piped up that I was the best candidate to oversee the volunteers because I managed the most volunteers in the church in the ministries I was responsible for. It was tabled before I could offer any protest, and I was tagged Volunteer Coordinator for the *Miracle on Merrick*. It did not take me long to realize that I had the heavy lifting as the volunteers were the guts of the actual operation. Everything else was preliminary, precursory, fore-planning.

The Coordinators were the foot soldiers. They would receive the foodstuff overnight, repackage everything in individual hampers, place these in strategic locations, set up the distribution points, welcome the public, hand out the food/gift items physically, collect the tickets for reconciliation, and closeout and clean up at the end of the night. We had a 24-hour non-stop shift. Before the actual event, we had to devise a means of distributing the tickets to the public, screening and training the volunteers, and plotting a schedule that accounted for their availability, abilities, and competencies. We also had to consider their safety and security, identification, and maintenance (food and breaks) while they worked in rotating shifts in the bitter cold of December outdoors. We only had a few months to execute this by the week of Christmas Day. Despite the gigantic task, I took comfort in knowing that we were doing enormous good work for mankind and our community. It was a witness that spoke volumes to the entire city and country in the most tangible ways. Many did not have the means of providing for themselves or having anything special given at Christmas, the time we celebrate the greatest gift of all. I could not say no to my Pastors even though if I did, they would understand. Thus I squared my shoulders for my last big task before I took my leave from my beloved church in the shadow of the Flakes, which was looming large all over the state and country in a magnanimous act of charity.

In weeks, my trusted Administrative Assistant, Stacy, and I sat down and hammered out a strategy to ticket the public, invite, screen, and select the volunteers needed. The Discipleship Ministry leaders were tapped and responded commendably as usual. As the word went out across the media, the switchboard was inundated with calls by people trying to acquire tickets for the hampers or gift baskets of over 40-50 lbs. of food and toys. We sprang into action to help the office staff overwhelmed with calls that made ordinary and necessary business almost too difficult to conduct. Alphabetical lists were drawn up, and the volunteers were prepped to distribute at the designated times.

We placed a message on the PBX that routed people to collect tickets at specific times by their last name on a first-come, first-served basis. Thus, we had a record of those obligated to serve, a gauge of the distribution's enormity, and the unique needs of those ticketed. Tickets set aside for other churches, ministries, and non-profit organizations such as shelters and programs that cater to the poor could now be better allotted. The training was arranged for the hundreds who volunteered, both Allen members and non-members, and by and large, we were blessed with noble people. We moved so quickly that we were a few steps ahead of Bro. Erve Francis, the Chief Coordinator of the event. We humbly apologized and met to ensure that all the assigned groups were on the same page. The General Staff was grateful for our effort, which relieved them of the deluge of calls too overwhelming to handle while maintaining Allen's Ministries and corporation's management.

The Miracle on Merrick

Merrick Boulevard was closed for several blocks to accommodate the "Miracle on Merrick" on the eve of the event. Rerouting traffic on Merrick Blvd. was a major City endorsement because it connected the traveling public from Long Island to Manhattan. This should have signaled us that our event was more prominent than we thought, but I was too busy with logistics to see the bigger picture unfolding before us in real-time. A central command station was established at the Shekinah Youth Church. We checked in the volunteers reporting for duty, gave them IDs, luminescent vests, plus their assignments to the various post. We broke down the volunteers into specific teams: Receiver Teams to offload the trucks, Distributor Teams to handout the hampers at the stations on the street, Ticket Receiver Teams to ensure ticket holders were served as promised, Assistants to help the elderly and disabled, Re-stocker Teams to replenish the distribution stations, and Team leaders over each with radios to convey information on operations on the ground. These teams rotated in four-hour periods to relieve them from the cold and have coffee breaks or replace them when their shifts were over. Bro. Chung and his crew had Shekinah's kitchen humming with offerings of hot soup, tea, coffee, juices, sandwiches, and light meals for the volunteers to keep them going.

At first light, we were shocked to see that the line was already several blocks long as people braved the bitter cold to collect the precious supplies. We began implementing and executing the Miracle on Merrick in a bevy of activities too much to detail. During the long hours that stretched relentlessly into the evening of the following day, people of all ethnic and economic groups were graciously served packages of food, toys, books, games, shoes, and even water. Interlopers had to be removed, bogus tickets had to be rejected, double-dipping had to be intercepted, conflicts with the unscrupulous had to be resolved, and the lines had to be kept moving. Thousands streamed down Merrick in a river of humanity that often threatened to overflow its banks on the four-lane highway. Given the onset of harsh economic conditions that impoverished many, the community was grateful for the relief others' kindness had provided. My mind catapulted to the feeding of the five and four thousand in the Scriptures by Jesus and His Apostles. I marveled that the story seemed so pat and benign in its description in the sacred text, but it must have been rawer like the near mayhem before us. Like the beleaguered disciples, we were trying to manage the masses. I had a new appreciation for the miraculous. Ironically we had dared to call our event *Miracle on Merrick*. I remarked to one of my co-volunteers that I never knew that a miracle demanded so much work; Jesus had made it look so easy!

At the end of the night, when we were forced to close at the City's curfew time, people were still coming, many with tickets and in a desperate hope of receiving something. Eventually, I had to shut the depleted distribution points and retreat to a supply area where extras were stored mainly with books, bottles of water, and shoes. People clamored at the fence for something, but the site was not set up to properly serve them in any meaningful and equitable way. There was no way to inspect the shoes for sizes or the books for age appropriateness. Therefore I had to make the executive decision to close the space and reserve the supplies for distribution the next day to shelters, children's programs, or other suitable agencies as the Project leaders had determined. The late crowd was upset and voiced their disapproval. Some volunteers who came late in the evening were also urging me to give in to the rowdy crowd's demands, but I observed that among them were those who merely wanted to acquire the merchandise to hustle it on the streets the next day.

I recognized the hustlers from my community involvement and Prison Ministry instincts. Many were even willing to storm the fence, giving way under their surge. Policemen were present, but I observed that they were unwilling to restrain the group. It was as if they were saying, 'We're not going to be trampled by this crowd.' I looked to them for assistance, but they were set to leave at their appointed time. I felt as though they were saying, 'These are your people; you handle it. I would not allow the event to be brought into disrepute or the Church slandered because of some unfortunate incident. I just knew reporters would want to carry the regrettable sale of give-aways on Jamaica Avenue the following day by hustlers in the media. I would not give the NBA players and other benefactors a reason to feel that their gracious gifts were inappropriately distributed and did not get to the people they intended. I would not allow Allen and its Pastors to be the subject of poor press after a whole day of utter benevolence. Therefore, I ordered the area closed and dismissed the crowd. A few dejected souls were somewhat defiant. One man stood in the staging area and stated that he will not leave. Some of the volunteers closed in, sensing a confrontation, but I had faced this desperate defiance before. My experience in the shelters working with the homeless and in group homes for children informed me that I was dealing with some psycho-social issues, so I approached him calmly, showing that his refusal to leave the area was not the issue. He was there to acquire a basket, and they were all gone. I assured him that if he returned the following day to the church, we would assist him with any supplies that would be suitable for his needs.

I also informed others who lingered that our feeding program distributed food twice weekly so that there was no need to stand in the cold at that late hour for items that may not fit or would be useless to them. One by one, they left, and we all breathed a sigh of relief that nothing unpleasant occurred. As my defiant friend slowly departed, Bro. Richard Sarumi came alongside me and whispered, "Don't worry, Rev. I was right here. He couldn't have touched you". I smiled and thanked him for his assurance; his tall, imposing frame and deep black eyes gave a determined stare that conveyed a sense of security over the few remaining volunteers. His father and mother were close friends; I appreciated the reciprocal care he was extending as I had served them in their bereavement. His mother had recently passed away.

My daughters soon became concerned for me; I was absent from home since the prior evening. My wife was concerned for my well-being. I hadn't slept since the day before and was now managing the clean-up. The mobile street sweepers from the Sanitation Authority moved in to restore order to the streets. Palettes of leftover merchandise were squeezed into the Cathedral and Shekinah Youth Church corridors for next-day distribution. Finally, we took a well-deserved exit from the Cathedral to our warm and desired homes at just past midnight. My final assignment was completed, my burden was discharged.

As the New Year dawned, I peered down its dim corridors of time with great trepidation, conscious of the enormous task ahead. There was much to do: accounts to close, debts to defray, business to conclude, people to engage, and scores to settle or amortize. More importantly, I needed to make transitional plans for Lorraine and Candace. The two older girls and our niece, Tania, would stay behind to manage the home. As can be imagined, a whirlwind of doctor visits and arrangements were made to ensure that systems were in place for Lorraine and connections were made in Barbados in case they were needed. Copies of files and documents were obtained to present if necessary. Extra supplies of necessities like vitamins and other food supplements were shipped if they were unavailable or too expensive in Barbados. Then arrangements were made for Candace to be transferred to my Alma Mater, Ellerslie Secondary School, which gladly welcomed the opportunity for her to study there in Barbados. Slowly, the exit from Allen and America began to take shape. All the paths of my life that converged there were now separating.

Strangely, what was desired in my youth was now being achieved. A mental list emerged, and I began to tick off life events with deep contemplation. I responded to the call to preach and was a full-time preacher as I had bargained. I gained a Seminary education in the USA as I longed for. I was going home to help my people in more ways than I had planned. I would be involved in global marketing- the packaging, branding, and positioning of the most fantastic service to mankind: life, eternal life. Gone were the feelings of frustration and victimization. I was confirmed in my purpose beyond man's intrigues; I was affirmed within myself beyond any prejudice; I was resolved to minister to a people wounded by years of misfortunes and stymied by repeated failures that forced them to keep starting over. I now had to assume a large torn and thread borne, stained, and faded mantle, yet it felt sturdy. The smell of Cassia and Myrrh still lingered in the waft of its delicate weave. It needed only mending, patching, washing, and drying in the wind of the Spirit to be donned by a humble servant awaiting the still small voice to speak above the bivouac of life to call a people to their destiny in the light of the Gospel of Jesus the Christ.

Casting A Shadow

Once my departure from Allen was announced, there was an overwhelming show of support, elation, and praise mixed with sorrow, shock, and regret from the congregation, especially those in the ministries my family and I served. Many brought cards, called or came by our house to express their sentiments. At the annual Christmas staff party, I was toasted, but the Pastors graciously allowed a service of appreciation at which many came to say their official goodbyes. The few remaining Sundays were challenging as we were stopped and greeted by all and sundry in the hallways. My ministerial colleagues rejoiced and cried with me at various intervals.

In a familiar twist, there was an unexpected turn of events. After the flights were booked and the itinerary set in place, Lorraine confided that she was not ready to leave! This caught me off guard. I expected Candace's resistance. She was a 15-year-old teenager who typically resented moving away from her friends she looked forward to graduating with. She feared the new culture she was unfamiliar with and the demanding academics for which Barbados was known. However, I did not expect a pullback from Lorraine. She, too, dreaded the loss of our precious friends. The love shown by a congregation that had embraced her and partnered with me in her care was probably overwhelming. We were blessed with good friends whom I came home some days to find cleaning the entire house and doing the laundry to lighten the load of my hands. Such love was hard to relinquish, I am sure.

Nevertheless, not even such Christian affection could squelch the burning I felt in my soul. Therefore, reluctantly, I had to leave my family behind and head to Barbados alone to fulfill my calling. Lorraine promised to be ready in a few more months. Candace would continue in school until spring break before joining us in Barbados.

On the first Sunday in February 2007, I mounted the pulpit of the First Baptist Church of Bridgetown, Barbados. Before me was a collage of eager faces intently gazing at the pulpit to hear the Word of the Lord from my lips. For some, I was Sis. Naomi Leacock's boy whom they had taught in Sunday School. I was the youth with whom some had grown up. For some others, I was the one they had only heard about. For all, I was the new Pastor. Behind me in the loft was the choir my father and mother served in for many years, of which I had been a member. Around me were four young men, Ministers in training. I stood in the bright tropical sunlight streaming through the windows, casting a shadow of my own but determined to stay in the shadow of the cross.

Other Books by Pastor Leacock

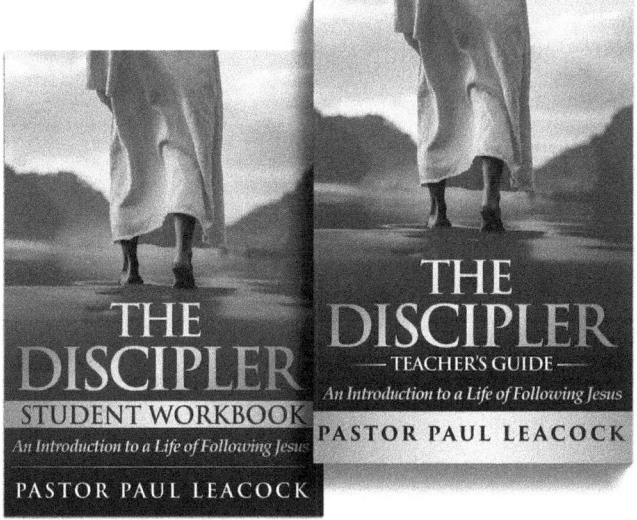

The Discipler Series
An Introduction to a Life of Following Jesus

Many churches lack a decisive program designed to mature members in the faith. *The Discipler Series* answers this need using easy to understand language – free from denominational dogmas but filled with the fundamentals of the faith.

Becoming a follower of Jesus Christ is much more than simply responding to an altar call or even joining an assembly. Christian discipleship is the God-ordained method of learning and living the truths Jesus taught.

The Discipler Series is twelve units of concise, interactive study designed to fulfill the mandate of the Lord Jesus to make disciples of all people throughout the world. It first defines Christian discipleship as the biblical method of learning and living out the tenets of the Christian faith. Then, it walks the believer from the call to discipleship to discipling others. Topics include:

- Defining Discipleship
- Repentance
- Baptism
- Church Fellowship
- Empowerment for Service to Christ
- The Gifts of the Spirit
- Stewardship
- Quiet time with God
- Evangelism
- Missions

The Discipler Teacher's Guide
ISBN 9781562293758 | 164 pages | 8.5" x 11"

The Discipler Student Workbook
ISBN 9781562293765 | 132 pages | 8.5" x 11"

Available wherever books are sold or from ChristianLivingBooks.com

Acknowledgments

Lest I forget the countless people who helped bring this work to reality, I must express my gratitude to all of them. Firstly, I thank my former Pastors, the Rev. Floyd and Elaine Flake, all the Assistant Pastors, and fellow Associate Ministers of the Greater Allen Cathedral of New York under whom and with whom I served. In addition, I am deeply indebted to my darling wife, Lorraine, who had never stood in the way of ministry even when it denied her access to her husband for the long hours I spent away from home and her. Equally denied were my beloved daughters Joanna, Samantha, and Candace, who may have often concluded that they were secondary to the members of the congregation. I am especially grateful to my eldest, Joanna, who skillfully and patiently edited this entire book, reliving many experiences; I hope they explained some mysteries she could share with her siblings.

Several others like Sis. Parker prodded me forward. Sis. Daisy Bernard listened carefully to early readings to help frame expressions appropriately, in whose blissfully peaceful home I spent many times of rest and recreation. Then there is my beloved mentor Sis. Iris Holder, whose spiritual insights and support have kept me on even keel. My Uncle, David Farnum, his belated wife, Hazel, and my cousins (Amanda, Karen, Shawn, and Monique) helped make life in New York possible for my family. Also, Allen's beloved members who welcomed me loved my family and me and provided the fertile soil for my growth in ministry, especially all the officers, Ushers, Stewards, and Stewardesses, to whom I will be eternally grateful. Bro. Charles Jenkins, Sis. Dixon, Bro. and Sis. Prescod, the late Mother Sarah Hurst, the late Sis. Sumler and the members of the Allen Prison Ministry, Sis. Willamae Woodson, the precious members of the Discipleship Ministry (too many to mention), those of the Hour of Power, the Mentors, mothers, and boys of the Rites of Passage, Sis. Eloise Hicks and countless others have all played vital parts.

I would be remiss if I didn't add my parents Cyril and Naomi Leacock, of blessed memory, the Leacock clan I am a part of, and all the early mentors of First Baptist (Barbados). I could go on, but this will still be an incomplete list.

Above all, to God be the glory for all He has done in my life, unworthy though I am. Nevertheless, He counted me worthy by putting me in the ministry, the ministry of those in whose shadow I was pleased to labor for the glory of His Son, my Savior, the Lord Jesus Christ. May these reflections be helpful to you in your ministry as you, too, serve Him in the vineyard.

Bibliography

Flake, Floyd H., and Donna Marie Williams. *The Way of the Bootstrapper: Nine Action Steps for Achieving Your Dreams*. San Francisco, CA: Harper Collins, 1999.

Hardy, Thomas. *Far from The Madding Crowd*. London: *Cornhill Magazine*, Smith, Elder & Co., 1874.

Leacock, Paul. *The Discipler Teacher's Guide*. Largo, MD: Christian Living Books, Inc., 2019.

Salaberrios, Dimas. *Street God: The Explosive True Story of a Former Drug Boss on the Run from the Hood--and the Courageous Mission That Drove Him Back*. Carol Stream, IL: Tyndale House Publishers, Inc., 2015.

Snyder, Howard A. *The Community of the King*. Downers Grove, IL: InterVarsity Press, 2004.

Strong, James. *The New Strong's Expanded Exhaustive Concordance of the Bible*. Nashville, TN: Thomas Nelson, 2010.

www.ingramcontent.com/pod-product-compliance
Lightning Source LLC
Chambersburg PA
CBHW071416150426
43191CB00008B/930